# Wasted

## *Why education isn't educating*

# FRANK FUREDI

continuum

Published by the Continuum International Publishing Group
The Tower Building, 11 York Road, London SE1 7NX
80 Maiden Lane, Suite 704, New York NY 10038

www.continuumbooks.com

First published 2009

*British Library Cataloguing-in-Publication Data*
A catalogue record for this book is available from the British Library.

ISBN 978-1847-06416-5

Designed and typeset by Kenneth Burnley, Wirral, Cheshire
Printed and bound by the MPG Books Group

# Contents

# *Preface*

This book is the product of both professional academic concerns and personal experience. As a sociologist my interest has focused on developments within the university system and in wider cultural and intellectual life. Like most people engaged with public affairs, I could not avoid reading and hearing about the 'crisis of education' and the numerous problems afflicting schools. Along with many colleagues in higher education I could not fail to note that far too many young people who enter universities lack the standards of literacy and numeracy expected of an undergraduate. But it was my own experience of discussing the concerns of parents and teachers that motivated me to undertake a study of why education finds it so difficult to educate.

I first became disturbed about children's education in 1999, when my wife and I sought to find a school for our son, then four years old. It surprised me that we had to look for a school in the first place. I grew up in an era where you automatically went to the school nearest to your home, and none of our family friends felt the need to look further. When our son turned four, my wife and I were bombarded with advice about which local school to avoid and which one to go for. Almost every parent we talked to appeared to be expert in the strengths and weaknesses of different local schools. We were left in no doubt that if we made a mistake, and chose the wrong school, our child's well-being would be compromised and his education would suffer. While I had no problem ignoring the advice of well-meaning friends, I was concerned by the informal guidance offered by the teachers we knew socially who echoed the anxieties of our acquaintances. Some of them had no inhibitions about recounting numerous horror stories about the failings of their own schools.

During our fact-finding mission a decade ago, I became aware that just about everything to do with schooling was transformed into a drama. We were always warmly welcomed by the teachers, but it struck us as odd that when they found out that we had a male child they tried to reassure us that they had a robust system in place for helping boys to read. Frequently, before we could ask any questions, teachers would inform us that they had a wonderful dyslexia unit and were experienced in dealing with boys' learning problems. I soon realized that twenty-first-century educationalists took it for granted that boys had 'special needs' and were unlikely to become good readers. During the next few years I also learned that such low expectations were not confined to how schools regard boys, but to how they regard young people in general.

In the end, what made me want to write this book was my personal frustration at the 'see no evil, hear no evil' attitude of officialdom. When questions are raised about the inadequacies of schooling, government ministers accuse critics of 'undermining the hard work of teachers' and being 'negative towards students' achievements'. Time and again the public is informed that the quality of teaching and the expertise of schooling is higher than ever before, and that 'the year-on-year rise in standards has come about because of hard work on the part of the students and their teachers'.[1] Such defensive responses transmit the misleading impression that the very questioning of educational standards constitutes an insult to the integrity of the teaching profession and denigrates the achievement of young people. This attempt to close down debate has the lamentable consequence of both polarizing and politicizing the discussion.

When education is politicized, the debate tends towards point-scoring and a focus on the symptoms rather than the causes of the problem. Regrettably, it also discourages thinking and discussion about fundamental questions, such as: What is it that we mean by education? What is the responsibility of adult society for the socialization of children? Many teachers, lecturers and parents are aware that something has gone wrong but are not sure of the source of the problem. *Wasted* was written to address this issue, by challenging the spirit of low expectations that influences much of current pedagogic thinking and lends the culture of schooling a narrow-minded and anti-intellectual character. The central focus of *Wasted* is what I consider to be the paradox of education: that the more society invests and expects of education, the less that schools and universities demand of students.

In the course of writing *Wasted* I was challenged and stimulated by the insights and research of numerous colleagues, teachers and parents. I have benefited from the work of Kathryn Ecclestone and Dennis Hayes on therapeutic education. Toby Marshall, Michelle Ledda and Shirley Lawes provided useful criticisms of early drafts. Conversations with my friend and collaborator Jennie Bristow helped to clarify my understanding of the dilemmas facing parents. This book is dedicated to the many inspiring teachers I have encountered who, despite all the pressures they face, insist on 'closing the door' and teaching a 'secret curriculum'.

# Introduction:
## The Paradox of Education

Education is the point at which we decide whether we love the world enough to assume responsibility for it and by the same token save it from ruin which, except for renewal, except for the coming of the new and young, would be inevitable. And education, too, is where we decide whether we love our children enough not to expel them from our world and leave them to their own devices, nor to strike from their hands their chance of undertaking something new, something unforeseen by us, but to prepare them in advance for the task of renewing a common world.[1] (Hannah Arendt)

It is tempting to find a scapegoat for the many problems that appear to afflict the institutions of education. Some critics point the finger of blame towards opportunist politicians, others target the numerous poorly conceived experiments with schooling, and teachers and parents are regularly denounced for their apparent failures. For their part, teachers blame government and its official inspectors. In private conversations, civil servants express the conviction that many teachers are simply not up to the job of educating their pupils. Condemnation is also directed at children and, by implication, at their parents. On numerous occasions I have been struck by the negative sentiments that teachers express towards their 'disruptive' pupils – some as young as six or seven years old – as well as towards their families. Education has become a battlefield on which often-pointless conflicts are fought. Such conflicts are not confined to any one country. They assume a particularly intense form in Anglo-

1

American societies, but in recent years I have encountered parents and teachers in Germany, Holland and Italy who are angry and bitter about this or that aspect of the way their education system works.

Education is about many different issues, but in the first instance it is about the exercise of adult responsibility. As Hannah Arendt, one of the leading political theorists of the twentieth century, reminds us, 'education is the point at which we decide whether we love the world enough to assume responsibility for it'. These days it is easy to overlook our responsibility as adults for the education of young people. Society continually communicates the warning: 'Keep Out – other people's children are not your business!' The task of educating children has been outsourced to the care of curriculum experts and pedagogues, and education is frequently represented as a discrete specialized activity that relies on their expertise. Of course it is that – but education is also much more than an activity that can be left to the care of a small group of professionals. As Arendt suggests, it is through education that adults ensure that the younger generation are prepared culturally, morally and intellectually to renew our 'common world'.

The term 'adult responsibility' can come across as a meaningless platitude. After all, most grown-ups have little involvement in the education of the young. Children are perceived as the responsibility of their parents or carers at home and of their teachers in school. Indeed, adults are encouraged to keep their distance from other people's children, and understandably draw the conclusion that what happens to young people is not their business.[2] But grown-ups are not just individuals: they are members of a wider world of adults. By their very existence they represent adulthood to the younger generation and through their behaviour send out very clear signals about what we expect from children. In a very real sense, adult authority is indivisible. The way grown-ups behave in everyday life does not go unnoticed by children as they head to school. If adults behave authoritatively towards youngsters at home and in their communities, it is likely that teachers will feel comfortable in exercising authority in the classroom. But if adults in general are reluctant or confused about giving guidance to the younger generation, the challenge facing the teacher in the classroom can sometimes become overwhelming.

Today, adults have become estranged from the task of taking responsibility for the younger generations. In March 2009 Bob Lightman, President of the Association of Teachers and Lecturers, complained that teachers were expected to teach children who 'seem never to have the opportunity to have a conversation outside school with an adult'.[3] The implication of this statement is far-reaching, because, as I argue in Chapter 3, an inter-generational conversation is an essential component of education. When grown-ups become disconnected from the young they cease to play an adult role. Adults are not simply biologically mature individuals. Although the state or quality of being an adult has many meanings, the sense of adulthood develops and gains its clarity through its relationship with the young.

Currently, ideas about adult responsibility tend to be expressed in a one-sided negative manner in relation to the question of education. Protagonists in controversies about schooling are happy to criticize parents, teachers or policy-makers for their 'irresponsible' behaviour. But such criticisms are often motivated by the goals of point-scoring and blame-avoidance. Typically parents are rounded upon to get involved and help the school get on with its job, and such exhortations often communicate a sense of disparagement towards the parent. A paradigmatic example of this approach was the highly influential American report *A Nation at Risk*. Published in 1983, the report warned American people about the threat posed by a decline in academic performance, and urged parents to be a 'living example of what you expect your child to honour and emulate'.[4] As one commentator observed: 'the initial portrayal of uninvolved and uncommitted parents in *A Nation at Risk* made serious mischief as it legitimized scapegoating parents, seemingly for everything'.[5] Similar sentiments are regularly expressed in Britain. 'It's no good blaming schools for deteriorating behaviour among young people when parents all too often set such an appalling example themselves', stated Tim Collins, a former Conservative spokesman on education.[6] In this case, censuring parents appears as a sensible alternative to blaming schools. Ed Balls MP, the Labour Government's Secretary of State for Children, Schools and Families, took a similar view, stating that 'parents should face up to their responsibilities' and be penalized if they don't.[7]

Far too many teachers adopt the attitude that the parent is the enemy. Mary Bousted, General Secretary of the Association of Teachers and Lecturers, writes that 'we know far too many children are behaving badly at school, even to the point of being violent to staff', adding: 'this is horrifying enough, but it is hard to be surprised since many children are just mirroring the behaviour of their parents'.[8] This sentiment is reinforced by John Dunford, General Secretary of the Association of School and College Leaders, who insists that 'in too many cases, the root cause of poor behaviour is a pupil's home life'.[9]

While some cast parents as the villains in the drama, others assign them the role of the saviours of education. In his capacity as Education Minister, Lord Adonis stated in August 2008 that more 'pushy parents' are required to force poor state schools to improve.[10] In March 2009, the British Government announced a scheme that would allow parents and pupils to use 'satisfaction ratings' to grade their schools.[11] Such calls for parental intervention are likely to reinforce the tendency for parents to vent their frustration on their children's schools, exacerbating the tensions that divide adult society without doing anything to improve the quality of schooling.

In passing, it is worth noting that parents are no less culpable than any other constituency of adults in pointing the finger of blame. Too often, parents adopt the role of their child's advocate and regard a teacher's criticism of their child as a slight on themselves. Instead of reinforcing and supporting the teacher's authority, parents inadvertently undermine it. Indeed, one of the most disturbing symptoms of the erosion of a sense of adult solidarity is an apparent lack of inhibition on the part of parents about criticizing teachers in front of their children. Such negative remarks undermine the authority, not only of the teacher, but of all adults.

Instead of representing a call for the assumption of adult responsibility, the 'blame game' often expresses an attempt to evade such obligations. Petty, divisive squabbles indicate that adults are not prepared to work together and assume a common responsibility towards the younger generations. Although most thinking people are concerned about the challenge of managing inter-generational relations, this is rarely conceptualized as a problem that needs to be addressed in its own right. Attitudes on this matter tend to be sectional – parents want school to exercise more authority and discipline, while teachers and politicians lecture mothers and fathers about their responsibilities. Such a narrow sectional approach does little to help revitalize an inter-generational conversation.

In debates about education, the concept of adult responsibility is rarely acknowledged as a significant issue, yet it influences virtually every aspect of formal education. Indeed, it appears that the very expansion of formal education can be understood as an attempt to occupy the territory vacated by the retreat of adult authority. So a recent review of primary education in England noted that schools need to respond to an ever-growing range of social problems, since 'society at large does not always live up to and exemplify the standards of behaviour it expects of its children'.[12] This call for taking an interest in the personal development of children is justified on the ground that 'society at large' is not setting a right example to young people. Yet schools can play only a limited role to make up for the failure of adult society to do this. The aim of this book is not to condemn the conduct of individual adults, because the problem lies with the inability of society as a whole to give meaning to the exercise of generational responsibility.

Sadly there is little public acknowledgement of the fact that the exercise of adult responsibility enjoys little cultural affirmation. Instead of explicitly addressing how to conduct an inter-generational conversation, society has sought to by-pass the issue by looking to motivational techniques and pedagogic expertise for a solution. Some of the gimmicks used to motivate children convey a sense of desperation. Some schools offer prizes such as iPods and game consoles to children who promise to behave. And when bribes fail to motivate, schools rely on professional crowd controllers, employing 'bouncers' to maintain order in the school.[13] The constant search for a substitute for adult authority is one of the main drivers of the expansion of the institution of education.

Education has become the repository of adult society's problems, and this is one reason why its role has expanded so dramatically. Unfortunately, schools do not possess the magical powers to fix the problems that have been assigned to them. Motivational techniques and pedagogic expertise cannot compensate for the ambiguous manner in which grown-ups in the twenty-first century exercise their authority. Worse still, through expanding the remit of education, the job of teaching becomes further complicated. When education becomes everything, it ceases to be education. Education needs to be saved from those who want to turn it into an all-purpose institution for solving the problems of society.

## Confusing the symptom of the crisis with its cause

There is little agreement about what issue constitutes the fundamental problem of education. There is widespread concern about the inability of schools to do very much about the apparent 'under-achievement' of children coming from poor or marginalized communities, but others claim that teachers spend far too much time indulging 'social misfits' and overlook the needs of 'bright' children.[14] Some policy-makers are worried about both the under-achievement of the economically disadvantaged and the lack of stimulation for the high achievers. School standards are a perennial subject of controversy. Critics lament the phenomenon of dumbing down while government officials insist that policies 'have helped to raise standards to an all-time high'.[15] Apprehensions about school discipline are widespread and, unlike the question of standards, nobody pretends that discipline is getting better.

Education and its meaning has always been a source of dispute. Should education be for its own sake? Is it right for schools to indoctrinate children with religious and national values? How much responsibility should schools assume for the socialization of children? Is the aim of the education to prepare children for the world of work? Such questions have been raised and re-raised through the centuries, so it is not surprising that the twenty-first-century public continues to argue about the meaning and aim of education. What is new, and in many ways unprecedented, is that the contemporary discussion of education is not confined to a debate on the basics but touches upon virtually every aspect of schooling. In recent times arguments about schooling have extended into an ever-expanding variety of specialized concerns. Even pedagogic matters to do with which techniques are most effective for teaching children to read, the role of assessments, exams and inspections, or the content of the curriculum, have become constant topics of debate.

Heated arguments about policy, pedagogy and the ethos of schooling are symptomatic of a culture where far too many of society's preoccupations and anxieties are refracted through education. Unfortunately such arguments rarely clarify matters. Invariably they tend to focus on the symptoms and confuse it with their cause. One of the key points argued in this book is that the different symptoms – unsatisfactory standards, confusions regarding the curriculum, uncertainties about how to socialize young people, lack of clarity about how to enforce discipline – are the outcome of a more fundamental problem, which is that of adult authority. As I argue in succeeding chapters, it is the reluctance of contemporary society to value and affirm the exercise of adult authority that undermines our capacity to develop the potential of the young people. Without the valuation of adult authority, much of teachers' hard work and effort and society's resources are wasted.

The ambiguous status enjoyed by the exercise of adult authority has a negative influence on education in five important respects:

1. The authority of adults is inextricably linked to the status enjoyed by the experience of the past. Historically their authority was, in no small part, based upon their capacity to transmit the legacy of human knowledge and cultural achievements. The ambiguous status of adulthood has fostered a mood where their knowledge, and the authority of academic subjects, is frequently called into question by educational experts. One unfortunate outcome of this process has been the growth of pedagogical

beliefs and practices that self-consciously question the status of subject-based knowledge, leading to the downsizing of academic learning in the school curriculum. Many policy-makers and curriculum engineers argue that learning from current experience is more rewarding than the study of subject-based knowledge. They often dismiss academic subject-based knowledge as 'narrow' and call for the 'broadening out' of the curriculum.

2. Paradoxically, although education is celebrated continually in our so-called 'knowledge society', the authority of formal schooling and education is questioned implicitly by policy-makers and curriculum engineers. The formal is often contrasted favourably with informal forms of learning. The widely acclaimed notion of 'lifelong learning' is presented often as a demonstration of the seriousness with which education should be taken. But, through recycling education as a lifelong project, the relative weight accorded to the formal education of the young diminishes. Indeed, some advocates of lifelong learning describe the education of children as the 'front-end model of learning' to signify that there are other potentially better models of learning. Implicitly, and sometimes explicitly, the authority of formal education is called into question.

3. The erosion of adult authority in general has a direct impact on the status of the teacher. During the past quarter-century the professional status of the teacher has undergone important modifications. Since the very term 'teacher' conveys a sense of authority, this term has come into question. There is a growing tendency to refer to all members of a school – teachers and pupils – as 'learners'. Many pedagogues insist that instead of acting as authority figures, teachers should assume the role of facilitators. The devaluation of the authority of the teacher is also reinforced through the loss of value accorded to subject-based knowledge. Many pedagogues regard the teaching of academic subjects in schools as irrelevant. Since the authority of teachers rests on their expertise in a subject, the current devaluation of academic subjects has a direct effect upon teachers'

professional status. The cumulative outcome of these developments is the decline of the status of the teaching profession.

4. Confusions surrounding the role and status of adult authority have led to a loss of confidence in society's ability to socialize the younger generations. The loss of authority undermines the claim that adults have something important to transmit to the younger generations. This crisis of adult authority frequently is experienced as an inability to communicate a shared system of norms and values with clarity and conviction. Often schools are charged with the task of taking responsibility for the socialization of their pupils, and it sometimes appears that schools are expected to find solutions to problems for which the wider society has no answer. As a result, the problems of society are frequently confused with that of education. It appears that as adult authority diminishes, the role of the school expands – particularly in the domain of socialization.

5. The confusions surrounding the exercise of adult authority have undermined authoritative forms of discipline. Since there is little cultural affirmation for the exercise of adult authority, schools and teachers are overwhelmed by a sense of disorientation when it comes to the maintenance of classroom discipline. The loss of nerve about the management of classroom discipline has become palpable. In many instances, teachers indicate that they are 'at risk' from the aggressive behaviour of young children – never mind teenagers. One observer has commented that 'adults are suffering from ephebiphobia – fear of young people'.[16]

Of the five trends outlined above, the only one that constitutes a topic for public concern is that of discipline. Issues like bullying, truancy and antisocial behaviour are difficult for society to ignore. Unfortunately, the question of discipline tends to be discussed in its more dramatic and violent manifestations. Discipline is not just about managing bad behaviour – it has a creative dimension in the cultivation and disciplining of young people's taste and sensibilities. The internalization of the habit of discipline encourages habits and attitudes that help children gain a sense of independence and self-mastery. Fundamental questions that bear upon the disciplining influence of academic and intellectual learning and of the formality of schooling are overlooked in the current public conversation on this subject.

Many of the current educational policies and pedagogic practices represent a semi-conscious attempt to compensate for, or evade, the difficulties surrounding the exercise of adult authority. Within teaching itself there is an emphasis on inventing motivational techniques that can by-pass this difficult question, and the new pedagogic vocabulary is full of terms that articulate an accommodation to the decline of adult authority. Terms like 'learning to learn', 'reflective learning', 'lifelong learning', 'e-learning' or 'experiential learning' signal a shift in emphasis from teaching to learning, and a shift in authority from teacher to learner. Although these terms touch on different dimensions of learning, they all communicate a common aspiration to promote and uphold a form of learning that does not depend on the authoritative leadership of a teacher. As an important study of this trend reminds us, 'all these pedagogic strategies can be seen as strands of an attempt to suppress hierarchy, or at least render it invisible'.[17]

The pedagogic project of suppressing hierarchy is often mis-interpreted as a move towards a more democratic way of managing education. Many schools claim that they are in the business of providing students with an opportunity to voice their views. Policy-makers also advocate the institutionalization of the student voice and sometimes transmit the idea that adult authority is no big deal. These initiatives are inspired by an ethos that is devoted to the project of motivating students in ways that are not reliant on authoritative adult behaviour, often through the use of behaviour management techniques. One of the unfortunate consequences of this approach is that its focus on motivation is at the expense of the content of the curriculum. As I note in Chapters 6 and 7, many of the motivational and behaviour management techniques used in schools foster an anti-intellectual climate in the classroom. One government-commissioned report, published in April 2009, proposed that teachers should try to hold their students' attention through adopting techniques from popular contemporary television quiz shows.[18]

The motivation of students in educational settings has always represented a significant challenge to schools. Historically, students become motivated to learn through a combination of different factors. Experience of life and the desire to improve one's life chances has often served to motivate children to take their education seriously. Within the school it is the authoritative guidance and, in some cases, the inspiration provided by teachers that has helped to motivate young people. The aspiration to learn and the motivation to study are outcomes of family and community influence and the authoritative leadership provided by schools and teachers. Motivational techniques are useful tools for encouraging students but, on their own, are rarely successful in fostering an effective learning environment. More to the point, the tendency to conceptualize motivation as a problem in its own right often leads to a one-sided reliance on techniques and gimmicks that distract children from engaging with a challenging curriculum. For example, in recent years, attempts to utilize information technology to capture the interests of pupils have failed to motivate the classroom. Nevertheless a recent review of primary education in England concludes that 'one highly promising route to meeting the demand for in-depth teaching and learning is undoubtedly emerging through ICT' (information and communication technologies).[19] The ease with which this report makes a conceptual leap from the need for in-depth teaching to ICT is testimony to the triumph of technique over the content of education

More worryingly, the pedagogy of 'motivation' often contributes to a deterioration of the academic ethos of a school, as well as to its standards of discipline. It encourages a culture where the question of how to keep children interested overrides the issue of what is the content of education that must be taught. For example, many curriculum engineers take the view that since it is not possible to motivate children to read books it is preferable to show them DVDs or give them simple worksheets. Recently Michael Rosen, the

Children's Laureate of England, noted that many pupils are going through their formative years in school without reading a single novel. He denounced the practice of giving children short extracts on worksheets as 'absurd' and 'pathetic'.[20] My own interviews with children aged seven to eleven confirm Rosen's concerns. Many schools have almost given up on the idea that children – especially boys – can acquire a love of reading. Recently a group of Dutch teachers complained to me about the way in which 'worksheet culture' alienates children from the world of books.

The imperative of motivation also has a corrosive impact on teacher–pupil relations in school. In January 2009, Ofsted, the regulatory authority for schools,  announced that it would crack down on 'boring' teachers, in response to concerns that the deterioration of pupils' behaviour was due to their lack of stimulation in class. Christine Gilbert, the Chief Inspector of Schools, justified this crackdown on the grounds that 'there was strong evidence' that there is a strong 'link between boredom and achievement'.[21] Every reader will have encountered a 'boring' teacher in their school years and understands that a state of tedium is not a desirable feature of school life. However, at a time when there is a manifest shortage of teachers who can teach maths, sciences, grammar or foreign languages, the focus on boring educators reveals a narrow-minded orientation. Another inane idea of Ofsted's is that it should write to children about their teacher's strengths and weaknesses. In one school, pupils as young as four received a letter from Ofsted which informed them that 'we have told your teachers they must try harder'.[22] The desperation with which the mission of motivation is pursued sometimes acquires a grotesque caricature. In some cases children are offered money or gifts to stay in school or to study for exams.[23]

Whether we like it or not, it is not always possible to motivate every student, and episodes of boredom are a normal feature of children's lives. When responsible adults hear a child say 'I am bored', they will not respond by transforming themselves into a clown. So too in education. The current one-sided obsession with motivation overlooks the fact that children too are responsible for their education. Chris Keates, the General Secretary of the National

Association of Schoolmasters Union of Women Teachers (NASUWT), was to the point when she responded to Christine Gilbert by stating that the 'chief inspector fuels the view that every lesson of every day for every minute has got to be packed with excitement, and education isn't like that'. On a more ominous note, she added that 'comments like this make teachers fair game for everyone, including pupils'.[24]

## The infantilization of education

Pedagogy, the science of teaching, should always be engaged in developing practices that promote students' enthusiasm for learning. However, the effectiveness of such practices depends on the authoritative leadership of educators. One of the ways in which adult society becomes conscious of the challenge it faces in exercising authority is through the difficulties it has in gaining the respect of the young. Parents and teachers can readily see this when young people respond positively to their guidance and embrace their ideas. That is why the problem of adult authority is frequently experienced as a motivational crisis. Uninterested pupils serve as reminders of the ineffectiveness of adult leadership. A current symptom of this crisis in education is the one-sided preoccupation with bored children.

The feeble valuation of adult authority indirectly leads to a disturbing loss of belief in children's capacity to engage with challenging experiences. In education the assumption that children need constant motivation has encouraged the institutionalization of a pedagogy that tends to infantilize them. Many pedagogues claim that children need to be taught material that is directly relevant and accessible to them. Too often children are treated childishly by educators who assume that playing is the ideal vehicle for learning. Back in the 1930s the American educational theorist Michael Demiashkevich warned that making mud-pies and dressing dolls were great kindergarten activities but 'the kindergarten must not be permitted to extend its domination over the secondary school and college'.[25] But in the twenty-first century the utilization of childish pedagogic techniques is no longer confined to the nursery. As we note in Chapter 7, role playing and a reliance on therapeutic techniques are increasingly used throughout the system of education.

The tendency to infantilize children even influences the way in which schools manage children's play. According to the prevailing wisdom, children are defined by their vulnerability and are characterized as 'at risk' from virtually everything.[26] Consequently, schools worry about the risks associated with playing and in some cases try to regulate children's physical activity carefully. In recent times many primary schools have drawn the conclusion that contact sports, and especially competitive sports, are not suitable activities for their pupils. In August 2008, Prime Minister Gordon Brown announced that the nation needed to have more competitive sports at school. He argued that his government had begun to 'correct the tragic mistake of reducing the competitive element in school'. However, his announcement is unlikely to undermine the powerful cultural crusade against children's aspiration to compete against one another. The ideals associated with a sporting ethos are bitterly opposed by a formidable army of educators, psychologists and health professionals who contend that competition threatens the emotional well-being of children. According to this view, children who fail to come first suffer long-term trauma and their self-esteem risks becoming damaged for life.

Many schools have introduced so-called 'co-operative games' in which there are no losers. Anti-competition campaigners advocate a carefully managed form of therapeutic sporting education for children. They believe that children gain great psychological benefits from co-operative sport since everybody receives applause and gains in self-esteem. In reality, children gain nothing from the manufactured forms of tokenistic rituals that accompany such emotionally correct gestures. When every child receives a prize for 'trying their best', the youngsters readily see through it. Even at an early age they understand that when nobody loses, nobody wins.

In part the attempt to immunize children from the experience of losing serves as an alternative to motivating them. To put it bluntly, many educators have drawn the conclusion that 'if you can't motivate them, at least make them feel good about themselves'.

Supporters of the therapeutic turn of education also subscribe to the illusion that if children are happy they are likely to feel motivated to learn. Experience shows that the project of abolishing failure in school infantilizes children and actually undermines their capacity to deal with the challenges they face.

Schools have become wedded to the idea that praising children and boosting their self-esteem is critical to children's well-being. The promotion of self-esteem has acquired the character of a crusade to the point that criticizing children is deemed to be 'bad practice'. Recently Dr Carol Craig, who is Chief Executive of the Centre for Confidence and Well-being in Scotland, has conceded that youngsters were being over-praised and had developed an 'all about me' mentality. She noted that 'parents no longer want to hear if their children had done anything wrong' and resent any criticism of their children. Most important of all, Craig warned that the self-esteem agenda has a detrimental impact on children's education. She stated that 'we are kidding ourselves if we think that we aren't going to undermine learning if we restrict criticism'.[27]

The tendency to treat children as vulnerable and fragile individuals has the perverse effect of discouraging children to develop their resilience and capacity to cope. Experience indicates that artificial attempts to boost children's self-esteem do not make them more confident, and that therapeutic education diminishes children's ability to deal with pressure. Time and again reports and surveys indicate that children are under more pressure today than ever before.[28] What these surveys actually mean is that children have become de-educated from being able to deal with difficult circumstances. To a considerable extent, children have been socialized to perceive pressure as a marker for a disease.

Whenever youngsters' existential insecurity is treated as a potential mental health problem, it is likely that this will encourage them to feel powerless and ill. Children fed on a diet of empty praise, who are rarely challenged and even more rarely forced to confront their failures, are poorly prepared to tackle the tests of life. Even relatively banal episodes will be experienced as a source of emotional disorientation. For example, during the past decade the transition from

primary to secondary school has been represented as a major traumatic event for children. Instead of depicting the process of starting
big school as an exciting experience, many children are offered
transitional counselling for what has been regarded as a normal
dimension of life for centuries. Transitional counselling, like many
forms of therapy, has a habit of turning into a self-fulfilling prophecy.
Once children pick up on the idea that going to secondary school is
a traumatic experience, many of them will interpret their normal
anxieties and insecurities through a psychological vocabulary. The
result is that a growing number of children reinterpret their anxieties
in pathological terms and become disoriented. One symptom of this
malaise is the growing number of referrals for a recently invented
condition called 'school phobia'.[29] Most grown-ups can recall numerous occasions when, as children, they felt that they hated school;
but today, children no longer hate school – they suffer from school
phobia. The addiction to diagnosing young people's anxious
response to the trials of life continues well into higher education. In
universities, students who are anxious about sitting for their exams
are diagnosed as suffering from 'examination syndrome'.

The tendency to infantilize education is not restricted to the
promiscuous distribution of smiley faces in the classroom or the
institutionalization of therapeutic rituals. As I note in Chapter 6, it
also influences both the teaching and the content of the curriculum.

## The paradox of education

The infantilization of education coincides with what appears at first
sight to be a contradictory tendency: that we take the institution
of education more seriously than ever before. In recent years, education has been the beneficiary of an ever-expanding expenditure
of financial resources, and the government is continually banking
on the capacity of this institution to deliver a range of positive outcomes. But paradoxically, the more that we expect of education,
the less we expect of children; and the more hope society invests
in education, the less we value it as something important in its own
right.

Throughout the western world, the education of children has become a continual source of concern to policy-makers and the media. Nobody complained when former Prime Minister Tony Blair told the 1996 Labour Party Conference that his three top priorities on coming to office were 'education, education and education'. Four years later, Blair still felt the need constantly to repeat the word 'education' when he promised that his 'government's passion' would be 'education, education, education'. Such zealous commitment to the cause of education is also constantly repeated in policy documents throughout Europe. An historian looking back on our time a couple of centuries from now may well infer that education was a dominant faith that inspired the European cultural elite in the twenty-first century.

Yet despite all the importance that newspaper headlines attach to education, it is not at all evident what is meant by this phenomenon. Indeed, it appears that the more that society talks about education, the less it is able to affirm education as a value in its own right. Education is frequently praised for its potential contribution to economic development, and upheld as a central instrument for encouraging social inclusion and mobility. People insist that education can promote values such as multiculturalism and environmental awareness. It often appears that the celebration of education has little to do with any integral qualities. Instead, education is interpreted as a means for achieving an objective that is separate and distinct from itself. That is what Tony Blair meant when in a speech on urban regeneration he insisted that education is 'now the centre of economic policy making for the future'.[30]

Numerous observers have criticized the tendency to treat education as a means for realizing economic objectives. Some have questioned the belief that money invested in education leads to a rise in economic efficiency and productivity.[31] Others take objection to the instrumental manner with which education is treated. In recent times numerous commentators have warned about the danger of perceiving education as an all-purpose policy instrument for solving the diverse problems facing society. 'We cannot deliver all the high expectations heaped upon us by society', argued Jane

Lees, President of the Association of School and College Leaders, in 2009.[32]

Many well-meaning people fervently believe in the capacity of education to minimize or overcome social differences and inequalities. Policy-makers and reformers believe that education is a powerful instrument of social mobility that will provide opportunities for people to improve their life chances and narrow social inequality. No doubt there are many individuals who have benefited enormously from their education and enjoy a social status that their parents could only dream of. However, research suggests that the institution of education has played only a limited role in promoting the mobility of children from poor families or from a working-class background. The constant expansion of the institution of education has led to the growth in educational attainment of people from all sections of society, but this growth in terms of credentials does not necessarily make people more mobile.[33] Expanding educational opportunities is a worthy objective in its own right but it 'cannot be used, on its own, to eradicate social inequalities'.[34]

Of course there is nothing novel or wrong about attempting to harness the potential of education to realize wider social and economic objectives. What is relatively novel and profoundly disturbing is that the mantra of 'education, education, education' coincides with a palpable sense of indifference to its content. Education is rarely upheld for its own sake, and all too often pragmatic interests and concerns are allowed to undermine the integrity of different school subjects. All too often the content of education has become negotiable. Frequently it appears that the political imperative of solving society's problems overrides the educational needs of young people. In many instances the problem of society is confused with that of education, and the school curriculum becomes a battlefield where the conflicting claims of competing interest groups are fought out.

The politicization of education even impacts on subjects such as physical education and music. Take the example of the UK's *Music Manifesto*. This manifesto is not so much about celebrating music as it is about using music to help realize a variety of social policy objectives. The imperative of social engineering leads the authors of the manifesto to proclaim: 'The time is ripe for a *Music Manifesto*.' Apparently the time is ripe because 'there is an increasing belief in the power of music to contribute to whole school development and community regeneration'. In other words, music is a useful tool for motivating people to buy into the agenda of policy-makers. Music is judged and evaluated by how well it contributes to community cohesion and economic development.

The tendency to confuse the problem of society with that of education creates the risk that schools become distracted from getting on with the task of cultivating the intellectual and moral outlook of children. A classroom that is subjected to the dictates of a policy agenda is very different from one devoted to inculcating a love and habit of learning. When education is perceived as providing an answer to everything, its distinct role and meaning become unclear.

In principle, education can serve as a vehicle for many different objectives. Some societies have relied on schools to help forge a distinct national identity and culture. Schools have been used to train young people for the world of work and for assuming their role in adult society. Schools have been used as centres of indoctrination by highly motivated ideologues. Schools have always been charged with carrying out activities that were motivated by the wider agenda of society. However, although education can be about many different activities, at a fundamental level it needs to be valued in its own terms. Education works when it is perceived as important in its own right and when children are taught to value learning for its own sake.

The paradox of education is that the more we expect of it, the less it is valued for its own sake. The reason for this paradox is that the main drivers of the expansion of education are motivated by objectives that are external to it. Strictly speaking, the idea that education is in crisis is inaccurate. As an institution, education has never enjoyed so much cultural and political support. Its social weight and economic role is on the increase and more and more people spend a greater amount of their life in educational institutions than in previous times. As the educational theorist Rob Moore argues, the crisis of education is 'specifically a crisis of *liberal–humanist education*'.[35]

A liberal–humanist education can be interpreted in a variety of ways, but fundamentally it is based on the conviction that education is important in and of itself. It has an intrinsic worth, and education is its aim rather than a means to another objective.

The statement that education is important for its own sake is not an appeal to some snobbish sentiment about valuing ideas in the abstract. What it refers to is the valuation of cultural accomplishments through which society renews itself and acquires the intellectual and moral resources necessary to understand itself and face the future.

In current times, the liberal–humanist ethos of education is often dismissed as an out-of-date elitist idea that is totally removed from the realities of the real world. Even in universities, the ideal of pursuing knowledge for its own sake is rejected as a pathetic expression of medieval prejudice. Education is endowed with the mission of fixing pressing practical problems. Many educators dismiss the liberal–humanist approach as inappropriate for the schooling of youngsters on the grounds that they are unlikely to be motivated by the love of ideas. What these criticisms imply is a marked preference for activities that are educational in form but not in content.

Yet experience indicates that the alleged benefits of a more practical and problem-fixing schooling are more apparent than real. Research and debate around the so-called 'education effect' finds it difficult to identify a specific causal link between levels and types of schooling and economic or social outcomes. A lack of consensus about the education effect is not surprising, since it is one of many other variables that influence economic and social life. Of course education does have an effect – a very important one, to do with its impact on individuals and communities – but this effect is intangible. The principal achievement of education is an educated people and society. My argument is that a significant portion of the resources and energies devoted to the institution of education is wasted when society loses sight of the importance of young people's education as an intrinsically worthwhile activity. Wasted opportunities, wasted potential and wasted youth are symptomatic of adult society's inability to give meaning to its authority and education.

# 1

# *Throwaway Pedagogy*

Politicians love to fiddle with the workings of the education system. It's September 2009, the start of a new school year and yet again teachers are confronted with a stream of new policies that affect their lives. As usual the curriculum has been reviewed and changed, as has the system of national exams. In England, pupils who started secondary schools in September 2008 were the first cohort to be legally required to stay in school until they are 17. The government has also introduced major changes to the curriculum for 11- to 14-year-olds as well as new diplomas for subjects such as construction and engineering. Since more than 20 major education acts have been introduced by successive governments in the previous 20 years it is not surprising that leading teachers complain that it is almost impossible to keep up with the constant stream of new policies that impact on their lives. John Dunford, the head of the Association of School and College Leaders, noted that the 'very last thing schools and colleges need is more change'. He added that 'heads and principals are weary of this annual treadmill of education bills and need time to implement the legislation that is already in the statute books'.[1]

One of the most striking symptoms of society's obsession with education is the speed with which new policies are introduced, implemented and then modified or withdrawn. The compulsion to invent new policies and initiatives dominates the educational landscape. Since 1987 the government department responsible for education in England has changed five times. What was once simply the Department for Education has now excised the word 'education' altogether, and its role is split between the Department for Children, Schools and Families, and the Department for Innovation, Universities and Skills. In the UK this addiction towards hyper-policy-making has acquired a pathological character. Some educators are so hooked on innovation that they constantly demand even more. We need an 'education epidemic' which can 'catch on quickly throughout the system' argued the educationalist Professor David Hargreaves. His pamphlet *Education Epidemic*, published by the think-tank Demos, suggests that the problem is not too much change but too little.[2] On a more ominous note Hargreaves stated that change needs to be an 'open-ended process' and warned that 'the most important characteristics of this process are not yet clear'.[3]

Since the 1980s the doctrine that the system of education requires radical alteration has been echoed by leading experts and policy-makers. Back in 2003, this obeisance to the paradigm of chaotic change was advanced forcefully by former Prime Minister Tony Blair when he stated that 'piecemeal change is not enough to build a first-class education system for London'. He added that 'radical structural reform is essential, not only to raise standards in existing schools, but to reshape the system around diversity, choice and the new specialist principle'.[4]

The principal justification for the constant demand for the incessant transformation of education is the claim that schools and universities risk becoming irrelevant to people living in a rapidly changing world. Virtually every policy initiative in the domain of education is prefaced with the remark that we live in a rapidly changing world. Change is frequently represented as an omnipotent force that, by its very nature, renders prevailing forms of knowledge and schooling redundant. In such circumstances education has no choice but to transform itself to keep up with the times. From this perspective educational policies can only be justified if they can keep up with or adapt to change. Since they are likely to be overtaken swiftly by events, such policies have a short-term and provisional status. So a report advocating 'personalizing learning' observes that the 'education system is already changing in response to the challenges of the twenty-first century', but adds that 'this will and must continue, testing ways in which the challenges of a still uncertain future can be tackled'.[5] The instability that afflicts the education system is turned into the normal state of an institution that needs to be responsive to the uncertain flow of events. As former Schools' Minister Estelle Morris writes: 'We've become used to change over the past 20 years and it's probably fair to say that there's been more of it in these two decades than in any other', adding that 'it's not just that schools are different; the attitudes and expectations of parents, politicians and wider society have changed as well'.[6]

Constant change is not merely portrayed as a fact of life that educationalists need to live with, it is also upheld as the decisive influence on the school curriculum. Charles Clarke, a former Secretary of State for Education and Skills, directly linked his party's pedagogic preferences to ideas that emerged from change. He wrote that:

> Over the last 60 years, a fundamental recasting of industry, employment, technology and society has transformed the requirement for education and training – not only driving the education system, but introducing new ideas about lifelong learning, personalised education, and self-directed learning.[7]

In the worldview of the educational establishment, change has acquired a sacred and divine-like character that determines what is taught and what is learned. It creates new 'requirements' and 'introduces' new ideas about learning. And it encourages the mass production of an easily disposable pedagogy.

## The fetishization of change

Typically change is presented in a dramatic and mechanistic manner that exaggerates the novelty of the present moment. Educationalists frequently adopt the rhetoric of breaks and ruptures and maintain that nothing is as it was and that the present has been decoupled from the past. Their outlook is shaped by an imagination that is so overwhelmed by the displacement of the old by the new that it often overlooks important dimensions of historical experience that may

continue to be relevant to our lives. The discussion of the relationship between education and change is frequently overwhelmed by
the fad of the moment and with the relatively superficial symptoms
of new developments. It is often distracted from acknowledging that
the fundamental educational needs of students do not alter every
time a new technology impacts on people's lives. And certainly the
questions raised by Greek philosophy, Renaissance poetry, Enlightenment science or the novels of George Eliot continue to be relevant
for students in our time and not just to the period that preceded the
Digital Age.

Policy documents on education conceptualize change as the principal influence on the curriculum. From their perspective the design
of the curriculum is less influenced by any intellectually driven logic
than by amorphous influence of change. So the English Qualifications and Curriculum Authority (QCA) argues that it 'has to be
forward looking and responsive to the forces shaping the future of
education and schooling'. Indeed the QCA has become so responsive
that it upholds its willingness to respond as its core achievement.[8]
Typically for QCA the ability to respond far outweighs the values
and the intellectual orientation with which the future is to be
engaged.

Often change and social transformation is represented as if it is
a unique feature of our time, a phenomenon that never happened
previously. Assuming a portentous demeanour, the innovation guru
Bill Law makes this pronouncement: 'We may not know precisely
what shape the future will take, but we do know that the futures of
our current students will not much resemble those of our past
ones.'[9] But when did we last think that the future of our children
will resemble our own? Certainly not in 1969, nor in 1939 or even
1909.

Policy documents continually repeat the refrain that 'we live in
an age where the pace of change is more rapid than at any time in
history'.[10] This rhetoric of unprecedented change is just that:
rhetoric. It is not a conclusion that is based on a careful evaluation
of the way societies have experienced change in the past. In a mechanistic way this approach divides the world into two periods – the

past where either nothing or very little changed, and the current moment when change is incessant. Consequently, deliberation about the problems of twenty-first-century education is afflicted by a disturbing mood of historical amnesia. The insistence that our current experience of global change is unprecedented is all the more surprising since literally the very same argument has been a recurrent theme in pedagogic debates for over a century.

The proposition that we live in an era of unprecedented change has acquired the character of a timeless formula which is constantly offered as an argument for 'reforming' schooling and for altering how and what is taught in the classroom.

'But we should not forget why reform is right', stated Tony Blair in 1998 before reminding his audience yet again that 'the system must change because the world has changed beyond the recognition of Beveridge's generation'.[11] The world may have indeed changed since the publication of the Beveridge Report on education in 1944 but it is useful to recall that, even in the early part of the twentieth century, the refrain that 'the world has changed' was used to promote the cause of transforming schooling. Even before the outbreak of the Second World War the fetishization of change had a widespread presence in pedagogy. At the turn of the twentieth century the renowned American philosopher of education, John Dewey, echoed Blair's judgement about the magnitude of social and economic change. In an essay published in 1902 his argument for educational reforms rested on his diagnosis of rapid change, which led to the 'relaxation of social discipline and control' but also to the expansion of knowledge and technological innovation.[12]

During the succeeding decades, the argument that the world was constantly changing became the foundational premise for educational reform. As an important study of the history of American school reforms noted, 'The case for changing the curriculum has been the same since the beginning of the twentieth century: society is changing, and the schools must change too.'[13] The pedagogue, Michael Demiashkevich, writing in the 1930s, characterized the advocates of this dogma as neo-Heracliteans, who, like the Greek philosopher Heraclitus, insisted that change was the only constant in life. Heraclitus, who put forward the proposition that 'you could not step twice into the same river', insisted that change was the only reality. Heraclitus' thesis of ceaseless change continues to enjoy the status of a foundational truth in much of modern pedagogy.

Demiashkevich asserted that the neo-Heraclitean perspective leads to 'an exaggerated degree of pedagogical chaos'.[14] Sadly his prognosis of what he characterized as 'organised pedagogical anarchy' would turn out to be an accurate representation of events. By the 1960s an advocate of educational reform would self-consciously entitle his book *Technology and Change: The New Heraclitus*. Its author Donald Schön, one of the leading early theorists of the idea of a learning society and of lifelong learning, noted that the 'loss of the stable state means that our society and all of its institutions are in a *continuous* process of transformation'.[15] In 1972, when UNESCO issued its influential report *Learning to Be*, change was depicted as an autonomous and dramatic force that would render formal education increasingly obsolete and irrelevant. It predicted that 'progress in human knowledge and power, which has assumed such dizzying speed over the past twenty years, is only in its early stages' and that future prospects were at once 'exalting' and 'terrifying'.[16] Leading educationalists embraced the ideas contained in *Learning to Be* and concluded that schooling needed to be radically transformed if it was to keep up with the dizzying speed of change. According to one account, 'the central question to which we repeatedly return' is 'whether schools and colleges and universities can learn to adapt themselves rapidly enough to the changing world around them to avoid becoming, like the dinosaur, museum pieces'.[17]

Since the 1980s, but especially the 1990s, the attachment of educational policy to the fetish of change has acquired the form of an unquestioned dogma. Policy-makers and educators self-consciously transmit a restless sense of confusion and disorder. 'We stand on the brink of a new age' cautioned former Secretary of State for Education and Employment, David Blunkett. He continued his Heraclitean interpretation of the future by declaring that 'familiar certainties and old ways of doing things are disappearing'.[18] Through projecting a future of unrelenting uncertainty, British policy-makers and their experts present the task of dealing with this chaos as the main challenge faced by schools. As Tom Bentley, a leading New Labour adviser, noted in 1998, 'The main task of a contemporary education system is to prepare its students for a world in which there is less order, less predictability and more chaos, where old solutions are running up against complex, apparently insurmountable challenges.'[19] By the turn of the twenty-first century the language of chaos and uncertainty served as a main framework through which British educationalists interpreted the issues facing the classroom. 'The fact is that wherever we look – science, history, management, politics – systems are giving way to chaos' asserted Michael Barber, another educational adviser to the New Labour Government.[20]

## The flight from the past

The dramatization of change renders the past wholly irrelevant. If we continually move from one 'new age' to another then the institutions and practices of the past have little relevance for today. Indeed, the ceaseless repetition of the proposition that the past is irrelevant serves to desensitize people from understanding the influence of a legacy of human development on their lives. Of course the constant reiteration of an argument – decade after decade – should at the very least lead an inquiring mind to question just how novel is the latest version of the 'new age'. However, every new generation of school-reformers imagines that they face an unprecedented period of perpetual socio-economic transformation. Their neo-Heraclitean perspective invariably associates change with chaos and uncertainty.

The idea of ceaseless change tends to naturalize it and turn it into an omnipotent autonomous force that subjects human beings to its will. This is a force that annihilates the past and demands that people learn to adapt and readapt to radically new experiences. From this standpoint human beings do not so much make history as adapt to powerful forces beyond their control.

Although the narrative of change has gained the status of an incontrovertible truth, it is rarely supported by a conceptually elaborated argument. Indeed, the dramatization of change works mainly as a rhetorical device for signalling western society's estrangement from the legacy of its past. In previous times the perception of an accelerating pace of change encouraged a disposition to embrace the past. In the nineteenth century many people – especially those of a conservative sensibility – looked to the past as a source of security in an alien world. Although many still seek security through an embrace of old traditions, the dominant tendency in western societies is to flee from the past. This sensibility has been thoroughly assimilated into pedagogic policy which is continually fixated with novelty and innovation.

The association of the past with obsolescence is conveyed through a rhetorical strategy of naturalizing change. Through the naturalization of change, any educational policy that seeks to draw on the cultural resources of the past is ruled out of the question. Like the Thatcherite imperative of 'There Is No Alternative' (TINA), the objectification of change shuts down discussion of any alternative to the agenda of perpetual policy innovation. Staying still is not an option in a world where survival depends on the capacity to adapt. A phenomenon that works like an act of nature puts itself beyond debate. It can only be treated as a fact of life. From this standpoint the only educational policy that makes sense is one that can claim to keep up with change through helping people to adapt to it. 'In the discourses of professional development, change is said to be everywhere and we are urged to be prepared to deal with the uncertainties it engenders', contends a critical analysis of this rhetorical strategy.[21] It adds that 'the irony of this is that rhetorically change and uncertainty are positioned as certain'. In a world of uncertainty, one fact is certain – the inevitability of yet more change.

It is important to note that the fetishization of change offers a distinctively passive version of its true meaning. Policy-makers present change as a powerful and chaotic force that works at a relentless pace and beyond human control. The role assigned to educators is to keep up with it or at least not fall too far behind it. It not only decouples society from its past, it also turns the future into a strange, unpredictable territory. According to this fatalistic model, change is rarely the outcome of human intent, it is something that happens to people. So the role assigned to education is not to help people to make decisions about how to achieve desirable objectives, but to learn how to adapt to a force that is not of their making. This position was forcefully put by Dewey in 1897:

> With the advent of democracy and modern industrial conditions, it is impossible to foretell definitely just what civilization will be twenty years from now. Hence it is impossible to prepare the child for any precise set of conditions. To prepare him for the future means to give him command of himself; it means so to train him that he will have the full and ready use of all his capacities.[22]

This assessment of ceaseless change made over a century ago has been turned into the one eternal truth in a world where 'it is impossible to foretell' anything of great significance. One review of Dewey's work writes that his contribution has 'lost none of its point in the intervening hundred years'. Why? Because a 'democratic society must be a restless society; it must be an innovative society'.[23]

Calls to modernize, reform and innovate education often tend to mystify their objectives. The policies of modernization are usually unspecific about the agenda they are trying to achieve. This is not surprising since the imperative to modernize or reform does not arise from problems that are integral to the system of education. Frequently such policies represent a response to issues that are entirely external to the workings of schools and colleges. For example, the call to 'personalize' learning is not solely motivated by the concern that 'impersonal' learning impedes the work of schools: it is offered as a solution to countless problems that have been identified outside the school gates. A report promoting personalized learning points to the need for schools to respond to: an 'ethnically and socially diverse society'; 'far greater access to, and reliance on, technology'; a 'knowledge based economy', with 'demanding employers'; a 'sharper focus on sustainability'; and 'complex pathways through education and training'.[24]

Calls for educational reform are often couched in a dramatic language that appeals to the instinct of economic survival. Warnings about the economic consequences of being left adrift in an increasingly complex and technologically innovative world provide the main rationale for reform. According to a study of the 'epidemic' of school reforms, the necessity for new education policy is 'largely cast in economic terms and particularly in relation to the preparation of a workforce and competition with other countries'.[25] That is why the problems associated with schooling are frequently interpreted as a threat to economic welfare and prosperity rather than to the intellectual life of society.

## The authority of the new

The rhetorical dissolution of society's relationship to the past is fuelled by the search for new forms of authority. Authoritative institutions and traditions in western society have been contested for some time. However, it is only in recent decades that the political and cultural elites have become so cut off and estranged from their own past. In such circumstances there is a temptation to perceive historical change as simply one of discontinuity and breaks with previous experience. The tendency to obliterate important continuities with previous experience is rhetorically expressed through a succession of 'post-' terms. Words like 'post-industrial', 'post-modern' or 'post-material' signify a new world that has left the old one behind. This cult of novelty dominates official thinking on education. Terms like 'knowledge economy', 'information age' and 'learning society' convey the idea of a world where education needs to confront issues that are unfamiliar and qualitatively different from the past.

Hannah Arendt described the tendency to elevate the sense of historical discontinuity as the 'pathos of the new'. The argument that society is fundamentally different from the past creates its own demand for new policies and institutions. That is why so many educationalists who assert that we live in a new kind of society conclude that a new approach to education is needed. There may be a difference of opinion about which policy should be introduced, but there is agreement on the fundamental principle that it has to be new. This attachment to the novel leads to what Cambridge education theorist Rob Moore has called the 'tradition of the new'. He argues convincingly that 'the strategy of discontinuity, of schism, the rejection of tradition, is itself a tradition'.[26] An example of the eternal truths associated with the tradition of the new is Dewey's 1897 statement about lack of continuity between the present and the future which meant that it was impossible to prepare children for the future. This vision of discontinuity has turned into a pedagogic truth that has almost a sacred status. In education policy the celebration of discontinuity has become something of a tradition. From this perspective the call for an epidemic of new policies makes perfect sense.

The thesis that we inhabit a new kind of society usually rests on the claim that economic change has fundamentally altered the world we inhabit. The highly publicized 1983 report, *A Nation At Risk*, published by the National Commission on Excellence in Education is paradigmatic in this respect.[27] It warned the American public that 'history is not kind to idlers' and that the nation was literally 'at risk'. It observed that 'our once unchallenged pre-eminence in commerce, industry, science, and technological innovation is being overtaken by competitors throughout the world'. The key argument of this influential report was that American schools had not kept up with the dramatic transformation of the economy and society, and the nation risked falling behind its competitors.

In recent decades the cult of the new is frequently transmitted through focusing on the allegedly unprecedented changes unleashed through globalization. Typically it is argued that globalization has created a qualitatively new environment that is 'increasingly complex and sophisticated' and one that poses a qualitatively new demand on education. This is a world that requires far more education and sophistication. 'So education, training, scholarship and research can be seen as the necessary tools for successful globalization in whatever field' goes the argument.[28] Calls for radical educational reform are almost always linked to the plea that schools need to catch up with new economic realities. The demand for radical change is invariably presented as a call for improving the quality of education. According to one account, 'transformation is needed in the next stage of educational reform' for as 'we enter a knowledge-based economy, more people should be educated than ever before'.[29]

At first sight the claim that the new knowledge economy requires the construction of a sophisticated learning society appears as a positive cultural endorsement of the role of education. The Blairite motto of 'education, education, education' signals the idea that education has acquired unprecedented significance to the new society. However, on closer inspection it becomes evident that the fixation on the new is dominated by narrow, short-term, economically focused concerns. Education tends to be depicted as a tactic to be used to realize the far wider objective of economic innovation. Indeed, one of the consequences of the pursuit of the new is the tendency to downsize the independent status of education. 'In all countries *knowledge and applied intelligence* have become central to economic success and social well-being' explains one advocate of reform.[30] From this perspective education is one-sidedly perceived as an economic resource to be used in response to changing market conditions. Tony Blair summed up this instrumental approach when he observed that 'education is the best economic policy we have'.[31]

Until the 1970s education possessed considerable independence to develop practices and institutional arrangements through the exercise of professional judgement. However, since that time the independent status of the institution of education has become gradually undermined. Paradoxically, the expansive rhetorical importance that education has for society has led to the diminishing of its own independent significance. According to the sociologist John Beck, the line that used to separate education from the domain of economic life has become indistinct, indeed it has been 'stripped away by direct intervention'.[32] In a sense the loss of autonomy of education discourages educators to exercise their judgement in accordance with criteria that emerge within their own professional and institutional environment. The loss of educational autonomy is frequently presented as a step in the right direction since the role assigned to this sector is to respond to a rapidly changing world. According to Beck the origin of the emphasis on the servicing role of education began in further education but has 'recently been extended much more widely, partly in response to the perceived need to functionalize education for a world in which the futures are held to be increasingly unpredictable and where the capacity to react rapidly and appropriately to changing market demands is at a premium'.[33]

Currently education is principally valued for its ability to respond and adapt to a world of ever-accelerating competition and change. It is worth noting that the goal of adaptation is far from new. The capacity to adapt has been upheld as a challenge facing education throughout the post-Second World War era. For example, a 1971 textbook on the state of education in Britain observed that 'qualifications are not, however, as durable as they used to be: new knowledge reaches the workshop with astonishing rapidity, and techniques and processes are constantly changing' and therefore 'adaptability is going to become more and more important'.[34] However, the author of this text recognized that nevertheless education should be valued in its own terms and argued that what was needed was a 'good general education'.

Contemporary culture no longer regards adaptability as merely a useful attribute of personhood but as a defining characteristic of a competent individual. That is why policy statements often convey the message that education is not so much about the teaching of a particular subject but the cultivation of the habit of adaptability. The capacity to adapt requires people to change so that they can develop the ability to respond to new developments. Donald Schön argued that children need to develop an 'ethic of change' in order to cope with the fluid reality they inhabit.[35] Consequently it is not what people know that is important but the possession of the mental capacity to adapt and respond to new circumstances. This is one reason why behaviour management and therapeutic techniques have become part of the landscape of schooling. 'Effective change in a field as dependent on human interaction as education requires millions of people to change their behaviour', argued David Blunkett

in 1997.[36] As the discussion on the ascendancy of therapeutic education in Chapter 7 argues, the institutionalization of behaviour
management is one of the most significant developments in
contemporary Anglo-American education.

The reconfiguration of education around the valuation of
novelty, innovation and adaptability lends it an unstable and
short-termist character. Yesterday's classroom lessons soon become
irrelevant to a world that never stands still. Many experts contend
that what children and young people learn in school cannot educate
them for their lives as adults. Those who uphold the authority of
the new assert that, since knowledge swiftly becomes obsolete,
schools should place less importance on academic subjects. They
regard the formal knowledge learned in school by young people as
insufficient for ensuring that individuals acquire the habit of adaptability to change. This fixation with adaptability and change has led
policy-makers and innovators to call into question what they often
describe as the 'front-end model of learning'.

One unfortunate by-product of the devaluation of the so-called
front-end model of learning is that the intellectual content of
schooling becomes negotiable. The schooling of the young as a
decisive phase in education loses its meaning according to a model
which suggests that learning is for life. What children are expected
to do in school is but a variation of what grown-ups can learn two
or three decades down the road. In such circumstances there need
not be any essential subjects, or even basics, that children have to
study in school. As one proponent of this short-termist perspective
states, 'If we want people to be able and motivated to learn throughout their lives' then 'we should be confident that knowledge of a
wide number of subjects is not essential for a 16- or 18-year-old it
might once have been.'[37] Such pragmatism towards the acquisition
of knowledge by teenagers is symptomatic of an outlook where what
you know is deemed to be far less important than how you react
and behave.

Since the emergence of modern, formal, compulsory education,
society regarded the schooling of its youth as the foundation for
preparing the young generations for adult life. It regarded this phase

of formal schooling as the decisive moment in the education of its youth. However, in recent times this association of education with the schooling of children and young people has been called into question by the short-termist outlook that informs policy. Numerous experts take the view that in a world of constant change, what children learn in school soon becomes obsolete and will therefore be irrelevant to their future. Critics of the front-end model of education advocate 'lifelong learning', a model that advocates continuous training and skill acquisition. Although lifelong learning is promoted as a model for upgrading the status of education, its premise rests on a shallow and short-termist view of the role of young people's schooling and education. Even the central role of the school in education is under question. The report aptly entitled *Learning to Change* predicts that in the future the role of the school is 'likely to alter profoundly' and while its 'provider role will not entirely disappear' it will be one institution among many providing educational opportunities.[38] Outwardly, this model of a world where educational opportunities multiply and spring up throughout society appears as a celebration of education. But as we shall see, when education becomes everything, it loses its purpose and meaning and this leads to the hollowing out of education.

Formal education has little value from the neo-Heraclitean worldview. Critics of the 'front-end model' of learning implicitly question the importance of the formal education of children. They argue that, to be sure, schools are important but are not the only place where learning takes place. Frequently the very formality of education is criticized for being too preoccupied with the traditional subjects that it transmits in the classroom and insensitive to the forces of change. That is one reason why many pedagogues prefer the term 'learning' to 'teaching'. They claim that since learning takes place in response to people's experience it has a unique capacity to engage with change. Back in 1995 Sir Geoffrey Holland, a former Permanent Secretary at the Education Department, was adamant that the 'priority for schools' should be 'learning not teaching' since in a changing world children will not live in a world of 'didacticism' where there are 'certain answers'.[39] Holland's call for a reorientation from didacticism of the classroom to learning about a changing world represented a call for down-sizing the role of teachers and argued for a 'fundamental reversal of the traditional role of the teacher'. He called for the metamorphoses of the teacher into a supporter for the 'learner', who now has to make 'her or his way for herself or himself'.[40]

The demotion of the authority of the teacher to that of a role of a supporter or facilitator logically follows from the obsession with the new. In a world where knowledge has a short shelf-life, teachers have little 'relevant' wisdom to convey. Their role is to 'facilitate' the process whereby 'learners' learn to learn. This shift in role is strikingly captured through the rhetorical strategy of renaming teachers as learners. In an era of constant change where there are such few 'certain answers' there is little to teach other than the need to learn.

## The invention of the learning age

The rhetorical acclamation of education is vividly captured through the description of our era as that of a 'learning age' or a 'knowledge society' or 'knowledge economy'. In line with the Blairite exhortation of 'education, education, education', these terms communicate the message that contemporary society attaches an unprecedented significance to the pursuit of knowledge and learning. But, on closer inspection, it becomes evident that, like many newly invented pedagogic terms, the 'learning age' lacks conceptual clarity. Indeed, the term 'learning age' is not so much an analytically informed concept as a rhetorical idiom designed to communicate the message that education needs to be taken seriously.

In practice, the term 'learning age' is used to sensitize people to the pseudo-Heraclitean reality of constant change. From this perspective, embracing the age of learning is a matter of national survival. 'If we do not create a learning society', warned Kim Howell, the then Minister for Lifelong Learning in 1997, 'we will fail to develop our most important resource – our people – and we will fail as an economy in this globalised market.'[41] Typically the idiom of learning is oriented towards fostering a spirit of economic competitiveness. Publications promoting the 'learning age' show little interest in education as such. The 1998 Green Paper, *The Learning Age*, simply echoes the tired old mantra that 'we are in a new age – the age of information and of global competition'. In a series of descriptive passages it repeats the old story that 'we must equip ourselves to cope with the enormous economic and social change we face'. But it does not pause and reflect on the meaning of this new age that we must equip ourselves for. Probably what's most significant about this discussion is its self-conscious treatment of learning as an afterthought. So, in passing, the Green Paper notes that 'our vision of the Learning Age is about more than employment'.[42] The promise that there is 'more than' just economic pragmatism is meant to suggest that the authors of this report have not entirely overlooked the sphere of education.

In recent years, terms like 'learning age' and 'knowledge economy' have been questioned by numerous academics for the narrow instrumentalist ethos they convey.[43] While there is little doubt that concepts like 'lifelong learning' or 'learning age' are dominated by the imperative of economic competition, they also serve to promote a form of pedagogy that systematically devalues the meaning of knowledge and of education.

Enthusisasts of the so-called knowledge society rarely reflect on what they understand as the content of knowledge. Their silence on this subject is not surprising since their interest is not with the content but the use to which knowledge can be put. Historically, a sound formal education was associated with the provision of knowledge that was not accessible to young people through direct experience of everyday life. In part, the value of such knowledge is that it 'enables those who acquire it to move beyond their experience and gain some understanding of the social and natural worlds of which they are a part'.[44] For the proponents of the learning age, this type of knowledge is far too irrelevant to the project of adapting to an ever-changing environment. In this vein, the author of a text sub-titled *Education for a Changing World* insists that 'our conception of knowledge must shift to include, alongside knowledge of what to say, how to say it, and knowledge of oneself, the *ability to do*'.[45] According to this model, knowledge ceases to have any independent significance and is simplistically transformed into a skill that helps people 'to do'.

The focus on 'the doing' serves to by-pass issues concerned with the meaning of knowledge. So the claim that 'learning how to apply knowledge in unfamiliar situations is more and more important' explicitly avoids deliberation on just what is the content of the knowledge to be applied.[46] Indeed, from this standpoint concern with the intellectual content of knowledge appears as both unnecessary and an obstacle to being able to adapt to change. Beck has remarked that this form of pedagogy is necessarily empty because its objective is the 'fostering of receptiveness to whatever set of objectives and contents comes along next'.[47] This subordination of curriculum content to its application is symptomatic of a simplistic instrumental turn towards the project of educating to adapt. One of the consequences of the reorganization of schooling around the principle of adaptation and application is that the only knowledge that is valued is one deemed relevant. But what seems relevant soon becomes outdated and the old knowledge must give way to the latest fad.

In many ways the throwaway pedagogy idealized by policy-makers is similar to the workings of management fads. Typically proponents of the concept of the learning age draw their ideas from business management manuals. Donald Schön, who was one of the most influential theorists of the learning society, self-consciously drew on the workings of the corporate firm as an example of a learning system. The necessity for businesses to ceaselessly transform themselves in response to changing market conditions is upheld by theories of the 'learning organization' as a model for schools. Policymakers and experts exhort schools to follow the example of business. One enthusiast of product innovation writes that 'business is well experienced in innovative processes and services from which education can learn'.[48]As Bentley points out, 'in other sectors of society, especially business, organizations are changing their form and their governing principles in response to a changing environment'.[49] The parallel that Bentley and others draw between the working of a business firm and a school is testimony to the policy establishment's indifference to substantive issues to do with the education of the young. The recycling of off-the-shelf management fads into the domain of education demonstrates that knowledge is regarded as a disposable resource of no inherent significance. It also indicates that current throwaway pedagogy draws its inspiration from experiences outside of the classroom.

Every future-oriented society is genuinely concerned about the development of knowledge. But proponents of the learning age are not interested in the development of knowledge as such: they are interested in knowledge of a specific kind; one that can respond to change, particularly economic change. That is why the educational establishment often displays its indifference, if not outright contempt, for abstract theoretical thought and the knowledge developed in the past. Both are frequently criticized for being either irrelevant or outdated; only new knowledge that can be applied and acted upon is seen to be suitable for the learning age.

In policy deliberations about education, the acquisition of subject-based knowledge is often dismissed as an old-fashioned practice. Formal education is equated with didacticism, and an emphasis on the intellectual content of classroom subjects is labelled an outdated form of scholasticism that has little significance in the modern era. When Bentley notes that 'scholasticism is a relatively narrow field of human achievement', the implication is that education should not be confined to the study of a subject-based curriculum.[50] The throwaway pedagogy of the learning society is peculiarly hostile to the teaching of academic subjects to young people. So-called modernizers regard the subject-based curriculum as far too rigid and formal for a school system that seeks to adapt to a constantly changing world. The QCA calls for an 'aims-led curriculum'. Although it pays lip-service to the need of the curriculum to reflect 'many enduring values', it does not mention any such values, and qualifies this statement in the very next sentence: 'However, the curriculum must respond to the demands of contemporary life and work if it is to provide a modern, world-class education.'[51] Anything that stands in the way of the ability to respond, such as a deep study of an academic subject, is often denounced as inappropriate for the 'curriculum of the future'.

The argument that a 'narrow' focus on academic studies limits students' ability to respond to economic opportunities is frequently reinforced by the claim that a subject-based curriculum is elitist. Modernizers argue that a knowledge-based curriculum is biased against people who either come from a disadvantaged background or who are not academically inclined.[52] These arguments often attract educators who are otherwise suspicious of the technocratic manipulation of the curriculum. In a curious way, an instrumental economic agenda has converged with an anti-elitist social engineering imperative, in a joint attack on academic, subject-based education.

## Conclusion

The idea that we live in a qualitatively different world serves as a premise for the claim that the knowledge and insights acquired in the past have only a minor historical significance. In education it is frequently claimed that old ways of teaching are outdated precisely because they are old. Knowledge itself is called into question because in a world of constant flux it must be continually overtaken by events. Consequently our preparedness to become adaptable lifelong learners is more important than what we now know. Policy has become so one-sidedly focused on keeping up with change that it has become distracted from the task of giving meaning to education.

Paradoxically, the very celebration of the age of learning has encouraged powerful anti-intellectual and anti-academic impulses. Novelty and change are preferred to the project of formal schooling that is based on academic subjects. The numerous critics of a subject-based curriculum transcend the traditional ideological divide, and a scorn for academic learning unites so-called progressive critics with advocates of economic instrumentalism. Back in 1969 Carl Rogers, a self-proclaimed liberation psychologist and proponent of progressive teaching techniques, remarked that 'traditional teaching is an almost completely futile, wasteful, over-rated function in today's changing world'. In line with his colleagues' addiction to the new, he asserted that 'no one should ever be trying to learn something for which one sees no relevance'.[53] Forty years later, Rogers' disdain for the 'irrelevant' subject-based curriculum would become the new 'new idea' among the educational establishment.

The objectification of change is symptomatic of a mood of intellectual malaise where notions of truth, knowledge and meaning have acquired a provisional and arbitrary character. Perversely, the transformation of change into a metaphysical force haunting humanity actually desensitizes society from distinguishing between novelty and qualitative change. That is why lessons learned through the experience of the past, and the knowledge developed through it, are so important for helping society face the future. When change is objectified, it turns into a spectacle that distracts society from valuing the important truths and insights that it has acquired throughout the best moments of human history. Yet these are truths that have emerged through attempts to find answers to many of the deepest and most durable questions facing the human species, and the more that the world changes, the more we need to draw on our cultural and intellectual inheritance from the past.

My critique of the current obsession with novelty is informed not by an underestimation of the significance of change, but by the tendency to objectify it. The objectification of change acts as a barrier to its understanding. Of course education and knowledge must be renewed, but always through developing the intellectual legacy of the past. The current project of confining the education of children to learning from experiences that are directly relevant to them disinherits the younger generations from their rightful intellectual legacy.

Probably the most interesting attempt to conceptualize the problem of engaging with change in education is to be found in an essay written in 1954 on 'The Crisis in Education' by Hannah Arendt. Arendt pointed out that, in a changing world, society finds it difficult to establish a creative balance between upholding the achievements and legacy of the past, and the provision of answers to new questions and challenges thrown up in the present. It is because it is so difficult to mediate between old and new that educators continually experience their professions as facing a crisis. She wrote that education 'never remains as it is but continuously renews itself' through the birth of new generations of children. Oriented towards their future, Arendt argued that the task of the adult world was to prepare them for 'undertaking something new'. However, her emphasis was not the novelty brought about through the process of objectified change, but on the constant renewal of our 'common world' through the education of the young. Arendt believed that the potential of the young for renewing the world required that they are educated to understand the world as it is. Schools should work to preserve the past for the sake of the new.[54]

The current trend to distance education from the past in exchange for relevant knowledge of the present irresponsibly deprives young people of the foundation they need to make their own way in this world. The Heraclitean approach confuses the need for society to respond to a changing world with the need to acquaint the young with the world as it is. 'For the child, familiarity with the world provides the existential security they need to have a chance of attempting something new', notes a commentary on Arendt's contribution.[55] The perpetual tinkering with the curriculum sends out the wrong signal to young people, and represents an act of irresponsibility on the part of an adult world that recycles its own uncertainties through the medium of educational reform.

One final point. Arguably, throw-away pedagogy has a most pernicious impact on those who come from economically or culturally disadvantaged backgrounds. One of the key markers of underachievement in school is children's relative lack of access to cultural and intellectual capital at home and in their communities. More than any other section of society, these children need to become acquainted with the cultural and intellectual legacy of the past in order to benefit from the educational opportunities available to them.

# 2

# *The Meaning of Education*

It is very difficult to have a grown-up discussion about contentious school-related issues unless there is a measure of agreement on the meaning of education. Unfortunately public debate on education rarely considers the fundamental question of its purpose. Instead, current controversies focus on issues such as how education should be used, how it should be delivered, or how it should be organized. Policy-makers are far better at deliberating about education's aims than its content. Controversies about selection, social inclusion, underachievement, assessment and standards are driven by a clash of opinion about process and procedure, and rarely reflect on education's meaning.

By comparison with today, the debates on education that followed the Second World War appear purposeful and intellectually informed. The 1940s education ethos was future-oriented and expressed a mood of optimistic hope. At the time, Ellen Wilkinson, Minster of Education, wrote of a new era of schooling that would be associated with 'laughter in the classroom, self-confidence growing every day, eager interest instead of bored uniformity'.[1] Today's debates about education are invariably driven by fear rather than hope. Mental health professionals and educationalists worry about the 'fragile identities' of children. They are concerned about the 'stress' placed on pupils by examinations or competitive sports. Policy-makers are apprehensive about 'falling standards', 'poor levels of literacy' and 'failing schools'. Parents fear just about everything: bullying, lack of discipline, children going to the wrong school, too much testing. Some educationalists are so concerned about the apparently fragile state of children that they advocate turning the school into an institution that, in all but name, functions as a clinic. One headmaster echoes the sentiment that 'the country has to wake up to the fact that far more attention needs to be given to the physical, mental and emotional health of young people', if 'academic performance' in schools is to improve.[2]

Anxieties about the experience of schooling often acquire a caricatured form. Take the fear of the recently discovered 'risk' associated with children's transition from primary to secondary school. Researchers claim that this transition is so 'unsettling, daunting, stressful' that it can de-motivate up to 40 per cent of 11-year-olds 'badly enough for them "never" to recover, thereby causing a marked dip in formal achievement'.[3] Numerous schools now provide transition counselling, and the primary–secondary school transition is sometimes expressed through a vocabulary usually associated with mourning and grief.

Many of the fears expressed about schools are in fact concerns about issues that are quite separate from education. Confusions about childhood and inter-generational tensions along with apprehension about antisocial behaviour are often recycled as school problems. Once the problems of the school become synonymous with the many problems facing society, it becomes easy to lose sight of what is specific about education. Matters are further complicated by the growing tendency to treat education as a lifelong quest that involves every learning experience. Such sentiments, expressed through the concept of lifelong learning, convey the idea that there is little to distinguish the work of the school from other educational opportunities. With such an unfocused representation of education, it becomes difficult to get a handle on what is special or distinct about formal schooling.

## So what is education?

Everyone wants their children to have a good education. But it is far from evident what we mean by a 'good education'. Most of the time, when education is discussed the focus is on different pedagogic approaches, techniques and their objectives rather than on the fundamental question of what education is. In Anglo-American societies the question of education is often dominated by concerns about how to motivate children to learn, and about the standards of their achievements. Pedagogy, the strategy of teaching, is invariably treated as synonymous with that of education. There is no doubt that the techniques adopted by teachers in the classroom are important subjects for discussion. Using synthetic phonics to teach children to read may or may not be an important aid to improve literacy; personalized learning may or may not be more effective than whole-class teaching. However, these are techniques designed to help children to learn and should not be confused with education as such. One philosopher of education refers to these techniques as aids that are *extrinsic* to education.[4] Such pedagogic techniques may well be linked to a distinct philosophy of education, but the two should not be confused.

It is important to consider the potential benefits of any pedagogic techniques. It is likely that they may work in some circumstances for some children but not for others. Teachers have their own distinct style of engaging with their classroom and some will achieve very different results using the same techniques as others. The dogmatic pursuit or rejection of any specific technique is unhelpful. However, a pluralistic tolerance towards different pedagogic styles requires both clarity and a consensus of what society means by education.

One reason why there is a lack of clarity about the meaning of education is because it is now used to apply to such a wide range of experiences. But what can a concept that deals with what seven-year-olds do in the classroom, or the work doctoral students pursue in a lab, or what a 45-year-old plumber does in an evening class, tell us about the meaning of education? Yes, learning can occur throughout life and in a wide variety of settings and contexts, but the knowledge gained through such encounters should not be interpreted as another variant of the education that children receive in the classroom.

Pupils and their parents experience education as a very personal matter. Society echoes this sentiment and insists that every child is different, with their own special individual needs. Of course, for an individual family this is very true, but education is most usefully understood as not simply the act of teaching or learning but as the process through which one generation initiates another into the ways of the world. Through education, adult society attempts to introduce children to the world as it is and provide them with the knowledge through which they can understand it. Today, when education is heralded as something an individual does throughout life, it becomes detached from this fundamental interaction between generations. Yet this generational dynamic is central for the meaning of education. It is through the institution of education that adults demonstrate their responsibility to the new generation, by introducing young people to the world as a whole.

Serious thinkers from across the left–right divide have recognized that education represents a transaction between the generations. Antonio Gramsci, the Italian Marxist thinker, wrote that 'in reality each generation educates the new generation'. Writing from a conservative perspective, the English philosopher Michael Oakeshott concluded that 'education in its most general significance may be recognized as a specific transaction which may go on between the generations of human beings in which newcomers to the scene are initiated into the world they inhabit'.[5] The liberal political philosopher Hannah Arendt regarded the 'realm of education' as a site governed by the 'relations between grown-ups and children', and she took the view that this relationship was far too important to be 'turned over to the special science of pedagogy'.[6]

Arendt was not exaggerating when she stated that education was far too important a subject to leave to the experts. She took the view that education provides an opportunity for society both to preserve and to renew its intellectual inheritance. According to this interpretation, education constitutes a critical phase in the renewal of humanity. What she meant when she concluded that the very 'essence of education is natality, that human beings are *born* into world', was that it is through education that society both preserves and renews itself. Arendt's concept of natality is not so much a biological but a cultural metaphor, signifying the capacity to preserve and develop humanity's understanding of itself.[7]

The birth of human beings continually demands that grown-ups assume responsibility for preparing them for a world they do not yet know or understand. John Dewey also stressed this point when he stated that the fundamental 'facts of birth and death' determine the 'necessity of education'. The young and the immature cannot be left to their own devices. Adults need to take responsibility both for physically preserving the young and also initiating them into the 'interests, purposes, information, skill and practices of the mature members: otherwise the group will cease its characteristic life'.[8] One of the purposes of education is to span the gap that exists between the undeveloped capacities of the immature and 'the standards and customs of the elders'.

One of the tasks of education is to teach children about the world as it is. Although society is continually subject to the forces of change, education needs to acquaint young people with the legacy of its past. 'Since the world is old, always older than they themselves, learning inevitably turns towards the past, no matter how much living will spend itself in the present', observed Arendt.[9] The term 'learning from the past' is often used as a platitude. Yet it is impossible to engage with the future unless people draw on the insights and knowledge gained through centuries of human experience. Individuals gain an understanding of themselves through familiarity with the unfolding of the human world.

The transition from one generation to another requires education to transmit an understanding of the lessons learned by humanity throughout the ages. Consequently the principal task of education is not to respond to a changing world but to preserve the past so that young people have the cultural and intellectual resources to deal with the challenges they face. This understanding of the constitution of education as renewal stands in direct contrast to the current focus of the curriculum one-sidedly on the future. When the QCA talks about how a 'curriculum fit for the twenty-first century should be flexible and adaptable so that it can meet the needs of all learners',[10] instead of acquainting children with the legacy of the past, it is devoted to cultivating an ethos of flexibility towards the future. Of course the capacity to adapt is a valuable asset to an individual. But the exercise of this capacity requires a sense of intellectual and moral grounding in an understanding of the world in which we live.

The question of the balance that education should strike between orienting towards the past and towards a changing world has been a constant source of debate. As noted in the previous chapter, policy-makers and pedagogues tend to be so fixated on the present that they continually attempt to distance education from the past. This perspective also motivated Dewey and other progressive educators, who argued that instead of teaching children about the world as it is, schools should take a lead in challenging outdated norms and practices. 'Is it a good thing to bring up the young with desires and habits that try to preserve everything just as it is today, or should they be able to meet change, to weigh up values and find good in the new?' was the question posed by Dewey rhetorically. He added, 'How much of the background and development of our civilization do children need to be able to understand what is in the world today?'[11] Dewey did not answer his question directly, but many of his followers responded with the sentiment, 'Not very much.'

Dewey, like his modern-day followers, attached little value to preserving the past through education. Their educational philosophy cannot take the idea of the inter-generational transmission of knowledge too seriously, for the simple reason that they consider that very little of the past needs to be transmitted. Indeed, from this perspective education is best promoted through distancing it from the influence of the outdated views of the older generations. The impulse to free education from the past is influenced by a prejudice that regards ideas that are not of the moment as, by definition, old-fashioned and irrelevant. Yet the project of preserving the past through education does not mean an uncritical acceptance of the world as it was; it means the assumption of adult responsibility for the world into which the young are integrated. The aim of this act is to acquaint the young with the world as it is so that they have the intellectual resources necessary for renewing it. In this sense, education 'never remains as it is but continuously renews itself through birth', explained Arendt.[12] Through the education of the new generation, all the important old questions are re-raised with the young, leading to a dialogue that moves humanity's conversation forward.

Education needs to conserve the past. Arendt was unequivocal on this point. 'To avoid misunderstanding: it seems to me that conservatism, in the sense of conservation, is of the essence of the educational activity', she argued.[13] Arendt's objective was not to conserve for the sake of nostalgia but because she recognized that the conservation of the old provided the foundation for renewal and innovation.[14] Indeed, Arendt went so far as to argue that 'education must be conservative' in order to create the conditions where children can feel secure to innovate and renew their world. It is only in relation to the world as it has been preserved that young people develop their understanding and potential for creating something new. Elaborating on this insight, Gordon wrote that in education 'It is precisely the authority relation and its corresponding conservative attitude that make room for renewal and innovation.'[15]

The characterization of conservation as the essence of educational activity can be easily misunderstood as a call inspired by a backward or reactionary political agenda. However, the argument for conservation is based on the understanding that, in a generational transaction, adults must assume responsibility for the world as it is and pass on its cultural and intellectual legacy to young people. An attitude of conservation is called for specifically in the context of inter-generational transmission of this legacy. Until recently, leading thinkers from across the ideological divide understood the significance of transmitting the knowledge of the past to young people. The conservative thinker Matthew Arnold's formulation of passing on 'the best that has been thought and said in the world' is virtually identical to Lenin's insistence that education needs to transmit the 'store of human knowledge'.[16]

From this perspective, education is a distinct activity that is informed by the way in which adults interact with children. Arendt argued that what goes on in education is not a model for how to conduct life in public or vice versa. Indeed, she went so far as to argue that a conservative orientation 'holds good only for the realm of education, or rather for the relations between grown-ups and children, and not for the realm of politics, where we act among and with adults and equals'.[17] The aim of preserving the legacy of the past is to provide children with the existential security they need to deal with an insecure world.

For her part, Arendt argued against the extension of conservatism into public life. She stated that in 'politics this conservative attitude – which accepts the world as it is, striving only to preserve the status quo – can only lead to destruction'. Why? Because the world is 'irrevocably delivered up to the ruin of time unless human beings are determined to intervene, to alter, to create what is new'.[18] This apparent paradox between a commitment to conservatism in education and radicalism in public life is mediated through the idea of natality: the process through which the preservation of the past provides children with the means to realize their potential to renew the world. So the argument for the necessity of introducing children to the world 'as it is' is motivated by the conviction that 'it is only in relation to this world' that students will 'come to an understanding of what needs to be challenged and transformed'.[19]

The experience of modern times indicates that the task of conserving the past through education faces formidable obstacles. As noted in the previous chapter, western society's obsession with change continually estranges it from its past. Historically the rejection of the past was associated with a radical temper. Today such an outlook is imbued with a conformist sensibility. Conservation, in the sense of nostalgia for a world that has been lost, exercises significant influence in western societies. But conservation as a project that gives meaning to the experience of the past enjoys little cultural valuation. At a time when an uncritical presentist mood is incessantly reacting to past traditions, education is continually charged with embracing novelty. In such circumstances the ability of education to mediate between the present and the past has become diminished. Conscious of this dilemma, Arendt observed:

The real difficulty in modern education lies in the fact that despite all the fashionable talk about a new conservatism, even the minimum of conservation and the conserving attitude without which education is simply not possible is in our time extraordinarily hard to achieve.[20]

The challenge posed by this problem requires deliberation on how twenty-first-century schools can be turned into institutions where the past has a legitimate status.

In the present day, the proper relationship between education and society has been turned upside down. Frequently education is used as the site where the unresolved issues of public life can be pursued. Too often, conservatism becomes the hallmark of public life, while the school is turned into the location for social experimentation. In public life politicians and policy-makers play it safe and tend to avoid substantive issues and serious debate. But often problems that are avoided in the domain of politics appear as a subject for the school curriculum. So the problem of political apathy and disengagement is accepted as a fact of life in public life only to reappear in the form of citizenship education in the schools. Solving problems and changing attitudes is assigned to the institutions of education.

## Important in its own right

Although the idea that education is fundamentally a generational transaction is rarely contested, there is a continual attempt to treat it in isolation from this process. Taken out of the context of inter-generation relations, education tends to come under the influence of agendas that are external to it. Yet precisely because education plays a unique role in acquainting children with the legacy of the past, this institution works best in isolation from external pressures. Politics and social pressures invariably intrude into the school, but such influences always work to the detriment of education. The introduction of new enlightened values or political objectives is often presented as a progressive attempt to take children seriously and give them a voice on the important issues of the day. However, the politicization of the curriculum distracts educators and children from coming to terms with the world as it is, and denies children the opportunity to develop their own ideas about what needs to be questioned and challenged.

Education needs to be insulated from politics if it is to carry out the transaction between the generations responsibly. 'Education can play no part in politics, because in politics we always have to deal with those who are already educated', insisted Arendt.[21] Politics assumes a relationship of equality between participants; education is founded on the assumption that children need to be treated differently from adults. Most fundamentally, the difference between the mature and the immature, the old and the new, the teacher and learner, assumes a relation of inequality that education seeks to transcend. When children are not yet educated there can be no political dialogue between equals, only an attempt at indoctrination.

The call to separate education from politics is informed by the understanding that the attitude we adopt towards children is different from the way in which adults relate to one another. The converse of this insight is that the rules that apply to the realm of education have no place in public life. Arendt remarked:

> We must decisively divorce the realm of education from the others, most of all from the realm of public and political life, in order to apply to it alone a concept of authority and attitude toward the past which are appropriate to it but have no general validity and must not claim a general validity in the world of grown-ups.[22]

Education involves the exercise of generational authority, which gives the institution a unique character. The exercise of such authority is inconsistent with the ethos of public life, where the relations between adults are managed on the basis of equality.

Modern educational theory confuses the role of politics and education, frequently portraying the school as the site where social inequalities and inequities are best resolved. This outlook was systematically promoted by Dewey, who regarded schools as essentially quasi-political institutions. According to one of his admirers, 'Dewey's notion of educational authority is inherently political because it views schools as those institutions that should teach students about social problems, political evils and industrial defects.'[23]

Since Dewey's time the tendency to subordinate education to a political or social agenda has become increasingly prevalent. Anthony Crosland, the former Secretary for Education, was scathing when he remarked in 1974 that a 'few people still think that social and political aspirations can, and should, somehow be kept out of education'. He added, 'but of course, they cannot and should not'.[24]

Crosland was more blunt than most. Many educators and policymakers have been more reluctant to acknowledge their commitment to imposing their political agenda on the curriculum. It is usually left to the more radical reformers to state the case for the politicization of schooling in explicit terms: those such as the radical educational theorist Paulo Freire, who argued: 'Neutral education cannot, in fact exist.' As far as Freire was concerned, all forms of educational activity represent 'political acts which imply an ideological choice'.[25] But in current times it is no longer merely radical pedagogues who demand that education ought to be politicized. Many politicians and educators are forthright in their advocacy of education as a tool of social or political reform. John Denham, the Universities Secretary of Britain's New Labour Government, stated in September 2008 that he 'profoundly disagreed' with the suggestion 'that universities, and by extension, education, is not an engine for social justice', and that he believed that, in fact, 'education is the most powerful tool we have in achieving social justice'.[26]

Political and social objectives are loaded routinely onto the curriculum, and even teachers who believe that schools should be instruments of social reform now find it difficult to keep up with the numerous policy objectives they have to promote. In recent years, teachers in Britain have been charged with training children to adopt, among other things, environmental values, become active citizens, embrace multiculturalism and diversity, fight discrimination, eschew homophobia, adopt healthy eating habits, and internalize government guidelines on relationships and sex.

Of course, as Freire argues, education never works as a neutral institution. Schools are subject continually to the influence of society, or at least a section of society. Prevailing cultural norms about how children should be socialized shape the way in which teachers instruct their pupils. Often, the institutions of education are organized according to principles that reflect vested and sectional interests and deny some children access to a positive class-room experience. However, the fact that education is sometimes used to promote narrow sectional interests does not detract from the importance of education in its own right. On the contrary, the unfortunate politicization of education represents an argument for depoliticizing it and for seeking to minimize the influence of the forces that distract it from providing children with the knowledge they need to understand the nature of the world.

From the perspective of an inter-generational transaction, edu-cation represents a distinct stage in the life of young people, and it has a beginning and an end. As far as the English philosopher Michael Oakeshott was concerned, education proper begins with the act of 'deliberate initiation'.[27] Through the term 'deliberate', Oakeshott pointed to the formal and institutional dimension of education. Unlike episodes of learning from life or through emu-lating the behaviour of others, education is an experience that is qualitatively different from the routine of normal life. 'It begins when the transaction becomes "schooling" and when learning becomes learning by study, not by chance in condition of direction and restraint', remarked Oakeshott.[28] Arendt added that 'education, as distinguished from learning, must have a predictable end'.[29] She insisted that this phase of the life-cycle had to be clearly delineated and distinguished from forms of learning that occurred later in life. She drew a distinction between learning and education, which was motivated by her conviction that this inter-generational transaction possessed features that were specific to it and it represented a par-ticular phase of young people's development.

The idea of education as a clearly delineated phase in young people's lives goes against the grain of contemporary thinking on the subject. The premise of lifelong learning is to contest the line that separates formal from informal forms of education. Its advocates contend that there is nothing that is intrinsically special or important about schooling as such. From this standpoint, formal schooling has no special purpose. It is seen as merely a variant of other forms of learning. Yet there is an important reason for distinguishing formal education from other forms of learning. Unlike the insights that a child picks up through interactions with friends and family and from other experiences, the knowledge gained through education is not directly related to his or her life. The knowledge imparted by a teacher is based upon an intellectual legacy of humanity as a whole and is often not directly connected to questions that are of interest to the child. This is knowledge 'which is *not* immediately connected with current wants or "interests" of the "learner"'.[30]

Today, critics of formal education object to the fact that it is too formal and not directly relevant to the lives of young people. They miss the point. Education is not, and should not be, reducible to ideas that are directly relevant to a pupil – it is about imparting the knowledge and insights gained through the experience others in far-away places and often in different historical circumstances. The main significance of formal education is that it provides people with the capacity for generalization and the acquisition of what Michael Young describes as 'context-independent or theoretical knowledge'.[31] This is knowledge that is distinct from the practical knowledge that people acquire through the experience of their everyday life.

The knowledge acquired through formal education is not always useful or directly relevant. Indeed, one of its characteristics is that it is the kind of knowledge that most people cannot acquire through their everyday existence. Often the knowledge provided through education is 'detached from the immediate, local world of the learner' and demands a redirection of interests away from the direct experience of the learner.[32] Education involves providing answers to questions that the young have not yet asked. One reason why this kind of knowledge is important is that it can help students to rise above their particular experience and gain insights into the wider world into which they are initiated. This type of formal education has as its premise the understanding that there are real limits to what can be learned from direct experience. Indeed, we often rely on knowledge gained through theoretical reflection to make sense of our own immediate experience. As Peters wrote, reflection on the world often involves the 'postulation of what is unobservable to explain what is observed'.[33] Since the way the world appears is often not the way it is, we rely on abstract theoretical knowledge to interpret it. In putting the case for a knowledge-based curriculum, Young observed that, 'because the world is not as we experience it, curriculum knowledge must be discontinuous, not continuous with everyday experience'.[34]

The purpose of education is to help young people develop their capacity for thinking, knowing, reflecting, imagining, observing, judging and questioning. At its best, such education provides students with an understanding of the past and with the knowledge to think about and engage with the issues of the present and the future. Of course formal education requires the acquisition of skills – reading, writing, counting – but these are aids that are necessary for acquiring knowledge.

## The search for meaning in education

Once the relation between education and purposeful inter-generation dynamic becomes diminished, its meaning becomes a focus for constant confusion and controversy. Throughout the past two centuries the purpose of education has been a subject of debate. Policy-makers have tended to emphasize the role of schooling as an 'instrument to achieve some other goal, only rarely as an end in itself'.[35] Government statements seldom demonstrate an interest in the content of education: they 'focus almost entirely on the *extrinsic* purposes of education'.[36] Educationalists tend to be preoccupied with innovating pedagogic techniques that can work to motivate children. In recent decades the imperative of motivating children has distracted educationalists from thinking about the fundamental meaning of their enterprise. Those who are most interested in what should be studied by children have tended to be conservative thinkers who are committed to upholding tradition. However, they, too, have tended to be concerned with goals extrinsic to education rather than its inner content. In their case, the political objectives of returning to basic values and to tradition divert their attention from a disinterested reflection of education as an institution in its own right.

It is true that education has seldom had an opportunity to flourish in its own right, and schools are continually subject to pressures from the labour market, government and wider cultural expectations. In many societies, teachers are perceived as civil servants – or at least as servants of a higher power whose main task is the socialization of children. However, the issue is not whether schools are subject to an externally influenced agenda but whether the ideal of education for its own sake retains cultural validation. What matters is the affirmation of the pursuit of knowledge as an endeavour to be encouraged among the young. Though such knowledge is not always useful or directly relevant, it prepares students to gain insights about what is true.

Historically the clash of views about the meaning of education has ranged from those who promote the idea of education for its own sake against those who regard it instrumentally as a form of training for the job market. By the nineteenth century, the tension 'between the academic and scholarly aims of education and the pragmatic and vocational aims' was palpable, notes Christopher Ray, headmaster of the Manchester Grammar School.[37] 'For over 2,000 years, debates about what to teach children took the form of a clash of views, usually between those who emphasized *education* and those who favoured *training*, namely between those who treated the child as the "heir to all ages", and those who treated the child as "job fodder"', claim Ecclestone and Hayes.[38] The history of this debate indicates that the devaluation of the idea of 'education for its own sake' serves as an invitation for a free-for-all. Some critics of this instrumentalism believe that this has precipitated 'the contemporary rush to produce new policies and practices that reflect an endless series of fads and fashions'.[39]

Education is continually in search of meaning. This is demonstrated by the constant attempt to formulate new goals and objectives for it. In recent times there has been a systematic attempt to call into question the ideal of a non-instrumental, disinterested form of education. Often a non-instrumental form of liberal education is castigated for being far too elitist for confronting the practical tasks facing society. One critic, John White, dismisses it as a throwback to eighteenth-century elite education and suggests that since 'there are many alternative candidates for central aims of education' it 'cannot be taken for granted that the pursuit of various types of theoretical understanding for non-instrumental reasons wins out over more practical pursuits, personal development, citizenship or promoting a strong economy'.[40] According to this shopping-list approach, academic knowledge is merely one of the many aims assigned to education. White seems to believe that an 'emphasis on the pupil's wellbeing, practical reasoning and preparation for civic life' would help liberate the curriculum from the stultifying influence of academic subjects.[41]

Current attempts to lend meaning to education emphasize a variety of diverse objectives. Some of the aims promoted by the official English curriculum are personal fulfilment, social and civic involvement, contribution to the economy, and practical wisdom. In a previous era such objectives would have been subsumed under the project of children's socialization. Implicity it appears that the purpose of education has been reduced to that of socialization. As Bentley states, the 'basic function of education is to prepare young people to meet the challenges of adult life'.[42] But what kind of challenges is society preparing young people to meet? It certainly does not mean the renewal of the world through understanding it and responding to it. It is evident that the challenges that Bentley has in mind are associated with the practical skills that adults need to have in order to participate in the job market and in other areas of life. Frequently this form of skills acquisition is directly contrasted to the learning of academic knowledge. The problem of education and indeed of socialization is implicitly redefined as the absence of necessary life-skills:

More broadly, evidence suggests that many people are not coping well with the tasks and challenges of ordinary life. This includes the inability to save money for the future, to understand and persevere in relationships, to plan and manage a career, to recognize and carry out obligations as a citizen, and to cope with stress, change and insecurity.[43]

The displacement of the appropriation of an intellectual and moral legacy and its replacement by training in basic life-skills is symptomatic of widespread failure to give meaning to education. The act of training people for an adult role avoids tackling the more basic question of how to acquaint children with their cultural and intellectual inheritance. Instead of relying on intellectual understanding, and the capacity to reason, some educationalists have opted for therapeutic techniques that promise to help youngsters to cope. This shift from education to training represents the downgrading of what adults expect children to achieve in schools.

It is important not to confuse the current advocacy of preparing young people for life with the idea of education as part of a generational transaction that is necessary for the renewal of the world. The former represents an implicit rejection of the ideal of education that provides the young with their inheritance of human understanding. The goal of preparing young people for adult life represents a form of training the objective of which is to facilitate the introduction of the trainee into society. This preoccupation with preparing young people for adult life coincides with an underestimation of the task of education. It by-passes the question of what the intellectual and cultural foundation should be upon which the preparation for adult life will take place. When the curriculum is fixated on the immediate practical questions posed by everyday life, it is difficult for teachers to cultivate an interest among their pupils in fundamental intellectual questions that have little direct connection to their circumstances.

Yet often education begins by reflecting on answers to questions never posed by the students themselves: questions that were crucial to the historical development of human understanding.

That is why Arendt insisted that 'the function of the school is to teach children what the world is like and not to instruct them in the art of living'.[44]

During the twentieth century the emergence of a socialization-led school agenda promoting the art of living has been associated with the upholding of a skills-linked curriculum. Pointing to the experience of 1950s America, Arendt pointed out that the 'conscious intention was not to teach knowledge but to inculcate a skill, and the result was a kind of transformation of institutes of learning into vocational institutions'. She wrote that these institutions were far better at teaching children how to use a typewriter or drive a car or the art of living than getting pupils to understand academic subjects.[45] Historically the provision of schooling in practical skills targeted the children of working people. What Oakeshott described as the 'substitution of "socialization" for education' had the objective of integrating the poorer sections of society. In nineteenth-century Britain it was 'geared to ensure that people were educated for the well being of the nation'. At the time, this type of schooling was perceived as independent of the 'educational engagement being pursued in schools and universities'. However, since the middle of the twentieth century the project of teaching life-skills and the art of living has acquired a powerful momentum and has expanded into all educational institutions, including the university.[46]

The ascendancy of skills-led pedagogy and the expansion of the imperative of socialization has been paralleled by the recent loss of authority of subject-based academic liberal education. It is worth recalling that, until the 1980s, many radical reformers demanded that the intellectually oriented curriculum that characterized the schooling of the elite ought to be made available to all sections of society. During the 1960s many egalitarian educational theorists 'wanted the working classes to enjoy the same curricular advantages as those from the elite'.[47] Numerous supporters of comprehensive education hoped that the new system would incorporate the best of the grammar school and extend it throughout society. Since the 1970s this positive endorsement of liberal education has eroded gradually. Some critics have denounced it as narrowly elitist and have castigated attempts to extend it into schools as the 'imposition of the middle-class curriculum on the whole nation'.[48]

The erosion of cultural support for the ideal of non-instrumental liberal education has had a disorienting impact on the life of schools. It has led to a fruitless and narrow search for meaning and purpose for education. Invariably policy-makers project their own concerns onto the sphere of education and lose sight of the importance of providing young people with the opportunity to gain a rigorous understanding of humanity's intellectual and cultural legacy. The most dramatic consequence of policy-makers' implicit disavowal of the objective of cultivating children's intellectual capital is the down-sizing of the significance of academic subject-based education. Time and again educational experts argue for a school curriculum that places the 'needs of the whole person' ahead of the academic or intel-lectual dimension of the school experience. In practice, this un-distinguished status assigned to academic learning means that policy-makers have adopted an attitude that implicitly disassociates education from academic learning. As we shall see in Chapter 6, this approach has led to the promotion of an anti-intellectual and anti-academic pedagogy.

In reality it is the difficulty that society has in giving meaning to education that is the source of the many school-related problems. The continuous attempts to invent 'aims' for education not only expose the absence of consensus but also highlight the confusion of the adult world about its responsibility towards the younger gen-erations. Society finds it difficult to acknowledge this problem and give it a name; instead, it has become resigned to a situation where the role and aim of education enjoys only a provisional status as it is constantly debated and revised. Yet there is no getting away from the fact that schooling only becomes education when it mediates a generational transaction through which the young become acquainted with their past and acquire the knowledge necessary to understand the present and engage with the future.

From time to time adult society is reminded of the necessity to take education seriously in its own terms. So Sir Jim Rose, who was asked by the British Government to review the school curriculum, was critical of the mindless process of subjecting children to inappropriate lessons about the art of living. He stated in October 2008 that 'we are terribly concerned about the ills that beset society and we have pressed them onto primary schools at an earlier and earlier stage'. Education has clearly lost its way when primary schools are charged with the task of dealing with the many social and moral problems afflicting adult society. Rose must have been all too aware of the futility of this project, which is why he felt compelled to remind the public that the question that needed to be posed was, 'Have we managed to instil a love of learning for its own sake?'[49]

The occasional reminder that education has meaning in its own terms suggests that we have not entirely lost sight of the central question at stake. To understand why this question is so rarely posed, it is necessary to examine the many confusions that surround the exercise of adult authority.

# 3

## Confusions about Adult Authority

Society is confronted continually with the question of what kind of values and meanings it should transmit through education. The act of generational transaction always raises questions about the view of the world into which young people should be initiated. Teachers preparing children for the world they face are most effective when they are able to transmit society's understanding of itself with clarity and purpose. 'Education is simply the soul of society as it passes from one generation to another', wrote the English writer G. K. Chesterton in 1924. But what happens if society finds it difficult to discover a language through which it can express its soul? Communication between generations becomes troublesome, and this undermines the ability of schools to possess an interpretative system through which they can guide the intellectual and moral development of their pupils effectively.

For some time, many western societies have found it difficult to forge a consensus through which they can affirm their past and the basic values they uphold. Traditional symbols and conventions have lost some of their power to enthuse and inspire, and in some cases have become irrevocably damaged. This development is illustrated strikingly through the constant controversy that surrounds the teaching of history. When a generation senses that the stories and ideals upon which it was brought up lose their relevance to a 'changed' world, it finds it difficult to transmit them with conviction to its children, and bitter disputes about historical rights and wrongs refract competing claims about conflicting interests and identities. How to continue an inter-generational conversation in such circumstances, is a question that society is hesitant to pose. Nevertheless policy-makers and educators intuit that this needs to be addressed and they are forced to respond to the demand for values and traditions that can be imparted to children. Such projects rarely succeed because, unlike the conventions organically linked to the past, these are artificial – albeit well-meaning – constructs that are open to challenge. Unlike customs and conventions that are held sacred, constructed values need to be regularly justified. The very fact that they were self-consciously designed and invented draws attention to the possibility of constructing alternative histories and traditions.

Back in 2006, then Chancellor Gordon Brown announced plans to launch a British Day in order to 'focus on things that bring us together'. However, spelling out just what binds society together has proven to be far too challenging a task and within a few years the Government quietly dropped the idea. The Government's quiet retreat on this represented an acknowledgement that national traditions able to inspire the public cannot be invented through committee meetings and consultation with 'stakeholders'. If society is itself unsure about what it stands for, it is not surprising that schools lack the ability to talk about its soul.

A new curriculum for 11–14-year-olds launched in June 2007 states that 'pupils will learn shared values and study national identity in the UK'. However, in the absence of clarity about what society's shared values are, teachers are uncertain about how to deal with this curriculum. Many teachers are worried about their ability to handle what they perceive to be a difficult and controversial subject. The author of a survey of teachers' attitudes to the teaching of patriotism noted that one reason for their apprehension is 'an uncertainty about how appropriate it is to promote patriotic attachment to Britain to immigrant students with existing attachments to their countries of origin'. This survey found that only 13 per cent of the teachers interviewed believed that schools should 'actively promote patriotism'.[1] The reluctance of these educators to promote 'patriotism' could be interpreted as evidence of their lack of attachment to British values. However, it is far more likely that their attitude expresses an anxiety about teaching what they perceive to be a confusing, troublesome and difficult subject.

The teaching of religion is no less fraught with difficulties. The Office for Standards in Education (Ofsted), the government body that inspects schools throughout England, fears that the existing examination system risks 'trivialising significant religious issues'. Motivated by apprehensions about the politicization of religion in the post-9/11 era, Ofsted's 2008 report urged that 'pupils should be taught that religion is complex' and not always a force for good.[2] No doubt this is true. But should adult society recycle its own ambiguities and conflicts about the role of religion into the classroom in the guise of religious education?

Confusion about what binds a community together acquired a caricatured form in 2008 when the Government's plan to publish a national songbook for primary schoolchildren was quietly dropped. Originally the Government attempted to publish a collection of 30 songs that every 11-year-old should know, but the idea was rejected as too divisive. Gareth Malone, a leading figure in Sing-Up, the organization charged with the realization of this project, noted that the experts could not agree on which songs to include in the collection. Malone described it as a 'hot potato culturally' and added that 'you have to be realistic' and you 'can't be too culturally imperialist about it'.[3] In the end, officials chose to evade the controversy that the publication of a common songbook would have raised and opted for establishing a 'song bank' of 600 songs.

The controversies that surround the subject of patriotism, religion and even what song to sing points to a critical problem facing education: the absence of clarity about how to guide the moral education of children. Experience indicates that it is not possible artificially to create a new tradition of core values that can inspire the younger generation, and that neither values nor meaning can be produced through the work of experts or administrators.[4] If teachers are less than convinced about a nation's story, they are unlikely to be able to guide their pupils with conviction, and the pick-and-choose approach towards inventing new 'traditions' for values education invariably fails to motivate. Since such values remain, to a significant extent, external to the experience of the older generation, they are unlikely to carry out their part of the inter-generational transaction successfully. Once adult society has lost the ability to recognize itself through the values to which it was social-ized, its capacity to educate children into a new system of meaning becomes diminished.

Yet teachers need to provide their pupils with an understanding of the human condition, and they need to do it authoritatively. The erosion of consensus about what kind of ideas to transmit not only compromises the inter-generational transaction of values but also diminishes the ability of the adult world to act authoritatively. Authority is not an attribute of individual behaviour: it is legitimized through shared ideals that provide a set of principles for the conduct of authoritative behaviour. Values, traditions and authority are closely connected to one another, and if one is undermined, so is the other. Yet the exercise of adult authority is indispensable for the running of an effective system of education.

In recent decades there has been widespread discussion about the problems that teachers have in exercising authority. Of course, the issue of maintaining discipline in classrooms has recurred since the beginning of formal schooling. It is interesting that, in more recent times, teachers tend to perceive the issue of discipline as a direct threat to themselves. A survey by the General Teaching Council issued in July 2008 concluded that bad behaviour was the biggest reason why teachers quit their profession.[5]

The issue of discipline is not confined to disruptive behaviour or to conflicts between pupils: one report published in February 2008 claimed that around half the teachers it surveyed in England indicated that they had been teased, abused or physically attacked by pupils. Some of them acknowledged that they were worried about reporting such incidents in case it made their schools 'look bad'.[6] A month later the Government pledged that it would take action to protect teachers from 'bullying' through the internet and mobile phones. The General Secretary of the teachers' union NASUWT, Chris Keates, responded by stating that she was 'pleased the government accepts that we need strong policies in schools which focus on teachers'. She warned that 'increasingly, teachers' lives are being destroyed by what pupils are doing', and added: 'Pupils who once had to content themselves with exhibiting poor behaviour when face to face with the teacher, now increasingly use technology to support their indiscipline.'

For many teachers, the threatening behaviour directed at them is not confined to rare episodes of hostile acts. Some feel powerless and easily disoriented in the school environment. The sense of insecurity experienced by a significant section of the teaching profession suggests that they not only feel insecure about the status of their authority, they also feel powerless to exercise it. The very idea of children bullying their teachers signifies an important reversal in generational dynamics. It suggests that the issue of discipline is not simply one that can be reduced to the individual behaviour of a child but is linked to the wider problem of gaining the respect of the children for adult authority. Discipline has even become an issue in primary schools. One report claimed that even at this early age a minority of pupils threw tantrums, swore and exhibited physical aggression.[7] The very fact that teachers can refer to children two to four years old as 'violent pupils' is symptomatic of the difficulty they experience in containing the behaviour of an age-group that is generally thought to be very responsive to adult guidance.[8] Many teachers acknowledge that they feel intimidated by the disruptive behaviour of six-year-olds. 'People often underestimate that young children can be as violent and intimidating as the older ones' writes one primary schoolteacher on primary schoolchildren.[9]

The feeble authority relations between adults and children acquire their most dramatic form in nursery education. Even when dealing with toddlers, adult carers and teachers often appear to be ineffective at drawing lines and maintaining authority. According to official figures, 1,540 infants were suspended from nursery schools during 2007 in England. Almost 1,000 of these infants were suspended for attacking teachers and other children. The difficulty that teachers have in maintaining control over the nursery school environment is shown by the fact that 20 children as young as two were suspended for physical and verbal assault. These figures

indicate that what appears to be a question of discipline is fundamentally an issue to do with the failure to give meaning to what it
means to be an adult and to be a child. Grown-ups who are either
not given the opportunity to behave authoritatively, or who cannot
do so, are forced to rely on administrative solutions that are entirely
inappropriate for toddlers. According to Mick Brookes, the leader
of the National Association of Head Teachers, teachers have opted
to suspend toddlers because they are concerned about losing their
jobs if they 'intervene to stop violent pupils'.[10]

Perversely, the consequence of this orientation is to treat two-
to four-year-olds as if they had the moral capacity to grapple with
adult issues. So, in this topsy-turvy world where the line between
adult and child is blurred, it should not be a surprise to discover
that a small number of three- to four-year-olds were also expelled
for racism, sexual misconduct and theft.[11] Ineffective attempts to
apply standards of adult behaviour to infants render adult authority
absurd. The helpless nursery worker or teacher in the classroom
personifies the general crisis of adult authority throughout society.
On both sides of the Atlantic, the problem of classroom discipline
has been a topic of concern for many decades. Since the late 1960s,
surveys in the USA have indicated that lack of discipline was
identified as a leading problem in schools.[12]

Concern about classroom discipline raises fundamental questions
about the capacity of teachers and adults to interact authoritatively
with children. However, apprehensions about discipline are only a
warning sign about a much more basic issue of authority.

The crisis of education is intimately linked to that of authority.
Whatever political theorists and commentators have thought about
the role of authority in the management of public life, its necessity
is generally recognized when it comes to the tasks of child-rearing
and education. In these spheres, 'authority in the widest sense has
always been accepted as a natural necessity, obviously required as
much by natural needs, the helplessness of the child as by political
necessity', wrote Hannah Arendt.[13] The fact that, today, relations of
authority in the domain of family life and schooling are often contested represents a major challenge to the effectiveness of education.

It is important to recall that the relation between adults and children, and teachers and pupils, is mediated through rules and guidelines that presuppose the authority of the grown-ups. This is not a relationship of equality but one where one generation assumes responsibility for a generation that cannot yet be responsible for the world. In this relationship, adults assume a role towards children that is very different from the one they adopt towards one another.

It is widely recognized that often parents need to behave towards their children in ways that are very different from the ways in which they would deal with another adult. From the moment of birth, mothers and fathers impose their will on their babies continually. Parents who would never dream of telling another grown-up it was time to go to bed have no problem demanding that their child should go to sleep on the dot at 8pm. Parents who check that their child's bottom is clean are unlikely to do the same to people their own age. Whenever they wash them, feed them, or read to them in bed, parents unthinkingly treat their children as children and not as adults.

Education, too, requires the conscious and regular imposition of adult authority. The role of the teachers is to direct and guide children's growth. Through the assumption of pedagogic authority, the teacher attempts to influence the development of a child. In the relationship between teacher and child, the educator needs to initiate, direct and set the terms of the relationship. Often a teacher will impose demands on children that go against the child's inclination. An educator will often insist that children study a topic in which they have no interest but which is nevertheless fundamentally important for their development. Teachers often have to set clear boundaries to help children acquire the habit of self-discipline and concentration and thus curb pupils' inclination to get easily distracted or to play. All authority relations are hierarchical, and the relation between a teacher and student is no exception. In education, a relationship of inequality founded on the primacy of adult authority is based on the recognition that only grown-ups can be genuinely responsible for the welfare of children and for the world. Education as a generational transaction presupposes the fact that the older generation has something important to impart that children need to learn.

Moreover, the act of learning and the very pursuit of knowledge requires the acceptance of the authority of the subject and of the teacher who represents it in the classroom. When children go to school, they rely on their teachers to guide them to comprehend new forms of knowledge. This reliance on the teacher involves a leap of faith which people only undertake if they accept the authority of the educator. 'Learning always involves a determination to grasp after what is as yet uncomprehended', observed Bantock. He added that in 'the pupil, the act of acceptance or the authority of the as yet unknown is an essential pre-requisite to learning'.[14] Indeed, it is precisely because venturing out to the unknown goes so much against the inclination of children's feelings that they need the authoritative guidance of the teacher.

'The problem of education in the modern world lies in the fact that by its very nature it cannot forgo either authority or tradition, and yet must proceed in a world that is neither structured by authority nor held together by tradition', wrote Arendt .[15] In other words, the crisis in education is often a symptom of a much wider one, and this is the difficulty that modern society has in giving a meaningful account of itself that can serve as the cornerstone for authoritative adult behaviour. Many conservative and traditionalist thinkers perceive the decline of authority in general, and in the classroom in particular, as the outcome of resistance and rebellion. For example, the author and journalist Melanie Phillips has criticized what she calls 'the fundamentalist egalitarianism' which has 'destroyed the hierarchy of authority between the generations'.[16] No doubt so-called child-centred pedagogues have played a part in promoting practices that attempt to contain the teacher's authority. However, the confusion surrounding the exercise of authority inside and outside the classroom is as much the result of the failure of those in authority to uphold their traditions as the outcome of resistance against it.

## The issue of authority

Western society has an ambiguous attitude towards authority and the exercise of authority. The emergence of modern western society has come about through a revolt against traditional authority. In the eighteenth century the pursuit of freedom required a challenge to the authority of the Church and the State. Since that time, questioning the right of traditional authority to determine how people conduct their life has become one of the defining features of modern culture. Moreover, the very assertion of authority is increasingly perceived as an encroachment on individual freedom. Ever since traditional forms of authority have come under question, all other forms have been challenged and sometimes castigated as arbitrary. Many people have come to regard authority as, by definition, the antithesis of freedom, and restricting its role is seen as the objective of movements fighting for the expansion of democratic rights. One consequence of this development is that authority in *all its forms* is often regarded with suspicion.[17]

It is no longer sufficient to appeal to the authority of the past. Since the Enlightenment, the major questions of our time have been subjected to the power of reasoning. What is true can no longer be affirmed through the support of sacred texts. Truth is arrived at through rational deliberation and reflection on the facts. Modern science is a profoundly anti-authoritarian enterprise that cannot accept truth as self-evident. It is not only science that refuses to accept age-old rules: morality seeks new answers continually and can only justify itself through appealing to reason. Society is prepared to accept moral principles as authoritative only as long as they can be upheld through the act of reasoning. And when authority needs to justify itself, its exercise invariably invites contestation.

In retrospect, the erosion of traditional authority has had many positive outcomes. Authority has less scope to behave in an arbitrary manner – it needs to account for its action. The questioning of moral codes gave some people the freedom to make their own way in life and to embrace new opportunities thrown up by a changing world. As Hannah Arendt argued, 'With the loss of tradition we have lost the thread which safely guided us through the vast realms of the past, but this thread was also the chain fettering each successive generation to a predetermined aspect of the past.'[18] Traditional authority was deeply hostile to change and to new ideas. It needed to be challenged by democratic forces in order for society to realize the potential benefits of change. However, the revolt against tradition has not always succeeded in developing alternatives that are consistent with contemporary aspirations for a meaningful and free life. Contemporary society is uncomfortable not only with traditional authority but also the very *idea* of authority. Terms like 'authority', 'authority figure' and 'authoritarian' are often used in ways that convey a negative connotation.

The progressive, Enlightenment-inspired questioning of tradition and authority has given way to a form of uncritical condemnation. In the twenty-first century it is not simply the arbitrary traditions handed down from the past that are questioned, but the status of the intellectual and cultural achievements of past generations. It is worth noting that the Enlightenment's advocacy of critical inquiry through the application of reason is itself a legacy that needs to be cherished. It is a tradition of sorts, but one which needs to be upheld through the further development of knowledge, rather than as an article of faith.

One of the consequences of the revolt against traditional authority is that in modern times all forms of authority have been called into question. If the authority of the king or the priest is interrogated, why not hold to account the status of the *pater familias*, the teacher or the professor? That is precisely what happened, gradually, during the past century-and-a-half. By the late nineteenth century, experts were making scathing remarks about parental competence and attempting to restrain the authority of the father and mother. At the same time, attacks on traditional education adopted an increasingly strident tone towards the exercise of adult authority in the classroom. By the turn of the twentieth century, the kind of criticisms that were directed at traditional political authority had expanded into what can be called the domain of the pre-political – child-rearing, family life and education.

The undermining of the legitimacy of pre-political authority was not confined to the new profession of educational reformers and parenting and relationship experts. The anti-authoritarian temper of modern times deprived many parents and teachers of the self-belief to engage confidently with the younger generation. They were told time and again that their authority rested on outdated assumptions and that they lacked the expertise required for their role.[19] Conscious of the difficulty of acting authoritatively, parents and teachers were often ready to embrace the suggestions and arrangements offered by educational reformers and experts. The explosion of new child-rearing and pedagogic fads was symptomatic of adult society's futile attempt to by-pass the question of finding some alternative to the workings of pre-political authority. The history of education shows that as the adult world found it difficult to celebrate authority and exercise it openly and enthusiastically, schools began to look for ways of skirting around the problem.

However, the exercise of pre-political authority cannot be entirely discarded.

Precisely because the welfare of children cannot be left to their instinct of survival, society has always assigned adults the responsibility for managing their affairs. Even the most radical critics of traditional education could not entirely dispense with the need for adults to teach and instruct children. In such circumstances they sought not so much to eliminate adult authority but to downsize and contain it.

In the field of education, the crusade against adult authority is usually associated with the movement for progressive pedagogy, and with its most well-known and articulate representative, the American liberal philosopher John Dewey. However, a closer examination of Dewey's work indicates that his main objective was not to abolish adult influence over schooling entirely, but to limit it. Dewey distanced himself from those reformers who rejected all forms of authority, and argued that they wrongly assumed that traditional authority was the only model. This led some of his supporters directly to counterpose freedom to authority. Dewey was concerned that if the very concept of authority was demolished, this would deprive 'individuals of the direction and support that are universally indispensable both for the organic freedom of individuals and for social stability'.[20]

Dewey sought to overcome the polarization of authority and freedom by attempting to reconcile the two. He concluded that what was needed was a 'kind of individual freedom that is general and shared and that has the backing and guidance of socially organized authoritative control'.[21] Dewey nevertheless remained hostile to the imposition of authority, even by adults in the classroom. He appeared to opt for a negotiated form of authority that relied on its voluntary acceptance. For his new model of authority, Dewey looked to the application of the scientific method, to what he referred to as the 'control of organized intelligence' as the 'working model of the union of freedom and authority'.[22] The personification of this form of authority was the expert.

Dewey was an important thinker in his own right, but many of his views about traditional education expressed the sentiments and prejudices of an era that had become disenchanted with authority. From this perspective, traditional education was perceived as unremittingly boring, didactic, autocratic and conformist. Traditional education was held responsible for thwarting the spontaneous curiosity of children and curbing the power of their imagination, and it was clear that traditional authority had to go. But how to manage the relationship between the generations in schools became a very tricky question for pedagogues. Their solution was to try to get around this thorny issue by redefining the meaning of a generational transaction. Adults would still have a role to play, but, gradually, their function would be downsized to what today is often called a *facilitator*. For example, Tom Bentley recasts this transaction as one between equals – a kind of partnership between the young and old. He states that 'we are torn between the desire to prepare young people properly for an uncertain future, and the recognition that we do not have all the answers for them'.[23] He believes that the failure of the older generation to possess 'all the answers' implicitly calls into question its capacity to 'prepare young people properly'. Lacking answers, it is far from evident what wisdom grown-ups can convey to their children, and only a very modest version of adult authority can be conveyed according to this model.

It is frequently claimed that Dewey and the progressive movement were driven by an egalitarian impulse in their crusade to restrain the imposition of adult authority in the classroom. From the evidence available it can be argued that their motives for questioning adult authority were more complex. It was often their own lack of confidence in the ability of adult authority to inspire and motivate schoolchildren that disposed so many reformers to embrace new pedagogic techniques. By the turn of the twentieth century many pedagogues reconciled their lack of confidence in authoritative teaching with the claim that a possible problem of schooling was that it was subjected to too much adult initiative. Dewey himself took the view that adult authority imposed a regime of conformist uniformity on children that deprived them of the motivation to learn and led to a 'lack of interest in the novel, aversion to progress, and dread of the uncertain and the unknown'.[24]

Dewey believed that traditional education stifled children's initiative and could not motivate them. In the twentieth century this belief acquired significant influence, and numerous educators have become wedded to the project of promoting students' motivation through limiting the influence of teachers' authority. Some have even drawn the conclusion that children learn best when adult authority is all but absent. More radical critics went so far as to depict the exercise of authority as a form of oppression. Paulo Freire outlined a form of anti-authoritarian pedagogy that demanded that teachers needed to reject the 'ideology of oppression' and adopt a modest view of their role and learn from their students. He proposed an anti-authoritarian partnership where both teachers and students were 'simultaneously teachers *and* students'.[25]

Freire's exhortation to demote the authority of the teacher is no longer regarded as the eccentric sentiment of a marginal radical. Teachers often refer to themselves as learners in a self-conscious attempt to distance themselves from the authority of their profession. Some American principals and British headteachers describe themselves as 'lead learners' to convey the view that they are not old-fashioned authority figures but leaders. The adoption of the managerial vocabulary of leadership betrays a profound sense of unease about appearing to take formal authority too seriously.[26]

The move to restrain adult authority has led to many situations where grown-ups have developed a feeble sense of responsibility for guiding the education of the younger generation. As Lionel Elvin, former Director of the University of London's Institute of Education, observed in 1969:

> The fight against the old authoritarianism led us to neglect the degree to which the teacher's function must be positive, and has left us in a poor mental state to deal with the different problem of our own time. Our problem is not too much guidance of the young but too little. This point is crucial. And all the fears we may have of being labelled 'authoritarian' must not prevent our saying it.[27]

The question implicitly raised by Elvin was how teachers could provide positive leadership without being accused of acting in an authoritarian fashion.

## Confusing the problem of motivation with that of education

It is only when anxiety about school discipline is debated that society comes close to reflecting on the problem of adult authority. For their part, policy-makers and pedagogues rarely engage with the issues raised by the lack of cultural valuation for the exercise of adult authority. On the contrary, teaching strategies that are based on an authoritative style of classroom management are criticized often for being rigid, inflexible and for stifling children's initiative. In policy deliberations the question of authority is displaced by the quest for techniques that can motivate young people. Developing pedagogic techniques to motivate children is an important and worthwhile objective: however, too often, the focus on motivation has encouraged an emphasis of techniques – many of which are psychological

– and distracted policy-makers and their experts from considering the kind of education with which they want to motivate children.[28] From pre-school to higher education, the dominant concern of policy-makers is to motivate young people to learn and to stay in school and university.

Historically, the elevation of the issue of motivation to the main challenge facing the school coincided with the development of mass secondary education in the United States in the early twentieth century. The introduction of large numbers of students meant that teachers and officials were confronted with a situation where many secondary school pupils were unenthusiastic about attending school and, as one account recalls, 'discussions of secondary education became more frequently interlarded with a new, decisive criterion of performance – "the holding power of the school".'[29] Since that time, some critics of mass schooling have accepted the view that widening participation must necessarily lead to a motivational problem. But it is much more useful to conceptualize the pedagogic problem of motivation as related to a lack of clarity about what education is for.

The central message transmitted by educators and policy advisers is that 'far too many young people are simply not motivated by what secondary school has to offer'.[30] In an influential book, endorsed by Tony Blair, Michael Barber states that when the curriculum is redesigned, 'the motivation of young people needs to be a consideration of the highest priority'. And although he qualifies his categorical assertion on the primacy of this priority – 'motivation, though important, is not the sole concern' – the overriding message is that it is perceived as the dominant problem.[31] Deliberations on the curriculum are preoccupied with the question of how to motivate more than what to teach, to the point that approval of course content is often judged on its capacity to motivate.

The problem of motivating students is invariably blamed on poor pedagogy, and the solution to it is presented as the adoption of more relevant or stimulating teaching techniques. As the American cultural critic Neil Postman notes, 'there was a time when educators became famous for providing reasons for learning: now they become famous for inventing a method'.[32] This discussion rarely acknowledges the more basic question of how to give meaning to education, and rarely touches on how to establish an authoritative regime of teaching. Studies that attempt to link the question of motivation to the exercise of authority conclude frequently that the problem is that there is too much, rather than too little, authority. The contribution of Tom Bentley is paradigmatic in this respect. 'There is considerable evidence to show that many young people are often bored by school', he writes, linking the age-old problem of classroom boredom to the insensitive and authoritarian behaviour of teachers. Bentley claims that 'evidence' of student complaints indicates that 'teachers fail to treat pupils with proper respect, the lessons are too often boring, and that young people do not have sufficient influence over where, when or how they learn'.[33] Bentley believes that too much of what takes place in the classroom is the result of teacher initiative that disempowers students from influencing the way they should be educated.

Bentley explicitly advocates that the adult world should acquiesce to its loss of authority. He writes:

[I]f we want our learning to reflect current reality, we must be able to question old assumptions, and to understand what it is really like to be a young person growing up now. This involves a fundamental shift of power between older and younger generations. It means recognising that we do not have all the answers, and that we can learn from the young as well as teaching them ... As adults and guardians, we have the power to control much of what young people are allowed to do. But we do not necessarily have the authority, and when power and authority come apart, the result is eventually alienation, hostility and rejection.[34]

For Bentley, the erosion of adult authority is a fact of life to which teachers must acquiesce. He notes that the 'young are less prepared to follow rules unconditionally, to follow instructions blindly, and to accept received wisdom without questioning and testing it for themselves'.[35] The lack of respect for adult authority is, in his view, a positive development brought about by critically engaged students who apparently refuse to 'accept received wisdom without questioning and testing it for themselves'. What is interesting about this idealized construction of a critically engaged anti-authoritarian student is that they are apparently unmotivated and bored – even while they are continually questioning and testing received wisdom. Even more paradoxical is the belief that this representation of critically oriented youth helps the reader to understand 'underachievement' in schools.

Despite his own biological maturity, Bentley appears to support young people's scepticism of adult authority. He notes that there is 'less reason to trust and accept what those in authority say', and that for the young, 'there is a growing disjunction between the *power* of adults and institutions, and their *authority*'.[36] The conclusion he draws is that it is unrealistic to expect young people to be likely to accept authority: 'expecting young people automatically to accept someone's authority because they are in a position of power is unrealistic, as well as unhealthy'.[37] Once the exercise of adult authority is represented as an outdated and unrealistic exercise in futility, the relationship between student and teacher assumes the form of a negotiated partnership, in which the teacher has 'authority in the whole subject' and a mandate to 'shape pupil's rule of engagement', but, 'the learner also has a particular kind of authority'. Why? Because the pupil 'knows best whether he understands the questions at hand, and what the most effective way it is for him to learn it'.[38] If indeed the student knows best how to learn, there is little point in upholding the authoritative status of the teacher.

Bentley, like other policy experts, cannot dispense entirely with authority. What he offers is a model where authority becomes individuated, and everyone – teacher, student, parent – possesses it. A century ago Dewey opted for science as the substitute for adult authority. Contemporary culture is much more uncomfortable with any form of external authority, and therefore science is rarely held up as a solution to confronting the problem of schooling. Increasingly authority is represented as the outcome of how people feel

about themselves and others. This emphasis on emotional experience lends authority a therapeutic form.[39] Bentley provides a clear
statement of a therapeutic framing of authority:

> Authority is often presumed to rest in its outward manifestations
> – the titles that we use to address people, the list of achievements
> or length of experience that individuals have in a particular field.
> But authority is in fact a product of inner value, the value which
> a person places in her own worth, in relation to a particular
> domain, and the value which others recognize and affirm from
> their own perspectives. Authority is not conferred by formal rules
> of differentiation and status, although it can be reflected by
> them.[40]

From this standpoint, authority works as an individual attribute. It
is an 'inner value' closely linked to emotional encounters.

New motivational techniques presuppose a shift from external
authority to an individualistic orientation to the self. In this therapeutic scenario there is a dramatic shift from the ideal of a teacher
inspiring children, to one of children becoming motivated through
enjoying the freedom to develop themselves in line with their personal inclination. The so-called 'child-centred' pedagogy, that has
as its objective a self-initiated process of personal education, was
coherently formulated by the therapist Carl Rogers. Rogers explicitly
rejected 'authoritarian teaching' and forms of education that were
focused on the intellect. He insisted that when teachers become
facilitators who don't stand in the way of their students, children
acquire 'confidence and self-esteem', and added that teachers learn
to realize that the 'good life is within, not something which is
dependent on outside sources'.[41] Rogers counterposed academic
education, which has no 'personal meaning' for students, to an education that motivates students since it involves 'feelings or personal
meanings'. He claimed that motivation develops through meaningful personal experience and that the role of the facilitator is to
provide a 'psychological climate in which the learner is able to take
responsible control'. The overriding emphasis on motivation

demands that the facilitator help 'de-emphasise static or content goals' and encourage a 'focus on process'. [42]

The primacy of motivation leads Rogers and others to subordinate the intellectual content of learning to the process of gaining fulfilment through experience. Not all advocates of education as motivation adopt the consistently psychological perspective of Rogers, but they embrace an approach where the imperative of motivation takes precedence over the content of education.

The intellectual content of what pupils learn is often presented as an issue that must be subordinated to the task of finding a solution to the question of motivation. Frequently it is claimed that children's feelings and experience should dictate not only how but also *what* they are taught, which is why the intellectual content of school subjects has become a negotiable commodity. If what is taught is assessed according to its capacity to motivate, then so-called 'difficult' and 'challenging' – often represented as 'boring' – subjects need to be transformed into ones that are likely to appeal to children. Content becomes secondary to the overriding focus of motivation. The pursuit of this objective has led to what Ravitch described as 'the century-long effort to diminish the intellectual purposes of the schools'.[43] Advocates of anti-authoritarian child-centred education are not self-consciously anti-intellectual. However, they tend to take a pragmatic orientation to the intellectual content of schooling, evaluating subjects according to their potential to motivate – and if certain academic subjects appear to have little potential for motivating students, they are prepared to downgrade them regardless of their intellectual significance. That is the implication of White's insistence that the 'true centre of correlation on the school subjects is not science, nor literature, nor history, but the child's social activities'.[44]

Of course pedagogues should always attempt to promote forms of teaching that enhance the appeal of a subject and stimulate the motivation to learn. How a subject is taught should always be debated with a view to innovating new techniques of teaching. However, what should be taught needs to be evaluated according to very different criteria. The content of a syllabus needs to provide students with an understanding of the subject. For example, at the very least, students of history need to have a knowledge of their past. Unfortunately the main motive for changing the history curriculum in England was not the objective of improving children's knowledge of their past but to make it more 'relevant' to their lives. So, in the 1970s, the teaching of history was indicted on the grounds that 'children found lessons dull and repetitive', and one survey indicating that less than 30 per cent of children 'considered studying history to be of any value' was used as argument to reorganize the curriculum.[45] A one-sided obsession with making history less boring led pedagogues to focusing on making the subject more directly relevant to children. Since 1990, the curriculum has been stripped of chronology, and a sense of historical process has been substituted by a thin gruel of story-telling and skills-led weighing-up of evidence. The outcome of this exercise is the disaggregation of history and a loss of meaning of the past. And, despite the best efforts of curriculum innovators to make history more relevant and make it come alive, children are no less bored with the subject today than when they were required to follow a chronological succession of events from Ancient Greece to the present.

In the US, the post-Second World War crusade against 'boring chronological history' has often assumed a self-consciously anti-intellectual form. Ravitch recounts the example of Alameda County, California, where policy-makers claimed that, since a course on world problems 'had degenerated into chronological history' it had to make way for something 'more important', which was 'driver education'. Apparently pupils could 'penetrate democratic living' through their learning experience with the automobile.[46] In twenty-first-century Britain, educators attempt to motivate students not so much through learning about cars but by providing information about 'diet, exercise and other aspects of health'.[47]

The sad experience of the history curriculum indicates that it requires more than clever pedagogical techniques to promote the motivation of students. Similar attempts to raise students' motivation by making science and maths more relevant to their lives also have failed to realize their objectives. All that a one-sided emphasis on motivation has done is to distract schools from facing up to the challenge of providing quality education to children. Worse, the pragmatic and casual orientation towards the intellectual content of education has undermined the status of academic subjects and, through that, the authority of the teacher. And yet experience shows that it is authoritative classroom teachers who possess the potential for inspiring young people. They may resort to effective motivational strategies, but in the end it is their authoritative style of teaching that fuels the curiosity and interest of their pupils.

## Sneaking authority through the back door

The erosion of adult authority is associated with, first, the estrangement of grown-ups from engaging in a deliberate act of generational transaction, and then with their acquiescence to its consequences. Many writers have argued that responsibility for this development lies with progressive pedagogues who promoted a child-centred and egalitarian philosophy to the detriment of all else.[48] This interpretation is questionable. To a considerable extent, it is the ambiguities that adults possess about the exercise of their authority that has encouraged its erosion. This development is particularly striking in the pre-political domain of education, where a palpable loss of adult confidence has encouraged a growing reliance on expertise and motivational techniques.

The flip-side of the demotion of adult authority is the inflation of the authority of the child. Often this shift has been perceived as a move in the direction of child-centred education. However, it is more accurate to see this development as a semi-conscious strategy to by-pass the problems posed by the decline of adult authority. In a world where authority as such had acquired negative connotations, the difficulty of exercising it by adults could be dismissed as a fact of life in a modern world. In such circumstances the decline of authority was experienced by many not as a loss but as the prelude to the long-overdue democratization of the classroom.

The tendency to castigate 'progressive' education often distracts from openly recognizing the fact that, in the first instance, it is the difficulty that adults have in behaving authoritatively that accounts for the crisis of adult authority. The orientation and techniques promoted by progressive educators are not in themselves responsible for the decline of adult authority. Indeed there is much to be said for promoting a less rigid and open-ended form of pedagogy that allows children the optimum scope for self-expression and for the realization of their individuality. Providing children with opportunities to experiment and with greater freedom to explore the world can yield tremendous benefits for the child. In many cases this form of risk-taking pedagogy is presented as anti-authority: however, if it is to work, it requires the input of confident and intelligent adults who are able to exercise influence over children in an authoritative manner. It is a solid and authoritative school ethos that provides the foundation for a free and open-ended learning process. The ability of children to express themselves depends on a degree of self-control, and unless they learned the habit of self-mastery it is far from evident what they will be expressing.

Although child-centred progressive education is often associated with egalitarianism, the two often contradict one another. With its emphasis on self-actualization and individual self-expression, progressive education is potentially anti-egalitarian. Indeed, it has tended to work best in circumstances where children enjoy the benefits of the considerable cultural capital of their prosperous parents. That is one reason why in current times a genuinely non-conformist child-oriented education exists only on the margins of society. We are preached the rhetoric of child-centred education; but in a world where education is assigned the role of serving society, education becomes anything but child-centred.

In contemporary times, child-centred rhetoric serves to legitimize and indirectly reinforce the loss of an open exercise of the teacher's authority in the classroom. Motivational techniques claim to encourage children to direct their own learning and give them a voice in the classroom. They exhort teachers to regard children as 'intelligence agents' or as 'active learners' who can from an early age 'convert their experience into assumptions and theories about the world'.[49] Policy-makers insist on celebrating the pupil's voice in education and advocate 'support for personalized learning'.[50] In some cases children are offered the opportunity to realize themselves through happiness and emotional education. But these are essentially motivational and therapeutic techniques designed to manage behaviour. As one study noted, 'Under the ambiguities of the rubric of student-centredness, choice and empowerment, progressivist aspirations have dovetailed with managerial priorities.'[51] Typically these techniques for managing behaviour are based on the premise that children respond to an initiative implemented and enforced by an adult, albeit indirectly.

More often than not, child-centred pedagogy turns into an indirect form of adult control. Dewey specifically endorsed this approach when he argued that the teacher should 'determine the environment of the child, and thus by indirection to direct'.[52] Burkard argues that those who advocate it opt for a manipulative form of control 'which sits more easily on their consciences than the more simple and honest expedient of giving direct orders'.[53] He states that:

> The fundamental myth of progressive education is the presumed removal of the teacher as the source of authority, with children being vested with the power to direct their own learning. In reality, the teacher is just as much in control as in a traditional school. There is an essential element of dishonesty, or at least self-delusion, involved. Direct authority is at least honest and open in its aims: the nature of the relationship is not disguised. The progressive educator exercises authority through manipulation.[54]

Burkard is right to point to the manipulative character of managerially inspired motivational techniques. However, whether the teacher is 'just as much in control as in a traditional school' is far from certain. Certainly the demotion of the status of the teacher's authority compromises the effectiveness with which a classroom can be managed. What the teacher achieves is not so much 'authority through manipulation' but a measure of control.

The question of asserting control through the application of motivational techniques will be considered further in my discussion of therapeutic education. For now, it is important to note that the self-conscious promotion of the student voice frequently serves to constrain the authority of the teachers and to even control their behaviour. It is worth noting that, since 2005, Ofsted inspections invite 'the views of young people' specifically on 'matters to do with the quality of teaching and learning'.[55] Some schools have embraced this practice to the point where students have been sent on training courses to learn how to assess the classroom performance of teachers. Children have also been encouraged to sit in on the interviews of teachers applying for employment. One north London school adopted a speed-dating style of interview procedure, whereby candidates for the posts of assistant head and deputy head were questioned for two and half minutes by 16 different pupils one after another. These interviews were justified on the grounds that they provided an opportunity for a large number of students to make an assessment of the candidates. After the interviews, the students rated each candidate and allocated each of them a point score.[56] Many officials and educators enthusiastically endorse this policy of providing children with the authority to assess the professional qualities of their teachers. They claim that this form of participation helps to inspire students to become more motivated about their studies. That this policy also has considerable potential to further erode the professional status of teachers is not considered a problem by policymakers: indeed, they have worked hard to fuel this process.

The project of using children to police teachers was given official recognition when the Government accepted a Liberal Democrat amendment to its Education Bill in November 2008. The aim of this amendment was to impose a new duty on schools to 'invite and consider' children's views. Advocates of this amendment pointed to the conclusions of an Ofsted survey, which found that a third of the pupils that it consulted felt that they were not listened to properly by their school. The imperative of listening to schoolchildren was spelled out by Children's Minister, Baroness Morgan, who told the House of Lords that 'as a minimum, schools should seek and take account of pupils' views on policies on the delivery of the curriculum, behaviour, the uniform, school food, health and safety, equalities and sustainability, not simply on what colour to paint the walls'. The significance that this politician attaches to the views of the child is symptomatic of the casual manner with which relations of authority are approached by policy-makers. The fact that the institutionalization of the student voice is supported by Parliament is likely to have a significant role in diminishing teachers' confidence in the assertion of their professional status.

Sections of the teaching profession have recognized this point. Chris Keates, General Secretary of the NASUWT, has argued that using pupils to interview teachers strikes 'at the heart of what constitutes an appropriate pupil/teacher relationship'.[57] Keates has also argued that the use of students to interview and monitor the performance of their teachers undermines teachers' status. 'It demonstrates a failure to respect the professional role and status of teachers and involves youngsters in a way which disempowers and deprofessionalises the staff', she said. To substantiate her point she gave the example of a teacher in the north-east of England who was taunted about matters that came up during the course of the interview by a pupil who had interviewed her.[58]

As one study suggests, the promotion of the student voice may be used as evidence for 'criticizing and controlling teachers'.[59] Such pressures reinforce the tendency of many teachers to adopt an even more defensive style of classroom management. The institutionalization of the student voice will have the perverse effect of fostering a climate where teachers will become ever more sensitive to the fact that they are on trial. Sadly, the one group whose authoritative voice ought to dominate education – teachers – is likely to be expressed in a hesitant manner. At a time when children experience less adult authority and control than ever before, it is singularly damaging to force teachers onto the defensive.

# 4

## Socialization in Reverse

The ambiguities associated with the exercise of authority in education are most striking in relation to the task of socialization. Socialization is the process through which children are prepared for the world ahead of them. This is a responsibility that is carried out by adults at home and their communities, and in the formal setting of the school. Although the purpose of education is to acquaint children with their intellectual and cultural inheritance, it also attempts to socialize them into the ways of behaviour of their cultural habitat. However, the devaluation of adult authority has complicated this task and called into question parents' capacity to socialize their offspring.

During the past century, responsibility for socialization has gradually shifted from the parent to the school. The depreciation of adulthood has been paralleled by the rise of professionals who claim that they are the ones who possess the expertise required to socialize children. What has emerged is a more pragmatic form of socialization that often relies on experts who transmit values by directly targeting children.

As noted previously, the argument that grown-ups do not have all the answers facing the world has been frequently used in the past to query the status of adult authority. In recent times this downbeat assessment of adult wisdom has mutated into an outright condemnation of the moral status of the older generations. 'Adults have ruined our world', is the headline of an article published by an online magazine targeting children. It warns that 'adults are ruining the world we are growing up in' and asks 'How is climate change going to affect us as the next generation'?[1] A similar message is communicated by the green crusader Jonathan Porritt, who informed children that 'your parents and grandparents have made a mess of looking after the earth' and added that 'they may deny it, but they are stealing your future'.[2] Instead of serving as role models, often adults are castigated for setting a bad example to children. One headteacher who was charged with carrying out a review of behaviour in English schools in 2008 pointed the finger of blame at adults for setting a bad example for young people. He observed that we 'live in a greedy culture' in which 'we are rude to each other', and 'children follow that'.[3] If, indeed, adults are so prone to set a negative example, how can they be entrusted with the task of preparing their children for the world they face?

The condemnation of adult behaviour is paralleled by a tendency to flatter children through suggesting that their values are more enlightened because they are more up-to-date than those of their elders. Marc Prensky, an advocate of digital learning, argues that, unlike adults, children are used to the 'instantaneity of hypertext, downloaded music, phones in their pockets, a library of laptops, beamed messages and instant messaging'. As a result they have 'little patience for lectures, step-by-step logic and "tell-test" instruction'. Prensky takes the view that as far as children are concerned the traditional curriculum is not interesting. Prensky's conclusion is that adults will have to change and become more like the young 'digital natives'.[4] This advice is congruent with the development of what can be described most accurately as socialization-in-reverse – a phenomenon where children are entrusted with the mission of socializing their elders.

## The problems of socialization

A lack of confidence in the capacity of ordinary adults to undertake the duty of socializing the younger generation has been evident since early modern times. According to one account, in the eighteenth century in 'all stations of society and in all sorts of countries the decline and feared disintegration of society was linked to the dire need to correct the manners of badly behaved adults, and sturdy appeal was made to the upbringing of children to prevent the future likes of them'.[5] The philosopher John Stuart Mill, the author of *On Liberty*, linked his call for the compulsory schooling of children to his distrust of parental competence. He regarded state-sponsored formal education as possessing the capacity to free children from the 'uncultivated' influence of their parents. He asserted that since 'the uncultivated cannot be competent judges of cultivation', they needed the support of enlightened educators to socialize their children.[6] Lack of confidence in parents' capacity to develop their children led many nineteenth-century reformers to uphold formal education as the principal institution of socialization. Others, such as Emile Durkheim, one of the founders of the discipline of modern sociology, argued that though the family had an important role to play in the socialization of children, so too did the State. Durkheim insisted that 'education consists of a methodical socialization of the young generation'.[7] Indeed, he took the view that the very purpose of education was to 'adapt the child to the social environment in which he is destined to live'.[8]

Durkheim's close association of education with socialization stemmed from his preoccupation with overcoming the fragmentary tendencies that prevailed in nineteenth-century industrial society. He looked upon education as a potentially powerful force for social integration. He was adamant that 'society can survive only if there exists among its members a sufficient degree of homogeneity' and concluded that 'education perpetuates and reinforces this homogeneity by fixing in the child, from the beginning, the essential similarities that collective life demands'.[9] The objective of social integration outlined by Durkheim was thought to be far too important to leave in the hands of parents. Institutions such as that of religion, which have traditionally contributed to this task, had lost significant influence in an increasingly secular modern world. In such circumstances the newly created institutions of public education were assigned a leading role in the socialization of children. 'Education,' noted Durkheim, 'far from having its unique or principal object the individual and his interest, is above all the means by which society perpetually recreates the conditions of its very existence.'[10]

The socialization imperative institutionalized through public education co-existed in an uneasy relationship with the family. Formally parents were still held responsible for cultivating the moral and social sensibilities of their offspring. Officially schools were given a supporting role in the realization of this project. The Hadow Report, published by the British Government in 1926, expressed the belief that the 'teachers of our country – given their opportunity – can bring the discipline of the school to aid the influence of home in making a new generation which alike in character, in tastes and trained skill will justify them abundantly of all their labours'. But although the Hadow Report embraced the project of socialization, in line with prevailing sentiment it did not go so far as to promote it as the principal end of education. In the first half of the twentieth century British schools upheld the ideal of strengthening character – both individual and national – which could 'serve to elevate the nation'.[11]

By the turn of the twentieth century many educators shared Mill's ambivalence about the influence of parents and the home upon children. They took the view that parents not only lacked the authority but also the intellectual and moral resources necessary for socializing children. At a time when many parents felt insecure about the task of rearing their children, they faced pressure from professionals to acquiesce to their expertise.

## The uneasy relationship between adult authority and experts

Since the late nineteenth century the exercise of adult authority has existed in an uneasy relationship with the claims of scientific expertise. At the very time that different forms of pre-political authority lost influence and legitimacy, the prestige of science was in ascendance. For many educators and psychologists, the success of the promise of the authority of science appeared as an effective and positive alternative to the apparently outdated child-rearing and teaching practices of the past. As one study of this process wrote:

'The vagaries of casual stories about children, the eccentricities of folk knowledge, and the superstitions of grandmothers were all to be cleansed by the mighty brush of scientific method.'[12] A new group of experts claimed that their science entitled them to be the authoritative voices on issues that were hitherto perceived as strictly pertaining to the domain of personal and family life. As one study of this group's ascendancy notes: 'The authoritative voice of "scientific experts" on child development advised repeatedly that the correct training of children required an expertise that few modern parents possessed.'[13] From their perspective, child-rearing, education and relationships needed to be reorganized in accordance with the latest finding of scientific research. The new cohort of experts possessed a powerful crusading ethos and did not confine themselves to the presentation of research and observations. Kessen writes that:

> Critical examination and study of parental practices and child behaviour almost inevitably slipped subtly over to advice about parental practices and child behaviour. The scientific statement became an ethical imperative, the descriptive account became normative. And along the way, there have been unsettling occasions in which scraps of knowledge, gathered by whatever procedures were held to be proper science at the time, were given inordinate weight against poor old defenceless folk knowledge.[14]

Nor did these experts merely provide advice. Often with the backing of official institutions they could impose their proposals on schools and directly influence the conduct of family life. As against the authority of science, the insights and values of ordinary people enjoyed little cultural valuation. This outlook was clearly communicated by a British expert, Jean Ayling, who observed in 1930 that 'most of the children of my acquaintance are already badly damaged at an early age'. Her solution was to limit the role of parents, since they have a 'strictly bounded domain of usefulness', and to assign the wider task of child socialization to the helping professions.[15]

    It is worth noting that the record of the science in the domains of child-rearing, education and relationships has proved to be one of ever-recurring fads that rarely achieve any positive durable results.[16] Nevertheless, at a time when adult authority was on the defensive, the scientific expert gained an ever-increasing influence over the conduct of inter-generational relations. Typically educational experts claimed that since their proposals were based on the findings of purely objective science, only the prejudiced could possibly disagree with them. Pedagogic techniques were frequently promoted on the ground that they were based on the latest psychological research into child development or new objective theories of learning. As far as Dewey was concerned, only an incorrigible superstitious traditionalist could object to the new scientific pedagogy. He could not comprehend how anyone could resist what the latest discoveries of the 'science of individual psychology' showed about the way people learn. He wrote that 'it was a little as if no one had been willing to put radios on the market, because it was obviously an absurd idea that sound can be transmitted through vast distances'. And with an air of impatience he exclaimed that 'although these psychological discoveries are as well established today as the facts of the radio, they are still temperamentally abhorrent to a great many schoolmasters and parents'.[17] Dewey, like many of his colleagues, clearly felt frustrated by what he perceived as the unholy alliance of prejudiced parents and unimaginative traditionalist teachers who questioned the new science of the curriculum.

The authority of experts rested on the claim that they possessed insights into the development of children and education that were far superior to the traditional practices of teachers and parents. These experts did not confine themselves to the advocacy of their science – they also implicitly, and in some cases explicitly, called into question the competence of parents. They regarded the 'old-fashioned' teacher with equal contempt and insisted that education had to be modernized along new scientific principles. One important theme advocated by the modernizing expert was the necessity for education to become more socially useful and relevant to a changing modern world. Their focus on social utility disposed them towards reframing education as the most important institution of socialization. This emphasis was further reinforced by an obsession with change and a dismissal of the past. For the new pedagogic expert, traditional education was outdated because it was traditional and therefore unlikely to be useful in a contemporary world. It also followed that knowledge which was not deemed to be socially useful could only be allowed a marginal role in the modern curriculum. The new pedagogy, wedded to the project of socialization, showed little interest in academic knowledge-based learning and regarded the cultivation of intellect as far less important than providing a curriculum that was socially relevant. Ever since the turn of the twentieth century this philistine fusion of education-as-socialization and an instrumentalist orientation to knowledge has had a significant influence over mainstream pedagogy.

Children do need to become socialized and gain an understanding about what it means to become a member of their society. But the way in which many education experts represented this issue was to turn the school into an institution where, through careful social engineering, the child was to be shaped to adapt to the demands of society. This approach was systematically formulated by Edward Ross, a leading American sociologist, who in 1901 enthusiastically argued that free public education was 'an engine of social control'. He stated that it was the mission of schools 'to collect little plastic lumps of human dough from private households and shape them on the social kneading-board'.[18] Not all experts embraced the rigid social engineering doctrine promoted by Ross. But they all shared a common conviction that the role of schools was to extract children from their family so that they could come under the influence of enlightened professionals. Socialization required saving children from the deleterious influence of their home life.

John Dewey, along with most progressive educators, took the view that schools should not simply socialize children to accept society's prevailing norms and values. Unlike Ross, he believed that the school had a duty to provide children with a more enlightened outlook; that 'it is the business of the school environment to eliminate, so far as possible, the unworthy features of the existing environment'. Moreover, he hoped that as a 'society becomes more enlightened, it realizes that it is responsible not to transmit and conserve the whole of its existing arrangements, but only such as make for a better future society'. Dewey concluded that the 'school is its chief agency for the accomplishment of this end'.[19] But he was no less insistent than Ross that the school had to correct the impoverished moral and intellectual influence that parents exercised over their children. His advocacy of nursery education was motivated by his belief in its potential for weaning children away from the negative influence of their life at home. 'They will forget to imitate the loud and coarse things they see at home, their attention will be centred on problems which were designed by the school to teach better aims and methods', he noted.[20]

The advocacy of educational expertise was transmitted through what Kessen has characterized as a 'salvationist view of children'.[21] According to this view, children were by nature innately good, with impulses that should be allowed to flourish and develop. In the 1920s, English progressive educators believed that children could play a vital role in the moral regeneration of the nation. 'This regeneration was to be achieved through developing the spiritual life of the child, primarily by means of promoting individual creativity', notes one study of this movement.[22] From this perspective the exercise of adult authority at home and in schools tended to be seen as a potential problem since it could serve as an obstacle to the spontaneous development of a child. Consequently traditional education was attacked not only because it was outdated, but because it was damaging to the development of the child. The salvationist view of the child was systematically promoted by advocates of what is often called 'child-centred education'. In 1926 Harold Rugg, one of the leading American proponents of this approach, declared 'the need for building the curriculum around the activities and interests of the children'. As far as Rugg was concerned the child-centred curriculum represented the future whereas the subject-based curriculum was steeped in the past.[23]

The salvationist perspective of children has often upheld their emotional well-being as a key priority for education. Experts argue that since unhappy children grow up into unhappy adults it is necessary to use the insights of the latest scientific discoveries to solve the emotional problems of childhood. Experts also claim to have a unique competence to deal with the emotional problems of children. As Ravitch notes, guidance experts in the US asserted that 'they knew how to "adjust" youngsters' personality; knew better than their parents how to turn them into the right sort of persons, with correct values, appreciations, attitudes, behaviours, and feelings: could, if only the curriculum was revised, shape society infinitely better than the one that existed'.[24] In more recent times, the call to introduce behaviour management in schools in order to offset the problems caused by emotionally illiterate parents is regularly voiced by experts.[25] Moreover the belief that parents lack the competence to nurture the emotional development of their children is far more widespread today than in the past.

Many proponents of the salvationist view of children believed that in adopting scientific child-rearing, the reform of education would lead to the reform of society. This sentiment, which was particularly influential among child psychologists, endures to this day. Kessen wrote that child psychologists, 'whatever their theoretical stripe, have taken the Romantic notion of childish innocence and openness a long way towards the several forms of "if only we could make matters right with the child, the world would be a better place"'. He adds that the 'child became the carrier, of political progressivism and the optimism of reformers'.[26]

Since the early twentieth century the tendency to bank on children as the vehicles of social reform has become more and more widely practised by policy-makers. Today, in the UK, all the main political parties are wedded to the idea of 'early intervention' in a child's life. In August 2006, Prime Minister Tony Blair announced that since potential troublemakers could be identified even before they are born, the Government would intervene to head off future problems. Early intervention through Government-run programmes like Sure Start is designed to offset the parenting deficit that apparently afflicts English families, and produce the kind of children that will turn into good citizens. Schools, too, have adopted this salvationist perspective.

The tendency for schools to assume responsibility for the

nurturing and socialization-related activities traditionally carried out within the family first became prevalent in the US during the inter-war period. These policies were originally developed to deal with the problems facing immigrant parents who found it difficult to socialize their children into the American way of life. Hofstadter wrote that 'immigrant parents unfamiliar with American ways, were inadequate guides to what their children needed to know, and the schools were now thrust into the parental role'. But the schools also took the view that their pupils could in turn help socialize the parents of immigrant families into the American way of life. Hofstadter noted that 'the children exposed to Yankee schoolmarms in the morning were expected to become instruments of Americanization by bringing home in the afternoon instructions in conduct and hygiene that their parents would take to heart'.[27]

The agenda of Americanizing the parents of immigrant children through the school was also observed by Arendt. She believed that this expansion of the role of schooling had a significant influence in the way in which socialization would be conceptualized. If the schools could successfully undertake the task of socializing immigrant parents through their children, what was to stop them from extending this project to other sections of society? Arendt argued:

> The political role that education plays in a land of the immigrants, the fact that the schools not only serve to Americanise the children but affect their parents as well, that here in fact one helps to shed an old world and enter into a new one, encourages the illusion that a new world is being built through the education of the children.[28]

The salvationist view of a new world built through the education of children was systematically promoted through the project of assimilating immigrant communities into the American way of life. However, in a world where the legitimacy of adult authority was constantly questioned, a similar model of socialization was soon adopted towards other parents.

In the early twentieth century educators and child experts sought to by-pass parental authority through assuming responsibility for the socialization of young people. It was only a matter of time before their conviction that parents had little to teach their children encouraged some to suggest that perhaps parents could learn from their children. As a result, children are encouraged to wean their parents away from outdated prejudices and to adopt the latest wisdom provided by expert authority. The outcome of this development is the encouragement of *socialization in reverse*. This is a reversal in authority relations, with dramatic consequences for inter-generational interaction.

The socialization of children involves a delicate transaction between parents and schools. Even the most complacent curriculum expert cannot be indifferent to the status of adult authority overall. Educators who are otherwise dismissive of parental competence understand that they cannot challenge parental authority too overtly without provoking a potentially damaging conflict. They know that unless parents successfully manage the behaviour of their children, the schools will be crushed by an impossible burden. Consequently the rhetoric of school–parent partnership prevails, and there is little open discussion of the relative weight of expert versus parent authority.

Back in 1967, the Plowden Report into English primary education drew attention to the reluctance of educators to speak plainly on this subject:

> An aim, which was hardly mentioned by head teachers and yet one which, if challenged, they would almost certainly have admitted, is the co-operation of school and home and, with it, that of making good to children, as far as possible, the deficiencies of their backgrounds. That this aim found so little expression is significant. The implications of the relationships between school and home have still to be worked out; some teachers are anxious about the extent to which the school is taking the responsibility for the child's welfare and thus undermining the responsibility, as some would put it, of parents.[29]

No doubt many educators are devoted to the cause of using schools to help children overcome the 'deficiencies of their backgrounds' out of a commitment to social justice and reform. Many of them are also sensitive to the danger that the expansion of the role of the school may represent to the exercise of parental responsibility. That is one reason why Plowden was able to report that teachers tended to be careful to cultivate good relations with parents. But that was in 1967. In recent times this restraint has given way to a far more aggressive affirmation of the role of expert authority.

Since the mid-1990s the implicit questioning of the ability of parents to socialize their children has become increasingly strident. As a result there has been a gradual shift in the way in which the uneasy partnership between family and school is portrayed by experts. Educationalists often assume that poor parenting and the fragmentation of the family is a fact of life which necessitates that schools assume responsibility for forms of socialization that were hitherto carried out in the home. This was the message communicated to the September 2008 conference of the Association of Schools and College Leaders by its General Secretary, Dr John Dunford. Dunford stated that 'schools have a much stronger role in bringing up children than in previous years'. He went on to argue that the school is 'the last moral force', and that for some children 'it is only the school that provides a framework that sets the line between what is and isn't acceptable'. His point was reinforced by the union's President, Brian Lightman, who asserted that schools were now often forced to parent children as well as teach them.[30] Dunford's and Lightman's perception that schools are the last 'moral force' is underpinned by a lack of trust about the capacity of adults – particularly parents – to act as positive moral agents. Such attitudes indicate that the relationship between expertise and the exercise of adult authority has become more complicated.

## Socialization as behaviour management

In recent decades there has been a gradual shift in the way in which the task of socialization is transmitted through formal schooling.

Historically, education contributed to the process of socialization by helping to introduce young people into the prevailing system of cultural values. This involved learning about 'rules of conduct and expectations about future behaviour' as well as the 'accumulated know-how for planting crops, making dwellings, dealing with sorcery or calculating logarithms'.[31] Those concerned with how socialization worked were mainly interested in issues associated with the transmissions of moral and cultural attitudes. These issues still retain their relevance. Indeed, as I discuss in the next chapter, the question of what values education should instil in children is arguably a more complicated and contested problem than it was in the last century. But there is one striking difference between the way in which schools see the role of socialization now and the way it was understood a century ago. Socialization is perceived increasingly as a form of behaviour management. It is less about indoctrinating pupils into an established way of life, or familiarizing them about a community's moral code, than it is about instructing them about how to manage their emotions and conduct relationships with others, and training them in so-called life-skills.

The gradual reorganization of socialization around the imperative of behaviour management has been influenced by three distinct but mutually reinforcing developments. First, adult authority has always found the management of young people's behaviour both bewildering and challenging. As a result, many parents have welcomed the support that schools and experts could provide. Second, the problems of individual behaviour and of emotional development provided a complex of issues where experts could assert their scientific authority. In the domain of emotions, psychologists could highlight both their expertise and claim authority for managing the behaviour of children. Consequently, experts had a real incentive to inflate and complicate the significance of the issue of a child's well-being and to introduce it into the domain of formal education. In a sense, the claim that experts could understand the problems facing children better than anyone else endowed them with authority. Finally, the elevation of the importance of a child's capacity to adapt to new circumstances resonated with the widely accepted belief that since change was constant, society required people who could respond flexibly to new conditions. This belief had a momentous impact on the way in which socialization was perceived. As one prescient study noted almost five decades ago, 'The fact that society seems to be changing so rapidly is thought to necessitate the development of flexibility of outlook in children rather than the acquiring of knowledge.'[32] In education, the value of flexibility has acquired the status of an ideology. Cultivating a flexible personality drew on the techniques developed by psychology and turned adaptability into one of the central aims of the curriculum.

By the middle of the twentieth century, many education experts argued that effective teachers needed to understand how to manage the emotional and personal problems facing their pupils. This standpoint was forcefully voiced by some American educators, who took the view that behaviour management was the key to the successful socialization of adolescents. Advocates of this 'life-adjustment' approach insisted that schools had to devote significant resources towards helping children deal with their personal and social issues. They believed that guiding students to cope with their emotions, personal problems and relationships would allow them to become 'fit and happy members of contemporary society'.[33] The rising influence of behavioural psychology acquired growing influence in the 1990s, when the traditional problems associated with education were gradually redefined as the consequence of different emotional deficits. On both sides of the Atlantic, children's low self-esteem was held responsible for virtually every educational problem. As one American study notes, 'by the 1980s, self-esteem was touted in the professional literature as both a means and an end of education.'[34] The UK followed suit and by the turn of the twenty-first century the socialization of schoolchildren increasingly assumed the form of emotional training. One Government advisory group on 'Education for Citizenship and the Teaching of Democracy in Schools' considered self-esteem to be a key core skill. Regularly policy documents convey the idea that self-esteem and emotional literacy is a value in its own right.[35]

The values and aims outlined by the 1999 National Curriculum illustrate the way that socialization is represented through the prism of emotional training. The document highlights the importance of education in reflecting the 'enduring values' of society. However, the enduring values that the National Curriculum upholds have little to do with the kind of moral, cultural or political principles that traditionally are transmitted from one generation to another. In line with the therapeutic ethos of our times, the weight of these 'enduring values' is towards emotional and behaviour management. First on the list is 'valuing ourselves', followed by valuing 'our families and other relationships'. Finally, the list calls for valuing 'the wider groups to which we belong, the diversity in our society and the environment in which we live'. The central role assigned to the value of 'valuing ourselves' is further reinforced in the discussion on the aims of the curriculum. It states that the school curriculum 'should promote pupils' self-esteem and emotional well-being'. Schools are also allocated the role of helping children 'form and maintain worthwhile and satisfying relationships'.[36]

The growing emphasis of the curriculum on behaviour management means that socialization is increasingly perceived in a highly individualized and personalized form. The shift from valuing your nation, your religion, or your way of life to 'valuing ourselves' is not simply one of emphasis. It represents an important reorientation from the idea that socialization involves the inter-generational process of values transmission to one that relies on techniques of behaviour management supervised by experts. How children feel about themselves constitutes the main focus of pedagogic interest. One supporter of the 1999 curriculum has observed that its aims 'place a good deal of emphasis on the pupil's personal well-being, practical reasoning and preparation for civic life'. According to his calculation, 60 per cent of the 'items in the list are about personal qualities we would like pupils to have' while 'knowledge aims' constitute 30 per cent.[37]

Advocates of the application of behaviour management techniques to the classroom recognize, sometimes explicitly, that their approach led to a form of socialization that is radically different from the past. 'While socialization is still vitally important, the challenge of socialization is not the same as it used to be', observes Bentley. Why? The answer offered is that, because we live in a constantly changing world where assumptions about the conduct of relationships are continually called into question, it is difficult to provide an authoritative guide to life. Under such circumstances, socialization needs to help people to acquire the soft skills necessary for conducting relationships and respond to events. However, there is one value – 'one of the most important of the values of younger people' – that must be addressed through socialization, argues Bentley; and that is young people's desire for 'authenticity'. From this perspective the servicing of the psychological drive for genuine self-expression becomes a fundamental objective of successful socialization.[38]

The primacy that the curriculum attaches to the promotion of pupils' well-being is often perceived as the response of a generous child-centred society devoted to nurturing its young. No doubt many psychologists and educators are seriously committed to the challenge of improving the emotional life of young people. But the refocusing of the process of socialization towards a more personalized and emotionally directed approach should not be interpreted as representing an enlightened response to children's emotional needs. As noted above, the embrace of behaviour management has been influenced by the weakening of adult authority and the ascendancy of the expert. In recent times the agenda promoted through behaviour management has also appealed to policy-makers and sections of business who uphold the ideal of a flexible workforce. Hence the growing tendency to depict personal attributes as 'soft skills' that are necessary for managing life in a changing world. In line with this development, official publications often prefer to refer to learning skills than studying subjects.

In contemporary times the project of socializing children through behaviour management is closely associated with the promotion of skills in the classroom. Virtually every personal attribute has been rebranded as a skill, and advocates of emotional education demand its further expansion. The fusion of the skills agenda with that of behaviour management was evident during a series of discussions charged with reviewing England's primary curriculum in early 2008. It was reported that those 1,500 people who attended the 60 seminars stressed the importance of skills training, and called 'for a focus on lifestyle lessons covering issues such as drugs, sex, healthy diets and thinking skills'. It was claimed that those who were consulted wanted pupils to 'study fewer formal subjects to allow more time for their social and personal development'.[39] The attachment to lifestyle and emotional management was most vehemently endorsed by John Bangs, the head of education of the National Union of Teachers (NUT), who claimed that personal development was 'shamefully neglected' in recent times.[40] There is now an influential lobby of policy-makers, pedagogues and school psychologists who are determined to redirect schools from academic subjects towards the provision of skills and emotional education. One leading advocate of this skills agenda, John White, wants the National Curriculum to be focused on skills such as team-building, public speaking and problem-solving, rather than what he scathingly dismisses as an 'encyclopaedic knowledge' of the world.[41]

Thankfully many parents and teachers understand the importance of providing children with a high quality academic education. There is a widespread awareness of the fact that schools that provide a solid background in the main subjects are necessary for providing children with the foundation to make their way in the world and to respond to new challenges. From time to time parents react against the latest behaviour management gimmicks, such as the recent introduction of emotional education and happiness courses. However, such reactions occur in a context where adult authority – particularly that of parents – is very much on the defensive. In such circumstances there is a temptation to leave education to the experts. But the experts are not prepared to return the favour. They know that if they are to assume authority for the socialization of the child, they need constantly to call into question the authority of the parent.

## Socialization in reverse

The ideals conveyed through behaviour management techniques constitute a distinct and key dimension of the way in which formal education goes about the business of socializing children. But socialization cannot confine itself to promoting ideals associated with the emotional well-being of children or the life-skills seen as necessary for coping with a changing world. Every society needs to transmit ideas about the conduct of life and about the ideals it upholds. In previous times, such ideals were communicated through the process of an inter-generational conversation about the norms of moral behaviour. However, as noted previously, with the erosion of adult authority the influence of the older generation's values has lost much of its force. This erosion of authority has also affected schools and their capacity to pass on the received wisdom of the past. Constant debates on religious, citizenship and values education indicate that the adoption of emotional and relationships education serves to divert attention from confronting the crisis of socialization.

Policy-makers and educators have sought to by-pass the problem of the inter-generational transmission of values by attempting to use schools to socialize children directly into values elaborated by experts and pedagogues. This approach has important implications for the inter-generational relations. In the course of teaching children the latest enlightened 'value', it is difficult to avoid concluding that these views are superior to the antiquated sentiments held by their parents. Implicitly, the direct socialization of children into expert-derived values serves to distance the young from the old. The view that the young know better than their elders has been a constant theme in the modern era. Recently, this sentiment has begun to be legitimized through the workings of the institution of education.

There are also powerful cultural forces which suggest that the young are also better people than their elders. Historically this sentiment was systematically conveyed through the child-centred salvationist perspective that represented children as the vehicles for progressive educational change. More recently this child-centred approach has gained cultural currency, leading to the elevation of the moral status and authority of the child. Consulting the student voice is not confined to schools: children are now regularly 'consulted' on many of the major issues confronting public life, and numerous advocates of children's rights claim that young people should be seen as equal decision-makers within the family.

The elevation of the moral status of the child stands in direct contrast to the steady depreciation of adulthood. Popular culture treats adults, and parents in particular, in an unattractive light. Films and television programmes portray parents as out-of-touch deadbeats who are insensitive to their youngsters' needs.[42] Politicians and policy-makers have internalized these sentiments and frequently blame parents for many of the problems that afflict society. Such views extend into the realm of education, where parents are charged with being complicit in the underachievement of their children. This trend has been particularly visible in the past decade. One study notes that in New Labour policy discussions 'lack of parental discipline is linked to problems of truancy, anti-social behaviour, offending and obesity'.[43] Current social policy is oriented towards altering the behaviour of parents, in an approach that has been described as 'New Labour's resocialization programme'. The project of re-socializing parents has precedents in the past. According to Gewitz it was promoted through the 'municipalisation of health visiting services for working-class mothers in the inter-war years' as well as through 'Plowden-inspired attempts to inculcate positive parental attitudes to schooling in the late 1960s and 1970s' and the 'Parents' Charter of the early 1990s'.[44] What has changed is that current policy initiatives are not confined to a particular group of 'problem parents', and they are far more intrusive than in previous times.

Arguably, the most important policy innovation in the project of re-socializing parents is the way in which it is directly linked to the socialization of children. In schools, children are often not only taught to act in accordance with the latest values that appear on the curriculum, but to encourage their parents to change their behaviour, for example to buy more healthy food or to recycle waste.

The main precedent for this approach is the experience of schools in the US which sought to Americanize immigrant parents through the schooling of their children. From time to time societies – particularly totalitarian ones – have attempted to use children to ensure that their parents conform to the officially sanctioned worldview. However, it is only in recent times that this form of indirect indoctrination has been used in liberal democracies in association with the self-conscious elevation of the moral status of young people.

It is important not to perceive the trend towards socialization in reverse as a process driven by a carefully elaborated agenda, through which the authorities are self-consciously manipulating children to police their parents. It is far more useful to interpret the trend towards socialization in reverse as just that, a trend, which is the indirect outcome of the growing confusion that surrounds inter-generational relations. Such confusions have encouraged a more fluid relationship between generations which, in certain situations, leads to a reversal of authority between old and young. In such circumstances the management of socialization through expertise can intensify the problem and contribute to a situation where the episodic reversal of generational authority has become culturally acceptable.

The process of socialization in reverse works through communicating the idea that children possess knowledge and competence about certain important issues and social experience that is way ahead of their parents. This idea has some basis in reality: young people are far more knowledgeable about the latest music and fashion than their elders, many adults are less able to manipulate new forms of digital technology than their children, and adults often complain that they cannot understand the bizarre language that youngsters use when texting or messaging one another. But these are examples of differences in generational experience and culture that are classically the stuff of a generation gap. When this generation gap is interpreted in a way that encourages adults to defer to the young, the issue of whose influence carries most weight is open to question. It is in such circumstances that the process of socialization in reverse can flourish.

Often this process draws attention to an uncontroversial example of the contrast between caring and responsible children and their uninterested parents. 'Parents "ignorant" on five-a-day' was the headline of a story published by *BBC News* in June 2008, reporting on a Department of Health poll that claimed that one in three parents indicated that their children knew more about healthy eating campaigns to promote the daily consumption of five portions of fruit and vegetables than they did.[45] In one sense this was a typical non-news story. The poll was based on a sample of 100 people and, in typical market research fashion, encouraged the respondents to give the answers that it sought. Close inspection of the poll indicated that the alleged parental ignorance was about the 'five-a-day' campaign specifically rather than healthy eating in general. Nevertheless, the aim of the poll was to validate the idea that children could be mobilized to help their parents overcome their ignorance. This message was reinforced by the Health Minister, Dawn Primarolo, who stated that 'we welcome the fact that children are absorbing our five-a-day messages and can teach their parents – and peers – to eat more healthily too'. Azmina Govindji of the British Dietetic Association was unapologetic about attempting to influence parents' behaviour through the pressure brought upon them by their children. 'If healthy eating messages can get through to children, then they have a lot of power in the home, and can ask their parents for the kind of food they need to be eating', she noted.

Sometimes children are self-consciously incited to chastize their parents for their apparently irresponsible behaviour. 'School Council teach parents a lesson' was the title of an article published by the website of School Councils UK, which stated that 'pupils at St Nicholas' Primary School, Lincolnshire, had had enough of naughty parents parking illegally in the yellow zigzag zones and decided to take control for themselves'. The article praised members of the school council for taking action by leafleting and petitioning parents as they were dropping off children.[46] At first sight this is a heart-warming illustration of how idealistic children take action against irresponsible adult behaviour. However, this is also a story about role reversal in inter-generational relations. The parents are infantalized – 'naughty parents' – and brought up short by their morally superior youngsters who 'teach' them a lesson.

During the 2008 US Presidential Election, some schools mobilized their pupils to teach their parents about the importance of voting. Candidate Kids described itself as a group of committed Danvers High School students who are 'dedicated to teaching kids to teach their parents about the importance of informed voting'. In a letter entitled 'Children, teach your parents well' it informs students that teaching children to teach their parents is a great way of assuming civic responsibility.[47]

There is nothing natural or spontaneous about children educating their parents; some officials, advocacy organizations and educational experts have adopted the practice of harnessing the well-meaning idealism of children to chastize their parents. So, in April 2007, the Home Office organized a competition for children that involved encouraged them to embarrass badly behaved adults. The Home Office circular explained that 'the competition and activities, such as designing posters that challenge bad behaviour and taking part in neighbourhood litter picks, help educate children about acceptable behaviour while at the same time they are encouraged to use their "pester power" in a positive way – reminding grown ups – how to behave'.[48] This initiative, designed to harness the self-righteousness in children to the task of moulding adult behaviour, explicitly endorses the ideals of socialization in reverse. Louise Casey, a leading promoter of this initiative, was unapologetic in her advocacy of using children to embarrass adults publicly. 'We want to remind people about what is, and is not, respectful behaviour and we are encouraging children to send this clear message to grown-ups', warned Casey.

What is interesting about this Home Office initiative is its positive representation of children's 'pester power'. Traditionally pester power has been depicted as a scourge of consumer society, and advertising which targets children has often been accused of manipulating children to nag their parents into purchasing the latest toy or trainers. However, in recent times, pester power has been rehabilitated as a potentially positive force when used by children to modify the values and behaviour of their parents. One marketing commentator praised the advertising campaigns of the car manufacturer Renault and the energy firm npower for targeting children and encouraging them to pester their parents to alter their behaviour. He noted that the campaigns are 'designed to get kids to change their behaviour and to persuade their parents to join in too', and praised npower's Greener Schools Campaign, which hopes to 'influence the parents to turn down the heating at home and buy energy-efficient white goods'. The author referred to this campaign as 'positive manipulation' and remarked that 'positive pester power' has many friends such as the National Schools Partnership and the Children's Food Campaign.[49] An article entitled 'Positive side of pester power' in *The Times* echoed this approach. It noted that kids are now much more clued up about healthy eating and 'they're nagging their parents to eat better food'.[50]

The representation of positive pestering sometimes acquires the character of a gimmicky marketing fantasy. The claim that children are pestering their parents to give them healthier food was based on a promotional survey carried out by a major British supermarket chain, which claimed that seven out of ten children have asked their parents to buy healthier food and more than half of them have asked for fruit instead of junk food. Like many public relations-led marketing surveys, the questions it posed were designed to solicit the answers it wanted. In this case the outcome of the survey served to legitimize the mobilization of pester power.

It is in the domain of environmental education that the project of using pester power to socialize adults is most systematically pursued. Many environmental educators self-consciously advocate pester power as a contribution to changing the behaviour of adults. David Uzell, a professor of environmental psychology at the University of Surrey, recalls attending an educational conference a few years ago where 'everyone was absolutely convinced' that pester power was 'the answer' to the problem of climate change.[51] Uzell's own research has focused on what he calls 'inter-generational learning through the transference of personal experience typically from the child to the parent/other adults/home'.[52] This casual reference to the transference of experience of child to parent illustrates the normalization of the practice of socialization in reverse. In the US, socializing children through the promotion of environmental education has been pursued systematically in schools for over a decade. *The New York Times* reports that 'eco-kids' devoted to green values 'try to hold their parents accountable at home' and notes that adults become defensive under the 'watchful eye of the pint-size eco-police'.[53] School districts across the US have sought to capitalize on the idealism of 'eco-kids' to integrate environmental values into whatever subjects they can.

Politicians and governments have embraced environmental education as a potentially effective instrument for influencing and managing the behaviour of the public. One Labour MP, Malcolm Wicks, argues that environmental values 'can act as vivid teaching aids in science lessons, civics lessons, geography lessons', and through absorbing these lessons 'children will then begin to educate the parents'. He adds that 'in this way we can start to shift behaviour'.[54] A similar aspiration was expressed by the Cabinet Minister, David Miliband, who argued that 'children are the key to changing society's long-term attitudes to the environment'. Miliband is convinced that 'not only are they passionate about saving the planet but children also have a big influence over their families' lifestyles and behaviour'.[55] The former Education Secretary, Alan Johnson, wrote that 'children have a dual role as consumers and influences' and therefore 'educating them about the impact of getting an extra pair of trainers for fashion's sake is as important as the pressure they put on their parents not to buy a gas-guzzling car'.[56]

A report entitled *The Role of Schools in Shaping Energy-related Consumer Behaviour* is devoted to elaborating a policy framework about this objective of promoting educational initiatives that impact on parental behaviour.[57] Andrew Sutter, who runs one such initiative – the Eco-Schools scheme involving 5,500 schools – believes that it provides an opportunity for children 'to be the teachers and tell their parents what to do for a change'.[58] This point is underlined in a Government report on energy, which states that the 'installation of renewable technologies in schools can bring the curriculum to life in ways that textbooks cannot'. Moreover, this report observes, 'with schools often being the focal point of communities, the installation of renewables could help to shape attitudes in the wider community'.[59] Not infrequently the mobilization of pester power to alter the behaviour of adults acquires the character of a frenetic crusade. The book *How to Turn Your Parents Green* by James Russell incites children to 'nag, pester, bug, torment and punish people who are merrily wrecking our world'. Russell calls on children to 'channel their pester power and issue fines against their parents and other transgressors'.[60]

In previous times, the practice of mobilizing children to police their parents' behaviour was confined to totalitarian societies. Authorities who attempted to harness youngsters' simplistic views of good and evil are reminiscent of Orwell's Big Brother. But who needs Big Brother when the then Prime Minister of the United Kingdom, Tony Blair, could assert that 'on climate change, it is parents who should listen to their children'?[61]

## Unresolved tensions

The disturbing phenomenon of socialization in reverse should not be seen as a self-conscious attempt to displace the authority of the parents. The willingness of experts to by-pass parents and socialize children directly has been evident for well over a century, and from its inception this approach represented falling confidence in the effectiveness of the inter-generational transmission of values. Expert-inspired forms of socialization arguably contributed to the further erosion of inter-generational relations, but that was not its intended purpose. With very rare exceptions, educators and officials have tended to be reluctant to provoke the sensitivities of parents through explicitly using children in this way. It is only in recent times that tactics associated with the phenomenon of reverse socialization have been explicitly endorsed by educators and policy-makers. However, it is unlikely that they welcome one of its unintended consequences: its contribution to the diminution of parental authority.

The diminishing of parental authority represents a problem for teachers as well as parents. In a fundamental sense, adult authority is indivisible and if the moral status of parents is undermined, so is that of the teacher and other grown-ups. The institution of education can only work if parents are able to exercise a measure of influence over their children. It is widely recognized that if parental authority is ineffectively exercised it can directly contribute to poor discipline in the classroom. So whatever private reservations educationalists have about the competence of parents, they still rely on the influence of the home to manage the behaviour of children. That is why there is a growing trend for schools to involve parents directly in their children's education. 'We must make it easier for parents to do more to help with the education of their child', argued former Education Secretary Alan Johnson.[62]

However, this involvement of parents is often accompanied by a ticking-off. Johnson's hectoring tone was reported under the head-line 'Parents must do better – Johnson', and his colleague, Children's Minister Beverley Hughes, followed him by blaming 'parents' behaviour and indifference' for damaging their children.[63] The infantilization of the parent implied by reverse socialization is reinforced by comments about parents' sub-standard child-rearing practices. Many educators have few inhibitions about reminding parents of their responsibilities, without thinking of the damaging consequences. Holding forth in this vein, Steve Sinnott, the head of the National Union of Teachers, accused parents of 'indulging or overindulging' their youngsters and called on teachers and schools to 'give parents advice'.[64] By positioning parents into a position of subservience, Sinnott inadvertently echoes society's lack of confidence in parental authority. That is unlikely to benefit the socialization of the younger generations.

This chapter has focused on the way in which tensions located within the exercise of adult authority bear upon the process of socialization. The project of attempting to socialize children through the application of behavioural management techniques does not provide an effective substitute for the influence exercised through authoritative adult behaviour. In the end, an effective form of socialization depends on transmitting a coherent system of values, or at least an orientation to the world. Appeals to therapeutic values that have as their stated objective the well-being of an individual only draw attention to a gaping hole in the curriculum, caused by the lack of a commonly shared understanding of life. The failure to provide satisfactory answers to the question, 'What are the values that we want to instil in our children?', has led to a situation where the entire process of education has become disrupted by this question.

# 5

## Social Engineering

An important consequence of the devaluation of adult authority is that greater and greater significance is attached to the role of schools in the management of inter-generational relations. In recent decades schools have extended their remit to deal with issues that in the past were catered for by parents, voluntary organizations or welfare institutions. As Martin Stephen, the High Master of St Paul's School in West London, wrote: 'We have shifted a whole load of society's conscience' onto the curriculum, 'making teachers and schools more and more responsible for preaching against drug misuse, teenage pregnancy and a host of other problems – in effect, we have sought to replace the Vicar of the Established Church by the teacher in the Educational Establishment.'[1] As a result the school has assumed a growing social significance relative to other institutions. Policy-makers now assign an unprecedented importance to education, and it has become regarded as the instrument for solving some of the most fundamental problems of society.

Yet the elevation of education into the policy-maker's instrument of choice inevitably breeds disappointment. The social evils and problems that education is invited to address, from economic decline to antisocial behaviour, continue to blight the social land-scape. Consequently education is blamed for the very problems that it is invited to solve, and a crisis in society is interpreted as a crisis of education. However, while the discovery that 'education is in crisis' leads to the demand that schools be reorganized; governments continue to insist that the role of schools in solving the problems of society should be extended. In this way schools are set up to fail.

Their response to this perceived crisis sets the stage for further failures. This chapter is devoted to an examination of the politicization
of the school and its impact on the curriculum.

## From socialization to social engineering

As discussed in Chapter 4, socialization deals with the transmission
of society's values to the younger generations. But, what if society
finds it difficult to articulate what those values are? In such circumstances socialization cannot be expected to transmit taken-for-
granted community ideals or reproduce the bonds that bind people
together. Today educators and policy-makers are sensitive to this
issue and deliberate constantly about what they refer to as the
problem of social cohesion. Nevertheless they find it difficult to
acknowledge openly their own uncertainty about what values and
ideals should be conveyed in the classroom. Indeed, policy-makers
hide continually behind the rhetoric of values, hoping that the repetition of the word will save them from the problem of having to
state what they mean. Policy documents repeat the word 'value' as
if its meaning is so evident that it requires no explanation. So the
Government-sponsored *Music Manifesto* initiative asserts that 'we
believe that music is important for the social and cultural values it
represents and promotes, and for the communities it can help to
build and to unite'.[2] The reader is left to ponder just what kind of
values will be promoted through music education and how these
are likely to unite communities.

But what values should schools uphold? Attempts to answer this
question have proven to be embarrassingly unsuccessful. In 1996,
the National Forum for Values and Education and the Community
was set up by the Schools Curriculum and Assessment Authority.
Its remit was 'to discover whether there are any values upon which
there is agreement across society'. After long deliberation it published a statement of values that has been described as a 'weak and
meaningless set of watered-down "politically correct" values'.[3] The
authors of this list had insisted that 'these values are so fundamental
that they may appear unexceptional'; they stated that the order in

which they were listed did not imply any priority or necessary preference, and shied away from taking a stand on 'whether there are any values that should be agreed upon across society'. In reality, what this list provided were not values but platitudes such as 'We value ourselves and 'We respect others'. The real importance of this embarrassing 'pick-'n'-mix' list of values was that it revealed the absence of clarity about what ideals bound society together.[4] The Statement concluded that 'there are some shared values but that there is no consensus on the source of these values or how they are applied'. Through attempting to address explicitly the question of what values, if any, are 'commonly agreed upon in society', the National Forum for Values and Education was forced to concede that such consensus was conspicuously weak.

From time to time apprehensions about which values should be encouraged in the classroom are explicitly addressed. So, an editorial of a journal devoted to the philosophy of education observed recently that 'we need to find the most effective way to harness whatever potent values are around – to the task of education'.[5] Note the inclusion of the word 'whatever'. The focus of this plea is not the utilization of values that we can take for granted, but whatever works. Regrettably, the public is exposed rarely to such a refreshingly open recognition that educationalists are at a loss to know what values to communicate to children. In policy circles, there is little appetite for a systematic attempt to forge a consensus on values; instead, policy-makers hide behind rhetoric. They acclaim 'diversity', 'multiculturalism' and 'plurality', and convey the idea that in this diverse, multicultural and plural world the meaning of socialization needs to change.

Historically, the challenge of socialization was perceived as one that focused on the most effective way of mobilizing existing shared values to promote social cohesion. This outlook was coherently expounded by Durkheim, when he remarked that 'it thus falls to society to remind the teacher continually of the ideas and sentiments that must be impressed upon the child in order for him to be in harmony with the environment in which he is destined to live'. For Durkheim the promotion of such ideas was necessary for the realization of social integration and consensus. He opposed the notion of diversity and warned that

> if society were not always present and ever-vigilant to constrain the teaching to be exercised in a social direction . . . teaching would necessarily be applied to serve particular beliefs, and the great heart of our country would become divided up, disintegrating into an incohesive host of fragmented petty creatures . . . undermining communality of ideas and sentiments, without which any society is impossible.[6]

Durkheim understood that, in a modern society, values were contested and that society was often divided by conflicting opinions and views. But he believed that 'in spite of all disputes, nowadays there exists, at the very foundation of our civilization, a certain number of principles which, implicitly or explicitly, are common to everybody and which very few people in any case dare to deny openly and outrightly'.[7]

Today, a lack of agreement about how to express 'communality of ideas and sentiments' has meant that the approach outlined by Durkheim is rejected as inapplicable to the working of twenty-first-century society. Some educationalists justify their hesitation towards the advocacy of an explicitly formulated system of values by arguing that such ideals might cause offence to those who do not subscribe to them. Some teachers feel uncomfortable about tackling highly charged, but pressing, moral issues. One government review of the 'Diversity and Citizenship Curriculum' noted that it was 'struck' by evidence that after the London bombings in July 2007 'there were many schools that chose silence as the best way of dealing with the complexity of the situation'; they 'simply did not know how to cope with the questions pupils were asking'.[8]

Many schools appear to be intensely defensive about potentially causing offence and prefer to cultivate diversity as an end in itself. Others contend that social cohesion cannot any longer be based on shared values – instead schools are asked to encourage students to have 'appropriate' attitudes towards communication and other people. What is important is how they behave. According to one Dutch account, 'education cannot contribute to the integration of society by passing on norms and values to children'.[9] Instead of teaching such norms, it proposes to instil in the young forms of social skills and behaviour that will help them deal with a 'complex and changing environment'. The authors of this account accept that their approach will foster 'diversity' instead of social consensus, but hope that through the acquired social skills students will develop a sense of connection to one another.[10] The perception that schools find it difficult to pass on social norms and values has led to a shift in focus from the inculcation of values to their clarification. As Standish notes: 'increasingly, values inculcation was replaced by values clarification, whereby the individual students were expected to determine their own values through an exploration of social issues'.[11] This reorientation towards values clarification has led to an emphasis on training children in social skills.

The shift in focus from the cultivation of values to the teaching of social skills is endorsed implicitly by numerous educators. Such skills, particularly as they touch on the conduct of relationships, are sometimes represented as the means through which more personal values can be expressed. So Bentley writes of the 'values of mutual respect, appreciation and curiosity' as values that can be transmitted through a skills-led form of socialization.[12] In this way basic personal attitudes and skills can be rebranded as 'personal values' and the challenge of giving meaning to shared values can be by-passed. In the US many schools offer children classes in 'empathy' and offer training in the skill of being a nice and considerate person.[13]

The absence of certainty about the capacity of society to achieve cohesion through cultivating its values to children stands in sharp contrast to the confidence with which this mission was regarded by educators in the first half of the twentieth century. Back in 1940, one leading English educator insisted that the 'bonds that hold England together are stronger than England itself'. Possibly this idealized version of the strength of English values was motivated by the goal of motivating people during the dark hours of the Second

World War, but it nevertheless represented a belief in the power of society's norms and values.[14] With the displacement of such beliefs, the very meaning and working of socialization has undergone a significant revision. Over the decades, education has embraced social engineering as one of the main instruments through which it attempts to socialize children.

There is a crucial difference between socialization and social engineering. Socialization does not merely involve the transmission of values to the younger generation: it proceeds by communicating values that are already held widely by the older generations in society. In contrast, social engineering is devoted to promoting values that are as yet weak, but which its proponents believe are necessary for society to move forward. This approach is sometimes inspired and justified by the conviction that prevailing values are outdated or wrong and that children should be instructed in more enlightened values to create a better world. But often social engineers themselves lack strong convictions, and their project is motivated by an awareness that traditions and values lack meaning and cannot be utilized effectively for the socialization of people. In such circumstances there is a temptation to construct new values to replace the old. The German social theorist Jürgen Habermas described this process as an attempt to regenerate values 'administratively'.[15] In education, social engineering has evolved through constructing values with a view to compensating for wider society's inability to cultivate social consensus.

The enterprise of regenerating values administratively is usually justified on the ground that attitudes have to be changed. Unlike socialization, which involves the transmission of pre-existing values, social engineering is devoted to gaining support for attitudes that as yet lack significant support in society. At the risk of simplification, this difference can be understood as one between mainly affirming prevailing attitudes (socialization) and changing them (social engineering). The emphasis of social engineering on changing values means that sometimes it self-consciously opposes attitudes that are associated with the older generations: for example, by encouraging children to question the behaviour and values of their parents, as discussed in the previous chapter.

From the standpoint of social engineering, schools represent a key institution for dealing with issues confronting society. Accordingly the cultivation of desirable attitudes among schoolchildren is harnessed to tackling problems that are external to education and socialization. It is wholly desirable that schools should strive to make a positive contribution to improve the quality of life of the wider community. But there is a fundamental difference between schools playing an active role in community life and being used to solve deep-seated social ills. Once schools are seen to possess the potential for compensating for the failures of society, they are charged with the mission of tackling a growing range of problems. This sentiment is frequently conveyed through the naïve belief that if schoolchildren can learn to internalize the attitudes propagated by enlightened experts, many of the problems associated with adult behaviour can be solved.

Unlike the ideals advanced through traditional forms of socialization, those communicated through social engineering often have little organic relation to community life: they are norms and values constructed through the work of experts, policy-makers and think-tanks. As a process, social engineering attempts to turn such administratively produced values into ones that can gain a wider resonance through their internalization by the institution of education. In this sense, social engineering involves the element of indoctrination. In previous times, attempts to alter children's attitudes were pursued through religious or ideological indoctrination; in the twentieth century, the uninhibited strategy of fundamentally altering the worldview of schoolchildren was practised in totalitarian societies like Nazi Germany or Stalinist Soviet Union. Contemporary social engineering has little in common with its more explicitly totalitarian counterpart.

In the twenty-first century, social indoctrination is not so much ideological as pragmatic. Although a large number of vested interests wish to advocate their strongly held views in the classroom, social engineering is essentially an instrumentalist enterprise. It lacks conviction and its main interest is in values that work. Policy documents that address the subject of values education often reveal an absence of purpose and meaning.

It is useful to distinguish the old ideological forms of hard social engineering from current practices. That is why I refer to its current form as *soft social engineering*, which is devoted not so much to changing society as it is to altering the behaviour of schoolchildren. Soft social engineering lacks a language through which it can talk meaningfully about societal values. This tentative and incoherent stance towards conducting a dialogue on broad moral and social issues is sometimes even evident in faith schools. As one prescient observer noted, 'Faith schools today are often only slightly different from ordinary state schools: and . . . the potent values we need in education are in almost as short supply in faith schools as else-where.'[16] Just because soft social engineering finds it difficult to convey potent values does not mean that its impact is without great significance. Soft social engineering plays a crucial role in contemporary education, and its main achievements are to politicize education and to distract schools from providing an intellectually stimulating experience for their students.

The tentative and pragmatic orientation of social engineers to their own administratively constructed values does not mean that they do not take their vocation very seriously. It often appears that, among policy-makers, the idea that education is the most effective instrument for solving the problems of society has acquired the character of an unquestioned dogma. Politicians and experts continually demand that the school should be used to tackle the problems of crime, drugs, obesity, racism, homophobia, antisocial behaviour, political apathy, etc. Embracing the school as an institution of social policy has meant that its educative role has been implicitly redefined – if not downgraded altogether.

## Social crisis perceived as a crisis of education

The relationship between school and society is a constant subject of debate. Some claim that schools have the potential for working as an engine of social change and play a central role in overcoming problems associated with inequality, discrimination or community fragmentation. Others regard schools as part of the problem, or as the source of inequality and discrimination. Historical experience suggests that the relationship between education and society is far from stable.

The relationship between school and society is subject to variations. In most historical periods education worked to conserve the institutions of society. But education has also contributed to the emergence of new ways of thinking and living, and has inspired people to adopt novel approaches to the problems facing society. However, attempts to utilize education to achieve wider social or political objectives are realized in practice rarely. Research suggests that the changes that were achieved 'were often inconsistent with the intentions of many of the agents who helped to bring them about'.[17] The experience of the past indicates that the goals assigned to education work best when they correspond to prevailing sentiment and experience. In such circumstances education may well serve as a means to realize social change. But as A. H. Halsey, one of Britain's leading sociologists of education, remarked:

> Education prepares children for society, transforming biological organisms into social personalities. Its capacity is essentially not to create but to recreate society, not to form structures of social life but to maintain the people and the skills that inform these structures. Education as a means of social change is secondary.[18]

A sound system of education is indispensable for the development of an enlightened and forward-looking society. Yet, despite the considerable potential of education to improve life, it exists in a relationship of tension with society. Often education is perceived as a mirror through which society becomes conscious of its blemishes. Schools are often seen as the source of a problem, the solution to the problem – or both.

Over the past 150 years, the difficulties facing society have often been interpreted as the fault of the system of education. At least in part, the perception that education is in a crisis is symptomatic of an absence of consensus about the basic values of society. Back in the early 1960s Arendt recognized the tendency to confuse the lack of moral consensus in society with the problem of schooling. There had to be a measure of consensus about the past before a system of education could affirm its virtues.[19] In other words, the crisis in education is often a symptom of society's inability to give a meaningful account of itself.

The periodic outbreaks of concern about the 'crisis of education' often represent a roundabout way of talking about a crisis in society. Modernizers have frequently blamed traditional 'elitist' education for the relative decline of British industry and economic power. In turn, conservatives have often charged 'progressive education', particularly as practised in the 1960s, as responsible for the nation's moral decline. Calls for new educational policies to overcome an alleged crisis of schooling are invariably associated with a political agenda. So-called educational reforms also often turn out to be counter-crisis policies that address problems which have little to do with the school. So, one of New Labour's leading educational advisers warned that the problems we face – global insecurity, environmental degradation – 'present a set of challenges more profound than any in human history', before noting that 'this is the justification for a radical programme of education reform'.[20]

It was during the Cold War that the so-called crisis of education became a regular topic of public concern in western societies. The launching of Sputnik 1 by the Soviet Union in October 1957 provoked a major crisis of confidence in the west about its capacity to adapt successfully to rapidly changing and challenging circumstances. The clearest symptom of this crisis of confidence was the defensive tone with which western governments and intellectuals responded to this event. Some went so far as to argue that the Soviet Union possessed the kind of formidable potential for innovation and dynamism that the west could not match. In the United States, leading commentators declared that the Soviet Union 'had found ways to mobilise the intellectual and economic capacities of its citizens while Americans frittered away their patrimony in mindless consumption and frivolous amusements'.[21] As is often the case in times of unease, anxiety about society's capacity to adapt was focused on the institution of education. It was widely believed that the Soviet Union's educational system was 'superior to our own in its ability to motivate youngsters and enlist them in the nation's enterprises'.[22] So when C. P. Snow concluded his highly acclaimed lecture on *The Two Cultures* with the warning that the public had to look at 'education with fresh eyes' and that there was a 'good deal to learn from the Russians', his audience would have known to what he was referring.[23]

In the 1980s, the publication of *A Nation at Risk* by the American National Commission on Excellence in Education showed that, more than ever before, socio-economic problems were being perceived as educational ones. This report, which warned of America's failure to maintain its economic and technological global 'pre-eminence', pointed the finger directly at its failing schools. 'If an unfriendly foreign power had attempted to impose on America the mediocre educational performance that exists today, we might well have viewed it as an act of war', the report warned, adding that the nation had committed an act of 'unthinking, unilateral educational disarmament'.[24] A careful reading of *A Nation at Risk* indicates that its outlook is influenced by a heightened sense of moral crisis and concerns about the ability of society to survive future threats. Education was perceived as both the cause of this problem and the institution that was most likely to reinvigorate American society.

Since the 1980s, perceptions of a social or moral crisis in the UK have influenced education policy directly. During the 1990s, public discussion about the social and moral development of Britain's youth frequently raised questions about the role of schools. Concerns about antisocial behaviour, crime, and unease about young people's attitudes and behaviour, were often expressed through an alarmist language. Eventually calls for values education led the Government to insist that 'citizenship education' should become a compulsory part of the National Curriculum. This innovation was advocated self-consciously as a response to the perception that the normal mechanisms of socialization had become ineffective, and was justified on the grounds that citizenship education would assist students 'to deal with difficult moral and social questions that arise in their lives and in society'.[25] As concern with young people's behaviour has intensified during the past decade, schools have become more and more involved with the problem. According to a recent review of the primary curriculum, 'deep societal concerns about such critical matters as drug abuse, obesity, sex and relationship education, violent behaviour, e-safety, financial capability and so forth, press for an educational response in primary schools with children at an ever earlier age'.[26] Although this statement is included in a review of primary education, its starting point is evidently 'societal concerns' which then 'press for an educational response'. An 'educational response' to the different manifestations assumed by a social crisis usually involves the inculcation of different personal and social skills, but it cannot entirely avoid the realm of moral norms and values. It also tends to be educational in form and political in content.

The mobilization of an 'educational response' to help solve a wider community problem is exemplified by legislation passed under the Education and Inspections Act 2006, which insists that schools have a duty to promote social cohesion. There are good reasons why ministers should be concerned about the relative erosion of the ties that bind us together. But can schools compensate for the failure of society to achieve social solidarity? According to the guidelines issued to schools, the duty to promote 'community cohesion' requires:

working towards a society in which there is a common vision and sense of belonging by all communities; a society in which the diversity of people's backgrounds and circumstances is appreciated and valued; a society in which similar life opportunities are available to all; and a society in which strong and positive relationships exist and continue to be developed in the workplace, in schools and in the wider community.[27]

This is a rather tall order. Charging schools with the duty to help realize government objectives for future society is based on the naïve idea that schoolchildren can compensate for the problems of adult society and serve as an engine for social change.

An 'educational response' to a political or social problem inevitably invites the politicization of the curriculum. The guidelines on the duty to promote community cohesion is essentially a political statement, that 'through their ethos and curriculum schools can promote a common sense of identity and support diversity, showing pupils how different communities can be united by common experiences and values'. Through the politicization of the curriculum, it is hoped that schools can achieve objectives that have so far eluded adult society.

The absence of a moral consensus in Britain today will not be solved by subjecting children to sanctimonious platitudes: which is why the guidelines about promoting cohesion can provide no real guidance. Informing schools that they must 'teach pupils to understand others, to promote common values and to value diversity' is unlikely to help educators who themselves don't know what 'common values' to uphold in the classroom. Often the guidelines issued by social engineers help teachers to internalize the rhetoric and to talk the talk. But the mere incantation of the rhetoric of cohesion is unlikely to help society overcome its sense of fragmentation.

## Fiddling with the curriculum

Values that are constructed through policy-making and deliberation cannot match the influence of taken-for-granted norms that have been cultivated for generations. As Habermas noted, socialization through social engineering has the perverse effect of diminishing rather than strengthening moral authority. Administratively produced values lack an organic relationship to a system of belief and shared experience. Such values are inherently unstable because they invite questioning and scepticism. The very construction of such values implicitly raises the question of why that value should be chosen, as opposed to another one produced by another expert. Moreover, Habermas argued, a 'cultural tradition loses precisely this force as soon as it is objectivistically prepared and strategically employed'. Once values are perceived as an act of administrative construction, even the influence of traditions that have managed to survive into modern times is likely to be undermined. Habermas pointed to curriculum planning as an example of a project of objectively constructing a narrative of socialization: 'whereas school administrations formerly merely had to codify a canon that has taken shape in an unplanned, nature-like manner, present curriculum *planning* is based on the premise that traditional patterns could as well be otherwise'.[28] Once values acquire such arbitrary and contingent character, they cease to possess any intrinsic meaning. Consequently such values become subject to contestation and ceaseless modification. This leads to what Habermas called the 'stirring up of cultural affairs' – that is, the constant tendency to fiddle with the curriculum.

Over the past two decades, schools in England have become the target of competing groups of policy-makers, moral entrepreneurs and advocacy organizations who wish to use the curriculum as a vehicle for promoting their ideals and values. As a result, pedagogic issues are continually confused with political ones. For example, in April 2007, the Equal Opportunities Commission dispatched 40 pages of guidance to headteachers and governors in England about how they should tackle inequality between the sexes. *The Gender Equality Duty* is the product of an imagination that regards the curriculum as principally a political instrument for changing attitudes and behaviour. 'The gender equality duty presents a fantastic opportunity for schools to make a co-ordinated effort to tackle inequality and ensure that all pupils are able to fully achieve their potential', declares the Commission.[29]

Instructions to schools about how to close the gender gap compete with directives that outline how children should be taught to become more sensitive to cultural differences. Everyone with a fashionable cause wants a piece of the curriculum. The former national chair of the Professional Association of Teachers wants pupils to 'learn about nappies' and has demanded the introduction of compulsory parenting classes for 14- to 16-year-olds.[30] Others insist that teachers spend more time talking to their class about sex or relationships or climate change or healthy eating or drugs or homophobia or Islamophobia.

The school curriculum has become a battleground for campaigners and entrepreneurs keen to promote their message. Public health officials demand more compulsory classroom discussions on healthy eating and obesity. Professionals obsessed with young people's sex lives insist that schools introduce yet more sex education initiatives. Others want schools to focus more on black history or gay history. In the recent widespread media outcry over the sordid scenes of moral and cultural illiteracy on the reality TV show *Celebrity Big Brother*, many demanded that schools should teach Britishness. The government hasn't yet announced any plans for introducing 'Appropriate Behaviour on Reality TV Shows' into the curriculum – but the hunt is still on for fashionable causes that could be made relevant to the classroom. In early 2007, the former Education Secretary Alan Johnson announced that not only had he introduced Global Warming Studies, but had made the instruction of Britain's involvement in the slave trade a compulsory part of the history curriculum.

For Johnson, the subject of history, like that of geography, must be subordinated to the task of transmitting the latest fashionable cause or value. Johnson is indifferent to the slave trade as part of an academic discipline with its own integrity; he sees slave trade studies as a vehicle for promoting his version of a multicultural Britain. 'This is about ensuring young people understand what it means to be British today', he said in defence of his reorganization of the history curriculum. Johnson's former title, Education Secretary, is something of a misnomer, as he seems to have no interest in education as such. Johnson could not even leave school sports alone, insisting that physical education lessons should stress the importance of a healthy lifestyle and raise awareness about the problem of obesity. So after children have received instruction on how to behave as green consumers, learn crucial parenting skills, and feel very British, they will be taught how and why to lose weight. A curriculum devoted to a total makeover of schoolboys and school-girls has little energy left for dealing with such secondary issues as how to gain children's interest in real education.

At a time when educators are unable to endow their vocation with real meaning, they turn to new causes in order to at least transmit some semblance of values. This was the intention behind Johnson's announcement, in February 2007, that 'we need the next generation to think about their impact on the environment in a different way'. Johnson justified this project, aimed at shaping the cultural outlook of children, through appealing to a higher truth: 'If we can instil in the next generation an understanding of how our actions can mitigate or cause global warming, then we lock in a culture change that could, quite literally, save the world.'[31] Saving the world looks like a price worth paying for fiddling with the geography curriculum, and using it to instruct children about climate change. But behind the lofty rhetoric lie some base assumptions.

Increasingly the curriculum is regarded as a vehicle for promoting political objectives and for changing the values, attitudes and sensibilities of children. Many advocacy organizations that demand changes to the curriculum do not have the slightest interest in the subject they wish to influence: as far as they are concerned they are making a statement through gaining recognition for their cause. That is what Nick Clegg, leader of the Liberal Democrats, was doing when he argued that education must tackle homophobia and that Ofsted inspectors should assess how well schools are managing the problem.[32] Sex experts continually demand that the amount of time devoted to sex education should be expanded. In July 2008 the Independent Advisory Group on Sexual Health and HIV noted that pupils were getting inadequate instruction because sex education was not a compulsory subject. The same month, the Family Planning Association and Brook argued that children as young as four should receive age-appropriate 'compulsory sex education', with sex and relationship education enjoying a position in the curriculum analogous to other compulsory subjects like maths and English. The emphasis of these advocacy groups on 'compulsion' is characteristic of the social engineering imperative. In this vein, the NSPCC has called for advice on emotions to become a compulsory part of sex education.[33] The ease with which the NSPCC makes the conceptual leap from advice to compulsion indicates that what it has in mind is a form of emotional indoctrination.

While the campaign to transform sex education into a compulsory school subject is sometimes questioned by traditionalist critics, many similar initiatives around different causes go by unremarked. In September 2008, the Government announced changes to the National Curriculum that will instruct boys as young as eleven on how to be good fathers. Children will be told that if they abandon their offspring they will face prosecution and a possible jail sentence. So where did this initiative come from? It certainly does not represent a response to a pedagogic problem identified in the classroom; rather, it emerged from the deliberations of policy-makers and experts who feel strongly that something should be done about 'deadbeat dads'. And when the question is posed, 'What should be done?', the answer is the now formulaic solution, that it should be dealt with in the National Curriculum. So Janet Paraskeva, chair of the Child Maintenance and Enforcement Commission, stated that 'there needs to be something in the National Curriculum to make children aware they will need to take financial responsibility for their children'. Paraskeva insisted that she meant business when she observed that 'this won't be a simple bolt-on to the National Curriculum' since 'we want to give children at a young age a good understanding of the financial commitment of becoming parents'.[34]

Over the years, successive governments have embraced the 'something must be done' orientation towards the curriculum. Among other initiatives, schools are now in the business of changing attitudes towards eating, relationships, sex, drugs, immigrants, smoking, exercise, public affairs, environmental issues and personal finance. Inspectors now assess schools on what they are doing to improve children's well-being and on how successful they are in realizing the agenda constructed by social engineers. According to one report, schools in England are 'amongst the most scrutinised in the world'.[35]

Social engineering has become wedded to the idea of what is referred to as 'early intervention', which, in everyday language, means influencing children as young as possible. From this standpoint, targeting four-year-olds with sex education makes perfect sense. In recent times the obsessive pursuit of early intervention has led moral crusaders to focus on the nursery. In July 2008 the National Children's Bureau published *Young Children and Racial Justice*, which noted that nursery staff 'must be alert for racist remarks among toddlers'. The goal of this 336-page guide is to change the outlook of toddlers, by sensitizing nursery workers to 'clues' that serve as markers for racist attitudes. One example of such a clue is when a toddler yells 'Yuck' and reacts negatively to a 'culinary tradition other than their own'. Apparently such a reaction to food that is alien to a toddler's experience may signify negative feelings towards the people associated with it.[36] Early intervention in Glasgow has assumed the form of instructing pre-school children with anti-racism education. A local councillor, Gordon Matheson, claims that 'the earlier you can pick up any tendency towards discriminatory or prejudicial behaviour, the better chance you have of tackling it'.[37]

## Citizenship without content

This ceaseless attempt to instil in schoolchildren currently fashionable values is symptomatic of a general state of moral confusion today. Instead of attempting to develop an understanding of what it means to be a good citizen, or articulate a vision of public good, Britain's cultural elites prefer to turn every one of their concerns into a school subject. In the classroom, the unresolved issues of public life can be transformed into simplistic teaching tools. Citizenship education is the clearest example of this corruption of the curriculum by the prejudices of social engineering.

Citizenship education represents an ambitious attempt to utilize the school to solve social problems. Schools have always sought to ensure that young people were intellectually and morally prepared for public life and understood their responsibility to their community and wider society, and they sometimes sought to cultivate a distinct view of the world to ensure that social values were transmitted to the child. One of the distinct features of citizenship education is that it combines this aspiration to indoctrinate with uncertainty about which values it should inculcate in children. It was in the 1990s that citizenship became an explicit objective of education. In 1997, the newly established Advisory Group on Citizenship was given responsibility to make recommendations for introducing this subject into the curriculum. The aim of this body was, as Standish notes, 'nothing less than to change the "political culture of the country"' by educating young people to have more 'socially responsible attitudes and behaviours'.[38] This was an ambitious social engineering project that sought to create citizens in the classrooms at a time when the idea of the responsible citizen had little meaning in everyday British society.

However, from the outset the proponents of this social engineering project were confused about the content of their mission. When citizenship education became part of the National Curriculum for English and Welsh primary schools in September 2000, many teachers were far from certain about what to instruct their students. Secondary schools, too, were in a similar position. As far back as July 2002, Ofsted inspectors warned that many secondary schools in England were ill-prepared for the introduction of citizenship teaching the following September. A year later, the inspectors complained that schools appeared confused and complacent. Standards were 'often low', with a lot of 'unsatisfactory management' of the subject. In a report published in 2005, Ofsted conceded that the 'implementation of citizenship has been beset by problems of definitions': in other words, educators were confused about the content of this compulsory subject.[39]

Time and again, school inspectors have criticized the teaching of citizenship, which is not really surprising considering that leading supporters of citizenship education seem to have little idea what the subject is, or ought to be, about. Nick Tate, former chief executive of the QCA, argued that citizenship education was 'about promoting and transmitting values', 'participation' and 'duties'. But the obvious question of 'Values about what?' was carefully avoided. Instead, those advocating citizenship education have cobbled together a list of unobjectionable and bland sentiments that are rebranded as values. Alongside fairness, honesty and community, even participation and voting have been turned into values.

A few years down the road and the meaning of citizenship is even less clear than when schools started teaching it as a subject. Back in January 2007, a review of how schools teach citizenship found that the subject failed to communicate any sense of what it means to be British. It showed that administratively constructed values invariably fail to capture the imagination.

Anyone with the slightest grasp of pedagogy will not be surprised by the failure of successive social engineering projects in the classroom. The absence of moral consensus will not be solved through subjecting children to sanctimonious platitudes. Those who are genuinely interested in educating children and inspiring them to become responsible citizens will instead look to real subjects that represent a genuine body of knowledge. Campaigns around the latest fashionable 'value' only distract children from learning. Values-led education has helped create a situation where children learn that the Holocaust was awful, but do not know which country suffered the greatest number of casualties during the Second World War. It will produce children who know that the slave trade was bad, but who are ignorant about how the right to vote was won in Britain.

In February 2008, the former Education Secretary David Blunkett warned that there were too few teachers to give the new compulsory citizenship classes.[40] Although he conceded that 'this is a new subject area, difficult to bring alive to pupils', he could not bring himself to admit that as an academic subject, citizenship has no meaning and that teachers themselves have little idea about the story they are expected to transmit. A couple of days after Blunkett's warning, a report based on a survey of 300 teachers by Michael Hand and Jo Pearce of the Institute of Education claimed that although teachers were far from clear about how to manage citizenship classes, they were fairly certain that patriotism 'should not be taught in school'.

As far as these authors were concerned, patriotism should only be taught as a 'controversial issue'; and Britain with its 'morally ambiguous' history should not become an object of children's love.[41]

What is particularly fascinating about Hand and Pearce's indictment of patriotism is that it offers, not a traditional critique of narrow nationalism, but a fundamental questioning of loyalty itself. They rhetorically ask, 'Are countries really appropriate objects of love?' before they counsel a form of implicit cultural hostility to 'national histories', which are all 'morally ambiguous'. Their advice is that 'loving things can be bad for us', especially when the 'thing we love is morally corrupt'. Implicitly, this perspective morally condemns the attempt to construct a British way of life. There is, of course, a respectable case for the argument that patriotism is usually the religion of scoundrels, and there is an honourable tradition of pedagogy that encourages people to embrace genuine universal values. But the critique of patriotism offered by Hand and Pearce has little to do with such a sensibility. It does not simply warn against the manipulation of patriotism, but counsels children not to feel good about their country. Three-quarters of the teachers surveyed in this report apparently agreed with this sentiment and stated that they felt they had an obligation to alert their pupils about hazards of patriotic feelings. From their perspective, citizenship will be taught as a form of identity with no particular community in mind and with no particular meaning. These two statements about what values children are socialized into were barely noted by the media; the idea that schools cannot provide children with a story about who they are and offer them a sense of wider loyalties is rarely acknowledged in public conversation.

The malaise that afflicts citizenship education should not be blamed on the teaching profession. It has been evident from the start that leading supporters of citizenship education had little idea what the subject was about. Debating the meaning of citizenship turned into an exchange of platitudes. Alongside fairness, honesty and community, participation and voting were turned into values. Professor Bernard Crick, who was a key adviser on citizenship education, stated that 'students must demonstrate a commitment to active citizenship, commitment to voluntary service and concern for the environment'. In other words, in the guise of studying an academic subject, schoolchildren have to adopt a particular form of behaviour demanded by the prevailing political code of conduct. The significance that the curriculum attaches to the value of participation is symptomatic of the subject's lack of moral and substantive content. According to the curriculum, pupils are required to 'take part in school- and community-based activities, demonstrating personal and group responsibility in their attitudes to themselves and others'. However, the exhortation to participate is not founded on any vision of what constitutes a good society or what it means to be a responsible citizen. Nor is it clear what kind of community-based activity pupils should engage in. Fox-hunting? Going to the pub? Protesting against the building of a new supermarket? The inability of the curriculum to endow participation with meaning suggests that the promoters of this subject cannot provide a convincing account of what it means to be a good citizen. Citizenship education is not an academic subject but a cause in search of an argument. It is therefore not surprising that 10 per cent of pupils polled did not know what was taught in citizenship lessons and another 17 per cent remarked that there was nothing memorable about them.

Citizenship education provides a paradigmatic example of the way soft social engineering works. Although its advocates boasted that citizenship education would change the political culture of society, it soon became evident that this subject lacked both clarity and content. As is the case with most forms of soft social engineering, it shifted emphasis from values education to values clarification. Citizenship classes are devoting a growing proportion of time to 'reflection' on personal values and behaviour. Its focus is on influencing individual attitudes rather than offering a wider vision of society. In this way, citizenship education advocates can claim that what they do is to help children learn to behave like future citizens rather than provide the intellectual resources necessary for becoming a citizen. Soft social engineering relies on the tools of behaviour management and therapy to influence children, and the values it upholds are those associated with approved forms of personal behaviour. As one proponent of this project writes: 'Citizenship education includes a specific body of knowledge and skills, but it is also an approach to learning, teaching and school life which fosters self-confidence, good relationships, responsible behaviour, enquiry, communication and active participation in the school and its community.'[42] Typically, this writer is far less specific about the 'body of knowledge' associated with citizenship education than with its numerous therapeutic benefits. What counts is its potential for influencing behaviour rather than intellectual clarity about what society expects of citizens.

## As engine of social change

There has been a steady increase in the political and economic expectations placed on schools during the past 30 to 40 years. Back in the early 1970s, the leading Labour politician Anthony Crosland was scathing about the idea of keeping politics out of education. 'A few people still think that social and political aspirations can, and should, somehow be kept out of education' he wrote, before asserting: 'but of course they cannot and should not.'[43] Crosland believed that ending early selection and introducing comprehensive education would 'lessen the early sense of failure'. Compared to the ambitions of social engineers today, Crosland's aspirations were relatively modest. Since the 1970s, the weight of expectations on education has increased steadily to the point where it is represented as the principal driver of social change. In current times education has become so politicized that policy-makers often appear out of touch with everyday realities in the classroom. In September 2008 the Secretary of State for Innovation, Universities and Skills, John Denham, stated that 'education is an engine of social justice, perhaps the most powerful tool we have'.[44] Indirectly, Denham's observation expressed a regrettable sense of defeatism about the ability of society to harness social and economic policy, cultural life or the dynamic of innovation to achieve positive change. It also represented an acknowledgement of a lack of faith in the potential of public and political life to achieve social justice. His characterization of education as the 'most powerful tool we have' conveys unrealistic expectations about the ability of schools to play the role hitherto assigned to public life.

Denham spoke the language of the social engineer when he described education as 'the most powerful tool'. According to his instrumentalist vocabulary, education is conceptualized as the means for achieving a goal which is external to itself. Once education is assigned this instrumental status, what is taught becomes subordinate to the realization of objectives that are external to it. Fiddling with the curriculum invariably leads to the devaluation of education. The destructive consequences of this process can be seen in the way that policies designed to overcome social inequality through schooling have led to the diminishing of the intellectual content of the curriculum.

Schools have an important role to play in helping children from disadvantaged backgrounds gain access to first-class education. A good education system strives to ensure that all children are encouraged to learn and that no barriers are placed in their way to develop and realize their potential. Most education systems fail in this respect, and children from working-class backgrounds are often forced to make do with an inferior quality of education to that enjoyed by their middle-class counterparts. This is a particular problem in England, where pupils from poor homes face considerable obstacles of getting into the best secondary schools.[45] There are many reasons why the attempts of successive governments to overcome social inequalities in educational attainment have failed to realize their objectives, and one is that schools alone cannot overcome social disadvantage. Another reason why the recent wave of education reforms has failed is that they rely on administrative solutions instead of educational ones.

In recent decades the failure to raise the achievement of pupils from disadvantaged backgrounds has led social engineers to tamper ceaselessly with the content of education. They have shifted focus from tackling the social and cultural barriers to a good education to representing education itself as the barrier to achieving social inequality. This change of emphasis is most clearly captured by the policy of social inclusion. In education, this policy demands the removal of any obstacle that stands in the way of including everyone. An inclusive curriculum is one that is not only open to all but also one that makes everyone feel included. That is why promoters of a so-called 'inclusive education' frequently decry the teaching of traditional subjects as a form of social exclusion, labelling them 'elitist' or middle class'. More challenging intellectually based subjects like physics and maths are often criticized by advocates of social inclusion because they are not readily accessible to every pupil. As Claire Fox, director of the think-tank Institute of Ideas writes, when promoters of social inclusion argue for removing the obstacles that stand in the way of children realizing their potential, they are 'not talking, as radicals did in the past, about removing the social barriers denying people access to knowledge and ideas'. Their aim is to remove the barrier of academic subject-based education and replace it with an education that includes anyone.[46]

The ascendancy of the social inclusion agenda is symptomatic of a loss of faith in the project of providing an intellectually challenging education for children from different social backgrounds. In previous times, the emphasis of reformers was on the elimination of the social barriers that prevented children gaining access to quality education. Today, the social engineering imperative of inclusion takes precedence over the content of schooling. That is why a growing number of policy-makers and curriculum experts regard academic education as a barrier to be overcome. It indicates that, despite its rhetorical celebration of the power of education, the social engineering perspective does not take the content of schooling seriously.

Social engineering is sometimes criticized for its tendency to politicize the curriculum and some educators are worried that this will lead to the devaluation of academic standards. Such concerns are all too often borne out by children's experience in the classroom. But, probably the most damaging consequence of social engineering is that it strengthens the power of anti-intellectual pedagogy over schooling.

# 6

## The Loss of Faith in Education

Many western societies have adopted a schizophrenic attitude towards education. Outwardly, education is celebrated to the point that its potential to change society is overestimated. Politicians extol the virtues of education and claim that their reform of schooling will help to transform the economy, thereby creating unrealistic expectations. However, while the potential of education to solve society's problems is overestimated, its capacity to inspire children to engage with intellectually challenging issues is underestimated.

The educational establishment finds it difficult to believe in the power of ideas. Instead of encouraging teachers to develop their expertise of their specialist subjects so that they can go on to inspire their students with the quality of their ideas, pedagogues prefer to put their faith in motivational techniques to manage classroom behaviour. So-called reforms and pedagogic innovations invariably skirt around how best to cultivate the intellectual development of young people. Instead, they draw upon market research and psychological techniques to devise schemes that promise to motivate students, investing hope in new psycho-pedagogy – learning styles, brain functioning, thinking skills, emotional intelligence or multiple intelligence.[1] The reliance of techniques has turned education into a territory that is hospitable to the latest fad. This pedagogy is fixated on learning styles but is devoid of interest in the knowledge to be learned.

The minor status that pedagogy assigns to knowledge reflects the

studied indifference that policy-makers display towards the intellectual content of education. All too often, new policies advocate the
devaluation of the role of knowledge acquisition and intellectual
development within the institution of education. Worse still, schools
are influenced by a pedagogy that has little faith in the potential of
education to transform and develop children.

Yet there appears to be no limit to the expansionary ambitions
of education as a social engineering project. In England, in March
2005, the Government launched a curriculum for 0–5-year-olds.
The Early Years Foundation Stage curriculum provides guidance
and targets for children's progress as they make their way from
gurgling to babbling sounds. Every child's development is to be
scrutinized against 13 assessment scales and divided between six
areas of learning and development.[2] The Government is confident
that, if this policy is implemented, children as young as 40 months
old will be able to participate in 'citizenship lessons' so that they
can comprehend that 'people have different needs, views, cultures
and beliefs, that need to be treated with respect'. Officialdom's
confidence in the magical powers of early learning stands in sharp
contrast to its uncertainty about the potential of young people
to engage with intellectually challenging subjects such as physics
or maths. Moreover, the claim that 40-months-old children will
be able to participate in citizenship lessons says more about the
trite content of this subject than it does about the conceptual
abilities of infants.

At first sight, this hyper-ambitious effort to formalize the care
of babies and infants and subject them to 'early learning goals' can
appear as the outcome of officialdom's strong commitment to the
power of education. In fact, it reflects the Government's confusion
and anxiety about the effectiveness of primary and secondary
schooling. This initiative is driven by the imperative that 'something
must be done', and 'the earlier the better'. Policy-makers seem to take
the view that if you wait till the ripe old age of six, it may be too
late for education to work. One of the regrettable outcomes of this
lack of faith is the tendency to infantalize education. A curriculum
drawn up for toddlers not only trivializes its meaning but also

threatens to provide the model for schooling young people in later years.

At a time when education has become the recipient of unprecedented levels of public expenditure and enjoys the continuous attention of policy-makers, the claim that there has been a loss of faith in education appears counter-intuitive. After all, policy-makers constantly promise a rise in standards and have set ambitious targets for the expansion of higher education. But this is a discussion that is driven by fear rather than hope, which is why it often assumes the form of a debate about who is to blame for failure. A language that dwells on failure to achieve targets, failure to raise standards, failed schools and failed teachers conveys the idea that something is seriously amiss. Implicitly, the conclusion drawn is that the problem lies with education itself – at least with education as it has been classically conceived. That is why the word 'education' has been displaced in numerous policy statements and pedagogic research papers by terms such as 'learning' and 'skills'. 'What messages or power relationships might be implied by the replacement of the term education by learning and skills?' ask a group of researchers, noting that the 'minimal use of the term education in recent documents referring to the post-compulsory stage seems to be a deliberate tactic'.[3] Whether or not officialdom's reluctance to use the term 'education' is deliberate or not is a matter of conjecture. However, it is beyond dispute that this shift in terminology is not confined to post-compulsory education. One of the most disturbing examples of this trend is a government-commissioned report entitled *2020 Vision* published in 2007, which attempts to outline what the implementation of official policy on 'personalized learning' should look like in 2020. The report offers a 'vision' where the word 'education' barely gets a mention. Its goal for the future is one where 'all children and young people leave school with functional skills in English and mathematics, understanding how to learn, think creatively, take risks and handle change'.[4] The report has a lot to say about information technology, but very little about academic learning. Its narrow technical focus and its goal of providing school-leavers with functional skills is symptomatic of the low expectations that policy-makers have of the institution of education.

The project of diminishing the intellectual content of education is signalled continually through a language that calls into question the central role of formal teaching of a subject-based curriculum. The Hurrah! word of experts is 'learning'. The preference for this term signifies a turn away from an emphasis on formal teaching to learning as a generic process. The shift in language towards learning points towards the affirmation of the extra-educational experience. Time and again, experts inform the public that what young people learn outside school is as, if not more, important than the instruction they receive in school. They claim that what people learn from life should be formally credited, while 'experiential learning' should be highly valued by schools. Ordinary, everyday routine learning has been rebranded as experiential learning, allowing educators to credit, and claim credit for, the routine insights that people gain from their work and life.

The credentialization of experiential learning is presented as a democratic gesture that values all forms of knowledge and experiences. But inflating the significance of the banal devalues the role of formal schooling. This sentiment is implicit in the tendency to depict the ideal of education as that of lifelong learning. Outwardly, advocates of lifelong learning appear to celebrate the importance of education, but in practice, the case for lifelong learning is often conveyed through calling into question the central role of the school in the education of the individual. The school is often depicted as but a brief phase before individuals get down to the challenging task of 'learning from life'.

It is important to note that 'learning' means something very different from 'education'. According to one definition, 'learning can be defined as an increase in understanding or capability'.[5] People learn from their experience in all kinds of different social settings, and learning from everyday life provides individuals with insight, skills and common sense. But while learning from experience is essential for personal development, it is not education. Education is a purposeful project that provides young people with the kind of knowledge and cultural legacy that society deems essential. Education is linked to people's lives and it plays an important role in assisting the 'systematisation and structuring of the child's experiences',[6] but the purpose of education is to provide children with knowledge that is not directly accessible through experience. It offers knowledge that is potentially universalizing and based on humanity's experience of the past. So education brings knowledge that is external to a child's experience into the classroom. It is precisely because this view of education is regarded as outdated that learning has become the axial concept in twenty-first-century pedagogy. The current tendency to uphold learning as the defining mission of education is influenced by a powerful impulse that seeks to minimize the relative weight of knowledge in the school curriculum. Nothing expresses the loss of faith in education more sharply than the decline in the valuation of the knowledge-led curriculum.

Whatever their original meaning, the terms 'learner' or 'learning' are now used to convey assumptions that are antithetical to the classical or the liberal humanist ideal of education. When curriculum engineers exclaim that 'we are all learners' they do not merely give voice to yet another banality – they implicitly call into question the idea of purposeful education carried out under the instruction of authoritative teachers. We may all learn from life on the streets. But learning from life is not simply a variant of the education that goes on in classrooms. And inside the school we need teachers who are teaching and not learning. Of course, if teachers want to learn, they can pursue that ambition by attending courses in further or higher education.

## Knowledge-based education as the barrier to learning

Education may serve a variety of different purposes, but unless a central role is assigned to the acquisition of subject-based knowledge it is not really education. As Young writes, 'The belief that the knowledge acquired through the curriculum is (or at least should be) cognitively superior to people's everyday knowledge has been the major rationale for the massive expansion of formal education in the past two centuries.'[7] It is regrettable that in the twenty-first century it is not always possible to assume that schools are prepared to uphold this sentiment. One reason why the central role of the acquisition of subject-based knowledge needs to be upheld is because so much of what goes by the name of curriculum reform and pedagogic innovation is designed to undermine it.

Most parents and non-specialists would be surprised to discover that many pedagogues have a very low opinion of a subject-based curriculum devoted to the cultivation of children's knowledge of history, literature, maths or science. These days, professional educators frequently refer to an academic curriculum as an irrelevant, elitist relic, taking the view that a 'subject-based mould' was 'outdated in the nineteenth, never mind the twenty-first century'.[8] Since intellectual and scientific development occurred and continues to occur through distinct academic subjects, it is far from evident why a curriculum based on literature, mathematics, history, geography, science and languages should be outdated. The knowledge that children gain through the study of these subjects is no more outdated today than it was 100 or 200 years ago. But the charge that an academic curriculum is outdated is rarely informed by a serious reflection on content of subjects. Such criticisms are usually justified on political or social engineering grounds. Specifically, a subject-based curriculum is perceived as inconsistent with the objectives of a social inclusion agenda. It is essential to note that the crass campaign against a subject-based curriculum is mainly motivated by a political and not educational agenda. This point was forcefully argued by Professor John White, one of the leading critics of subject-based curriculum, who asserts that this discriminates against children from poor homes because they are likely to struggle in a 'highly academic school culture'.[9]

White is right when he notes that children from poor homes are likely to face difficulties when they engage with a 'highly academic school culture'. Indeed, most children – including those from the middle classes – are likely to be stretched by an academic school culture. However, the role of educators is to establish an environment where children are helped to overcome the obstacles that stand in the way of attaining a good academic education. Decrying the value of such an education avoids confronting the challenge of how to provide quality education to everyone regardless of their social circumstances. It also significantly underestimates the human capacity for learning. The currently fashionable pedagogy of limits distracts society's energies from realizing the formidable potential that education has in 'helping people more fully to realize their humanity and powers'.[10]

There was a time when radical educational reformers sought to provide working-class people with the opportunity to gain access to a curriculum with a high level of intellectual content. As Entwistle recalls, the issue for these reformers was 'discovering ways of bringing to the socially and economically disadvantaged the benefits of the kind of education which has traditionally been reserved to the ruling class'.[11] This approach was forcefully argued by Gramsci, who believed that the problem with the kind of education monopolized by the elites was that the rest of society was prevented from gaining access to it.[12] In contrast to his valuation of the 'great works of European culture', today's reformers assume that such an education is elitist and therefore not suitable for a national curriculum. 'It is hardly surprising that in an age where education was the property of the privileged, the subjects thought worthy of inclusion in a curriculum were intellectual', states a report hostile to knowledge-led schooling. Instead of proposing that this kind of education should be available to everyone, the authors of the report acquiesce to the age-old prejudice that an academic education is not suitable for the mass of students. They insist that 'the classical and elite model containing a narrow range of intellectual knowledge and skill is inappropriate for an age of universal education'.[13] Intellectual knowledge that has a unique capacity to expand the mind and the imagination is caricatured as narrow, but paradoxically, these authors' polemic against the classical model is based on assumptions that are surprisingly similar to the elites that they criticize. Today's anti-subject crusaders implicitly agree with traditional hierarchical educators on one important point: an intellectually informed curriculum is only suitable for the elites, and not for the education of the masses.

Criticism of the 'knowledge model' of education often conveys the idea that, because of its historical association with the privileged, it was complicit in maintaining inequality. Such philistine critics often denounce the transmission of knowledge through academic subjects because of its alleged 'association with the values of the privileged classes'. They insist that because of its association with privilege, the academic subject is likely to perpetuate the differentiation of society on 'class lines'.[14] Advocates of the social inclusion agenda take the view that an academically specialized curriculum benefits the powerful and, by definition, excludes the poor. Yet the claim that an academic curriculum serves to perpetuate inequality lacks intellectual rigour. As Moore and Young observe, 'there are no grounds for claiming that the historical association of the two patterns, curriculum specialization and inequality, has a causal explanation'.[15] Curriculum specialization does not cause inequality, and its elimination will do nothing to overcome it. On the contrary – one way of narrowing inequality is through providing everyone with an opportunity to benefit from an academic educational culture.

Criticism of the 'knowledge model' of education is often expressed through statements that question explicitly the authority of knowledge. One recurring argument used to contest the knowledge-led curriculum is that it is quickly outdated in an ever-changing world. It appears that since 'what is known to be true changes by the hour', the 'rote learning of facts must give way to nurturing through education of essential transferable skills'.[16] Typically, 'truth' is represented as a momentary epiphenomenon and knowledge acquisition is caricatured as the 'rote learning of facts'. Such a philistine construction of educational knowledge is the flipside of the advocacy of the social engineering agenda. The representation of truth and knowledge as an unstable and transitory phenomenon has become an unstated core assumption of opponents of an academically based school curriculum. A position statement by one teachers' union asserts that 'a twenty-first century curriculum cannot have the transfer of knowledge at its core for the simple reason that the selection of what is required has become problematic in an information-rich age'.[17]

The claim that transmitting knowledge to children loses its relevance in an information-rich age fails to understand the distinction between knowledge and information. A society's knowledge gives meaning to new information, by allowing people to interpret new facts and by helping society to understand what significance to attach to them. Knowledge itself develops through the appropriation of new experience. But the latest knowledge is linked organically to that which preceded it. Implicitly scepticism towards the authority of knowledge calls into question the meaning of education itself. Once the knowledge of the past is rendered obsolescent, what can education mean? If 'what is known to be true changes by the hour', what is there left to teach? The alternative offered to the knowledge-based curriculum is an agenda that encourages students to acquire skills which allow them to adapt to a constantly changing environment. From this perspective, it is students' ability to adapt to new circumstances that is important, not what they know. So the proposed shift from academic education is not towards another kind of education, but towards training. The new pedagogy is less interested in students learning a subject than in acquiring the generic skill of 'learning to learn'. As Beck and Young remark, learning to learn is based on the assumption of 'the inevitable obsolescence of accumulated knowledge', and prioritizes the 'value of developing skills and flexibility to acquire and put to use whatever is needed next'.[18]

Learning to learn is an inevitable and, of course, necessary by-product of a good education. Once children have acquired the solid foundations of an academic subject, they are often able to use that knowledge to engage with new problems and acquire important insights from their experience. Unfortunately, learning to learn has become disassociated from the learning of the content of a subject. Learning to learn is branded as a stand-alone generic skill that is deemed more important than the content of learning. The current obsession with functional skills has fostered a climate in which a one-dimensional emphasis on learning to learn threatens to turn pedagogy into a sub-branch of management training. Increasingly, curriculum engineers perceive schooling as a process by which, when children are not learning to learn, they are learning 'thinking skills' and becoming 'reflective learners', 'independent enquirers', 'self managers' and 'critical thinkers'. Even knowledge has been deconstructed into four distinct types of skills-related activity: know what, know why, know how and know who. According to this formulation, knowing a subject is know what, and the other three are generic skills.[19]

There are two major problems with the one-dimensional emphasis on skills training. The first is that it distracts schools from educating children and encouraging their intellectual development. For example, the current one-dimensional focus on literacy skills deprives children of an understanding of the literary world and a familiarity with literature itself. One regrettable consequence of this approach is that many young people who arrive at university are functionally literate but quite estranged from the world of literature. Furthermore, training children in generic skills is ineffective in its own terms. It is through the study of academic subjects that children acquire the skills that are necessary for learning and for engaging with the questions and challenges thrown up by everyday life. The isolation of skills from the pursuit of knowledge-based subjects represents a form of training that tends to provide children with formulaic techniques that are far more likely to help them talk the talk than learn to learn.

## Devaluation of the subject-based curriculum

It has become fashionable to blame 'subjects' for the failures of education. Sir Ken Robinson believes that education 'is stifling the individual talents and abilities of too many children and killing the motivation to learn', and needs to 'eliminate the existing hierarchy of subjects'. Subjects, he believes, 'interrupt the flow of creativity', and he goes so far as to argue that the very idea of a subject needs to be questioned. Why? Because 'the idea of separate subjects that have nothing in common offends the principle of dynamism'.[20] Robinson's recycling of the tired old argument that subject-based schooling stifles creativity captures the mood of the times. Another argument against the academically based curriculum is that it does not address the lifestyle concerns that social engineers wish to promote in the schools. One call for a shift in focus from 'the current subject-based, or academic system' is based on the belief that we 'need a curriculum that helps young people cope with other pressing issues, including substance abuse, obesity, teenage pregnancy, bullying, gang violence, apathy and eroded nationhood'.[21]

The project of transforming the school curriculum into an all-purpose instrument of social policy is doomed to failure. This instrumental view of the curriculum fails to understand that studying academic subjects also helps to provide the moral and intellectual resources with which young people can make their way in the world. While history or literature do not provide tips on healthy eating, they help young people to gain ideas about their place in the world and about their responsibilities towards fellow human beings. The acquisition of academic knowledge provides children with a capacity to make responsible decisions. Most important of all, when children learn to take ideas seriously they also begin to take themselves more seriously and hence develop the potential for behaving maturely.

As noted earlier, the idea that the world is constantly changing serves to undermine the authority of the academic subject. Some argue that with the rise of digital technology, students may well know more than their teachers. 'It's no longer unusual for students to know more than their teachers about a particular topic because they have used e-mail and the web to delve deeply into something that engages their interest', observes one think-tank.[22] Another version of this argument against the subject-based curriculum is that the knowledge acquired has little use for young people as they make their way in the future: that 'little of what is learned in a classroom is used in life'. Such an outlook is founded on a lack of faith in the transformative potential of knowledge and knowledge acquisition. This author argues that 'what they learn in particular subject-based lessons might serve them for a year or two, perhaps a little longer', and what students need is to 'learn to learn' since the 'learning process serves them lifelong'.[23] But the knowledge of the past does not have a limited shelf-life. Intellectual progress is achieved through elaborating the understanding achieved by thinkers throughout history. In the same way, the knowledge-based achievements of society serve to stimulate the intellectual development of young people. The philistine idea that what children learn is likely to be outdated in a year or two may have some relevance to information, but not to knowledge. This regrettable confusion of knowledge with facts is one of the hallmarks of the dogma of learning to learn. Advocates of the idea of learning to learn believe that the key objective of schools should be to motivate youngsters, rather than the acquisition of knowledge. 'Developing the motivation, the depth of understanding and the personal discipline required to understand in depth is surely the most important priority for education during childhood and adolescence', states Bentley.[24] The implication conveyed by sponsors of learning to learn is that young people will be more likely to become motivated through the acquisition of skills than through knowledge-based subjects.

Opponents of subject-based schooling frequently argue that young people's experience provides a more reliable foundation for learning than academic subjects. At best, a 'subject is a convenient category, one way of organising knowledge'.[25] Others state that a subject-based curriculum is a poor way of organizing teaching. 'The institutionalisation of knowledge via discipline and subjects limits the possibilities for freedom or autonomy for teachers and students and the possibility of making meaningful connections across schooling', writes one curriculum specialist.[26] This point is often stressed in relation to primary education, and critics claim that subject-based teaching stultifies children's creativity. The main objective of critics is to shift the emphasis from curriculum content to the stimulation of the child. A report on the evidence provided for the 2008 English Primary Curriculum Review notes that 'there was a general call for a reduction in the number of subject areas'. The report caricatures the subject as rigid and counterpoises it to the ideals of flexibility, creativity and innovation. The unspoken assumption of the report is that the teaching of a subject-based curriculum represents the polar opposite to the cultivation of the child's well-being and personal development, stating that a 'move from segregated subjects into flexibility and creativity was a common call' and that this is 'already under way in several innovative schools'.[27] Those giving evidence to this review appeared to internalize the rhetoric of the curriculum engineer. The report remarks that 'phrases frequently used included flexibility, creativity, capacity building, cross-curricular planning with care for local progression, concepts and skills and local relevance'. One can be fairly certain that phrases that were very infrequently used were education, knowledge and academic learning. The one point of agreement among the respondents was the need to liberate the curriculum from the apparently pernicious influence of the academic subject. 'Almost all respondents strongly believed that a curriculum framework driven by key concepts and processes (including personal, learning and thinking skills) should replace a curriculum dominated by content', concludes this official analysis of evidence.

As the Primary Curriculum Review indicates, opposition to the subject is inextricably linked to the project of diminishing the role of curriculum content. Hostility to the subject signals scepticism towards its intellectual content. The turn against the subject is motivated by a sense of disenchantment towards academic knowledge and learning. The call for the elimination of the subject-based curriculum is sometimes advocated on the grounds that it will provide greater opportunity for cross-curricular teaching. Opponents of subject-based teaching frequently enthuse about the potential for stimulating children's imagination through engaging them in broad themes and projects. In principle, the teaching of issues and themes can provide children with intellectual stimulation and an ability to understand how different dimensions of a phenomenon interact with one another. But what the critics of the subject propose is not the replacement of one form of academic learning with another one. The aims of the subject-light curriculum are linked to lifestyle and social engineering objectives, and the themes they propose do not emerge through questions raised by deliberation about a subject-based discipline but are themes that are imposed on the curriculum by a politically driven agenda. Even the most philistine school curriculum cannot entirely rid itself of the provision of subject-based knowledge. But through adopting a half-hearted and sceptical attitude towards it, the authority of the subject is undermined.

There are very good reasons why academic subjects are not an optional extra to the running of an intellectually informed curriculum. Bantock argued that academic subjects 'have evolved as they have simply because they have proved to be the most economical and lucid ways of handling the undifferentiated mass of phenomena we experience in the natural and social worlds around us or in our internal life of feelings and emotions'.[28] This pragmatic view of the role of the academic subject is open to other ways of capturing and transmitting new knowledge. There is no reason why education should be confined to the teaching of academic subjects. Moreover, experience shows that the relative status and role of academic disciplines alters with the development of new knowledge. Children, especially in primary schools, can develop through the study of topics and issues that transcend any particular academic subject. The subject-based curriculum, like any aspect of education, needs continuous reflection. But academic subjects provide an intellectual framework through which students gain an understanding of how a subject works and through which their understanding can be deepened. Subject-based learning is not a barrier to creativity and cross-curricular innovation. On the contrary: children are much more likely to grasp the connections between the insights of different subjects if they have a firm grounding in core academic disciplines.

## The devaluation of the formal

Antagonism towards the 'knowledge model' of education is driven by the impulse to remove any barriers that stand in the way of inclusion. Experience indicates that once the project of removing barriers dominates policy, virtually any dimension of formal education becomes negotiable. Why stop with removing the academic subject?

What critics of subject-based education mean when they contrast it unfavourably to a curriculum devoted to promoting creativity, flexibility and innovation, is that an academic discipline is too formal to motivate children. The term 'formal' has acquired negative connotations and is generally regarded as a marker for stultifying teaching, rote learning and classroom boredom. The discussion about education conveys the idea that, because of its formality, schooling itself is the problem. Some reformers even go so far as to look for solutions to children's motivation outside the school, arguing that 'if we want to achieve a real shift in the chances of all young people, focusing only on what happens *inside* schools is misguided'.[29] Formal schooling is sometimes criticized for turning 'so many people off the idea of learning' and there is growing pressure to rebrand people's experience of everyday life as a valid form of certifiable education.[30]

There are many reasons why formality in education is regarded as bad practice by curriculum engineers. However, their fundamental assumption is that schools would work better if they were more like everyday life. There are numerous ways in which this sentiment is expressed. Teachers are often told to teach material that is relevant to their students. Pedagogues argue that there should be a close relationship between youngsters' prior experience and what they learn in school. One of the 'evidence-informed pedagogic principles' put forward by the Economic and Social Research Council's (ESRC) Teaching and Learning Research Project is the need to recognize 'the importance of prior experience and learning'. According to this statement of pedagogic learning, 'informal learning, such as learning out of school or away from the workplace, should be recognized as at least as significant as formal learning'.[31] That's another way of saying that formal education is not a big deal.

The cultural capital that children bring with them when they enter school, and the insights they gain through their experience in a variety of settings, have a significant influence on their intellectual and moral development, and good teachers will always seek to understand their pupils' backgrounds and experiences. But it is important not to confuse what children learn through their lives with their education in school. Indeed, sometimes a decent education requires that children *un*learn what they learnt in an informal setting. Gramsci argued that 'education is a struggle against folklore' and is often at odds with the common sense of everyday life.[32] As Young argues, different forms of learning need to be differentiated from one another:

> [T]he purpose of formal education is to enable students to acquire knowledge that (i) is not accessible to most people in their everyday lives, and (ii) enables those who acquire it to move beyond their experience and gain some understanding of the social and natural worlds of which they are a part.[33]

Once disassociated from its formality, education becomes merely a variant of folk learning. Yet its transformative potential lies in its ability to inspire students to go beyond their experience. Leesa Wheelahan expresses her concerns with the tendency to erode the qualitative distinction between formal and informal learning in this way:

> [A]ttempts to collapse the boundary between abstract, theoretical knowledge that is primarily available in education and everyday knowledge available in the workplace in the interest of making it more "authentic" or "relevant" robs students of the capacity to recognise the boundaries between different kinds of knowledge and to successfully navigate them.[34]

Many well-meaning experts believe that by placing a value on the student's extra-educational experience and background they are helping working-class, ethnic minority and other students from non-traditional bacgrounds gain status and recognition. However, bestowing an educational value on people's street knowledge does little to help them to deal with social and economic disadvantage. People need to be exposed to the knowledge that they do not encounter through their lives and they become educated when they are taught answers to questions they have not previously thought of asking. As Simon argues, without this knowledge, a 'high propor-tion of children, whose concepts are formed as a result of their everyday experiences, and as a result, are often distorted and incorrectly reflect reality, will never reach the stage where the development of higher cognitive forms of activity becomes a possibility'.[35] Without gaining access to knowledge-led education, many children risk becoming prisoners of their circumstance.

The tendency to erode the distinction between formal and informal learning has acquired the character of a pedagogic dogma. Bentley contends that 'learning can take place in any situation, at any time, and that to improve the quality of education we must overcome the historical mistake of confusing school-based instruction with the whole of education'.[36] Barber also regards formal schooling as one of many sites where education takes place, and argues that 'we should be aiming to shorten the formal school day and lengthen the learning day'.[37] Why shorten the school day unless you believe that it is a barrier to exploiting the opportunities provided by the informal learning day? Indeed, why go to school at all?

Schooling is often depicted as one of a number of different 'learning activities'. As a result, many pedagogues argue that the experience of informal learning activity should be given credit by an educational institution as a form of 'experiential learning'. One of the principles upheld by the ESRC's Teaching and Learning Research Project is that informal learning should be 'valued and appropriately utilized in formal processes'.[38] Informal learning is particularly advocated as a solution to the problem of adult education. So a report on further education claims that this sector has 'the potential to reach out to adults who can become new learners in their homes, in factories, in shops and offices, in the schools where their children learn and in a host of community venues'.[39] No doubt adults and children gain important insights about the world through a variety of settings, but the equation of these experiences with education invariably devalues its significance. Learning from experience is a lifelong process through which individuals become acquainted with the practices and customs of their community. This form of learning takes place spontaneously and is the by-product of life. In contrast, education involves a conscious and purposeful engagement to acquire knowledge that not only does not arise from everyday experience and sometimes even contradicts it. The formality of education follows inexorably from the need to present knowledge in a systematic and comprehensive way so that pupils comprehend the world of human achievement.

Advocates of lifelong learning are less interested in formal learning than in learning to learn. From their standpoint the school is not the obvious site for learning to learn. Consequently, the 'key educational question is no longer how certain materials can be taught as successfully as possible, but which learning environments can best stimulate self-determined learning: how learning itself can be "learned"'.[40] This emphasis reduces the authority of the educator. As Crowther writes, 'the educator's involvement in the curriculum is simplified to that of a facilitator of the learning process'.[41]

The turn from formal teaching towards learning and experience invariably encourages the downsizing of the intellectual content of education. Carl Rogers, one of the most passionate pioneer crusaders for experiential learning, demanded that 'the facilitator' helps to 'de-emphasize static or content goals and, thus, encourages a focus on the process, on *experiencing* the way in which learning takes place'.[42] This tendency to delineate the process sharply from the content of learning is one of the hallmarks of contemporary pedagogy. Yet both are inextricably linked, and exist in a dynamic relationship to one another. Regrettably, the polarized representation of process and content serves as a prelude to promoting process – learning to learn – over the intellectual content.

## Loss of faith in children

The current pedagogic imagination perceives education itself as the source of barriers that must be overcome. Some of those barriers are perceived to be the subject-based curriculum, the emphasis on knowledge, and the formality of education itself. Pedagogy's indifference to content lends teaching an arbitrary character. This arbitrariness is implicitly justified and promoted through the turn towards *personalized learning*. Although the concept of personalized learning lacks clarity and coherence, its main accomplishment is to shift emphasis from the curriculum to the individual child. Good teachers always attempt to assess the strengths and weaknesses of their pupils in order to get the best out of their work: but personalized learning is not simply an attempt to encourage teachers to develop greater sensitivity to individual students. Personalized learning represents an implicit attempt to minimize the significance of a common curriculum in favour of a more differentiated approach that claims to take into account the differentiated needs of children. From this perspective, children's aptitudes, rather than the requirements of the transmission of knowledge, shape what is taught in the classroom.

The Department for Children, Schools and Families (DCSF) demands that schools 'reflect a professional ethos that accepts and assumes every child comes to the classroom with a different knowledge base and skill set, as well as varying aptitudes and aspirations'. It states that teaching and learning should be focused on 'the aptitudes and interests of pupils'.[43] So the task of the teacher is not so much to develop children intellectually as to develop a strategy for catering to their differential aptitudes and interests. In this model of personalized learning, the aptitude of the child takes logical priority over the subject matter to be taught. Teaching becomes far less concerned with expertise in a subject. Since there are limits as to how far knowledge can be broken down to respond to the different 'skill set' and 'aptitudes' of children, the focus of teaching can be lost. It is worth noting that, when a Government-sponsored report demands that 'skills for personalizing learning' should be 'fundamental to teacher training', what it has in mind is principally Information Technology Training.[44] What the programme of personalized teaching demands are skilled technicians rather than educators who are specialist in an academic subject.

Personalized learning can be misconstrued as an enlightened attempt to respond sensitively to the unique qualities of the child. In reality, this strategy relies on behaviour management techniques that aim to motivate and engage rather than teach. Implicitly, the personalized learning agenda is underpinned by the belief that children possess some kind of deficit that needs to be addressed by teachers. 'The school system already recognizes that some children have "special needs"', writes one proponent, who goes on to argue that 'personalized learning would extend this principle, already implicit in the system, to all children'.[45] The proposal that special needs education serves as the model for all children makes explicit the embedded premise of personalization. Although proponents of personalization talk the talk of individual choice and personal needs, its main concern is to extend a system of special needs to a wider group of pupils deemed to be low achievers. And the high achievers – talented, bright, motivated students – because of their intelligence also have a 'special need'.

Publications preaching the virtues of personalized learning are almost entirely rhetorical and, even by the low standards of current pedagogic thinking, are unusually insipid, making no attempt to explain the concept itself.[46] Even leading supporters of personalization concede that this is a concept in search of meaning. Professor David Hargreaves, one of England's leading experts on personalized learning, recently conceded that it was a 'total waste of time trying to find a definition'.[47] Unfortunately, the absence of clarity about what personalization means does not inhibit politicians from adopting it as a central theme, and although it is not a pedagogically informed concept, personalization has an important ideological role to play. Many statements about personalization are actually calls to extend the model of special needs education to a wider constituency of low achievers. So one report argues for 'establishing an entitlement to personal learning' on the grounds that 'a significant proportion of low-attaining pupils from disadvantaged backgrounds' do not get the benefit of additional provisions. Throughout the report, the main concern of its authors is with pupils who are 'not achieving expected standards'.[48] Personalized learning is rarely devoted towards engaging with the needs of the top achiever. As one government-sponsored report concluded, many schools are reluctant to identify talented students for fear of being seen as elitist: 'there was relatively little for the talented' both 'in terms of how they were identified and the activities that were available to them'.[49]

The failure to provide a challenging learning environment for able students should not be seen as a temporary flaw in an otherwise sound educational system. Since personalized education is motivated by pessimistic assumptions about the capacity of children to benefit from a sound academic education, its energy is inevitably directed towards containing the problem of low achievement. Many supporters, and indeed critics, of personalized learning believe that this approach, and its claim to address the different learning needs of all, is motivated by the spirit of egalitarianism. In fact, the anti-intellectual turn of contemporary pedagogy demonstrates a lack of confidence in the capacity of children to acquire a good academic education. Such pessimistic conclusions are often couched in the language of pragmatism. 'We need a bit of honesty', says a report published by the Association of Teachers and Lecturers before stating that 'most people are not intellectuals'. Just as well, they write, because the 'world cannot survive only through thought'.[50] Their call for a practical, down-to-earth skills-based curriculum is presented in an anti-elitist form, but it captures the worst features of nineteenth-century differentiation between thinkers and doers. Worse still, it reproduces the outdated prejudice which believes that only a tiny minority can thrive through an academic education and that the rest can only benefit from training.

As an ideology, personalized learning intuitively appeals to our understanding of the fact that children develop in different ways, which most educators already recognize. Despite the claim by advocates of personal learning that they are engaged in a crusade against the 'one size fits all' approach, there are very few teachers who uphold the view that there is 'one way to learn, the right way, and either kids will learn it or it's too bad'.[51] The call to adopt special needs teaching as the model for all children conveys a pessimistic view about the capacity of schools to educate children together through a common curriculum. As the developmental psychologist Helene Guldberg states, 'Children have different strengths and weaknesses, and teachers have always had to adapt their teaching accordingly' – but the crucial question is, 'Do we really want to solidify and accentuate differences?'[52]

It is worth noting that the weight attached to the significance of individual differences among children risks obscuring the common features of their development. There is a body of educational theory that argues that 'in general terms, the process of learning among human beings is similar across the human species as a whole'.[53] No system of education can work effectively unless it is based on general principles that are capable of engaging with the needs of a cohort of children. An effective pedagogy must involve starting 'from what children have in common as members of the human species; to establish general principles of teaching and, in the light of these, to determine what modifications of practice are necessary to meet specific individual needs'.[54]

The fixation of personalized learning is founded on the assumption that what children have in common is less significant than their difference. In previous times this preoccupation with difference has encouraged a tendency to naturalize it and to perceive variations in children's intellectual development as the consequence of innate qualities. As late as the 1940s, official reports argued that there were three types of children – 'those that are good with abstract ideas, those that are good with their hands, and those who are simply good'.[55] The education system was organized in such a way that children with innate academic qualities were segregated from those who needed to be trained for a manual occupation. The hierarchy of educational opportunities, which reflected people's social circumstances, was legitimized on the grounds that children were fit for different roles in society. One argument used was that since children had different innate capacities as measured by IQ, academic learning was only suitable for a small minority. In the twenty-first century this fatalistic prejudice that associates children's achievement with their fixed innate abilities has little intellectual credibility. However, through the use of psychological research and diagnostic instruments, a new 'psycho-pedagogy' has emerged that labels and categorizes children according to the 'learning styles' or 'intelligences' they possess. As one critic of psycho-pedagogy, who is worried about 'the stultifying effect of labelling' noted, such stereotyping risks 'limiting learners' potential and opportunities'.[56]

Psycho-pedagogy has invented a veritable dictionary of labels that can be used to diagnose children's 'learning styles', 'aptitudes' and 'intelligences'. Some pupils have visual, while others have auditory and still others kinaesthetic learning styles. Learners are categorized as innovators, adaptors, reflective, pragmatic, etc. Policy-makers have invented the terms 'gifted' and 'talented' to categorize able students. Such terms are constructed to convey a sense of scientific precision. So gifted students are the top 5–10 per cent of pupils 'as measured by actual or potential achievement in the main curriculum subjects', according to the British Government's Excellence in Cities programme. Turning stereotyping into an art form is one of the legacies of curriculum engineers. Helpfully they provide a glossary of terms that can also be used to describe 'gifted' and 'talented' children. The glossary includes terms like 'able pupils', 'more able pupils', 'the very able', 'exceptionally able', 'gifted children', 'talented pupils', 'those with exceptional talent', 'pupils with marked aptitude'.[57] This addiction to stereotyping should not be seen as a rare or incidental by-product of an otherwise sound system of pedagogy. The pedagogy of personalized learning is transmitted through the provision of a diagnosis. Giving a child a label is as about as personal as it gets.

The belief that many children are not likely to be motivated by an intellectually based curriculum is given legitimacy by theories that claim there are different types of children with different profiles of intelligence. In previous times, pessimistic views of child development argued that their future was determined by their innate intelligence. In the first half of the twentieth century the claim that children's intelligence was genetically inherited and fixed served as an explanation for differential rates of achievement. From this perspective it could be argued that a significant percentage of children would not benefit from an academic education. In more recent times this fatalistic view of children's potential has been discredited. Unfortunately, some of the new theories of child development also convey an element of fatalism about the potential of children to benefit from an academic education. Howard Gardner's theory of Multiple Intelligences (MI) is widely seen as an enlightened alternative to the pessimistic views of the past, and exercises an important influence on twenty-first-century curriculum engineers. Gardner argues that there are 'at least seven different ways of knowing the world', to which he refers as seven human intelligences; he contends that each child has a different mix of intelligences and therefore learns in very different ways.[58] Many pedagogues have embraced the theory of Multiple Intelligences to argue for multiple approaches to learning. Of course it makes perfect sense to adopt teaching styles that take account of the different strengths and weaknesses of students. Unfortunately, the authority of the theory of MI tends to be invoked on the grounds that it encourages a more 'inclusive' curriculum than one that valorizes intellectual endeavours. One leading New Labour adviser enthused about this approach because it allegedly opens the 'room of learning, not just for the elite, but for everyone'.[59] The theory of MI is embraced because it provides an ideological rationale for a shift away from an academic subject-based curriculum.

The main reason why Gardner has become so popular with policy-makers is because he provides a coherent argument against a curriculum that is devoted to the teaching of academic knowledge. According to Gardner's model, 'logical–mathematical' intelligences shape the learning styles of some, but by no means all, children. He posits a number of other non-intellectual intelligences that can influence children's learning style. For example, bodily–kinaesthetic intelligence – the use of one's whole body or parts of the body to problem solve – has been turned into a learning style which, it is claimed, characterizes 'kinaesthetic learners'. These are children who learn best through physical activity – through 'doing' rather than 'thinking'. MI theory is frequently used in a template fashion to pigeon-hole children and categorize the way they think. Many parents have bought into this system of categorization. 'My daughter is not academic, she is an emotional learner' is not an uncommon observation these days.

At the end of the day, Gardner's approach shares the fatalistic assumptions of the now discredited IQ theorists he criticizes. As Guldberg argues, 'MI theory is based on the idea of pre-programmed modules in the brain that dispose us to learn in particular ways'.[60] Certainly, in the hands of curriculum engineers MI proves to be a surprisingly deterministic theory. So Bentley asserts that 'each of us has a different blend of intelligences' and therefore 'not only will we be more suited to some kinds of knowledge and understanding than to others, we will also be more suited to some kinds of *learning* than to others'.[61] The idea that some of us are 'suited' to some kinds of learning but not to others has the unfortunate consequence of closing off opportunities for those labelled with such a diagnosis. This fatalistic perspective overlooks the potential for the emergence of creative, flexible and imaginative thinking among the vast majority of children.

Psycho-pedagogy is less fatalistic than nineteenth-century biological determinism. It claims that some of the limits on children's capacity to learn can be overcome through matching a learner's aptitude with appropriate learning tasks. But invariably diagnostic teaching creates stereotypes that can assume a fixed character and close down opportunities for intellectual development, and the extent to which it is educationally beneficial, let alone viable to be able to determine whether a learner is an innovator or an adaptor, reflective or pragmatic, etc., is itself questionable.[62]

Fundamentally, psycho-pedagogy offers a far more pessimistic analysis of children's potential to attain high levels of intellectual attainment than nineteenth-century theories of innate abilities. The old elitist theories lacked faith in the capacity of the masses to benefit from an academic education, but they upheld its benefit for a minority of superior pupils. Current pedagogy appears to disavow the transformative potential of knowledge for all children – the most able included. What distinguishes current psycho-pedagogy from old-fashioned prejudices about innate abilities is that they are hesitant about endorsing a hierarchy of types. Nineteenth-century theories of innate capacities explicitly celebrated individuals who were deemed to be of a superior intelligence; today, schools are hesitant about identifying gifted children in case they are accused of the crime of elitism. Curriculum engineers have strong, albeit often unspoken, views about which form of intelligence should be prized above all others, but this has little to do with intellectual abilities.

Experts constantly uphold *emotional intelligence* as the most important attribute of an educated child by experts. After discussing different 'blends of intelligence', one expert states that 'emotional intelligence is perhaps more important than any other factor, such as social class or raw IQ, in determining a person's life chances: their success at work, the quality of their relationships, their personal wellbeing'.[63] Policy-makers are also enthusiastic about the merits of emotional intelligence. One Government statement on the importance of the emotional aspects of learning argues that 'research on "emotional intelligence"' suggests that 'emotional and social competences have been shown to be more influential than cognitive abilities for personal, career and scholastic success' and therefore they 'need to be central to school and learning to increase school effectiveness'.[64] At a time when the meaning of emotional intelligence remains far from clear, its advocacy simply means that policy-makers have more belief in the effectiveness of techniques of behaviour management than in the power of academic teaching.

## Conclusion: how broad do we want to go?

The multiplication of intelligences parallels the burgeoning of sites of learning. The cumulative effect of the expansion of the range of intelligences and learning styles is to minimize the significance of an academic education. The flip-side of the representation of academic intelligence as just one of a plurality of intelligences is that the meaning of learning is expanded. Schools are charged not only with providing academic learning – they also provide lessons in emotional intelligence and personal well-being.

The expansionary ambition of psycho-pedagogy means that too often the site of real education is lost. This approach is self-consciously endorsed by the 'evidence-informed pedagogic principles' outlined by the ESRC's Teaching and Learning Research Project. Its statement of principles states that it attempted 'to broaden the conception of what is to be learned, beyond the notions of curricula and subjects associated with schools'. It claims that 'effective pedagogy equips learners for life in its broadest sense'. And it calls for the adoption of a 'broad conception of worthwhile learning outcomes'.[65] The term 'broad' conveys the implication that a subject-based education is far too 'narrow'. The characterization of academic learning as narrow should be seen as a symptom of the disillusionment that pedagogy has in the power of education. Far from representing a genuinely innovative and experimental project, the constant attempt to broaden out the meaning of education is driven by the conviction that academic schooling is itself the problem. It is prepared to sacrifice far too much in order to uphold its promise of inclusion.

The tendency to broaden out the meaning of education has redirected the energy of schools towards the social and emotional aspects of children's lives. The mission of schools has become the well-being of the child. The school system often appears to be more concerned with the aim of 'educating' children to adapt than with developing them intellectually. In numerous policy documents, knowledge-based education has a relatively minor role compared to the emphasis on emotional, personal and social development. It appears that the more that society loses faith in the power of education, the more it looks for quick-fix therapeutic solutions. This turn towards the management of children's emotional lives does little for their well-being, and even less for their education.

# 7

## *The Unhappy Turn to Happiness*

With the exception of a small number of unimaginative officials, most people know that there is something amiss with the way we educate children. Time and again, reports demand that schools must be reformed or that the curriculum should be changed. There are numerous requests to add new issues and aims to the curriculum, and to 'broaden' it out. One of the more thoughtful contributions on the subject, the Cambridge review of primary education, published in February 2009, argues that children in England are receiving an education that is far too narrow.[1] Other pressure groups advocate educating the 'whole child' and call on Government to broaden out the curriculum to include instruction in emotional intelligence, happiness or well-being. On both sides of the Atlantic, governments have been responsive to these requests. In the USA, the 'No Child Left Behind' initiative endorses emotional and social learning programmes. The 'Social and Emotional Aspects of Learning' (SEAL) programme in England, which has been introduced in more than 60 per cent of primary schools, represents an ambitious attempt to train children to understand their feelings.

Concern with the 'whole child' and their 'personal and emotional needs' corresponds to our natural desire for children to have a well-balanced and content life. Young children in particular need physical exercise, benefit from sport, music and the arts, and it makes perfect sense for schools to provide an opportunity for children to explore and express the different aspects of their personality. Our instinct tells us that it is better to broaden out the school experience of youngsters and we take exception to a narrow curriculum.

Unfortunately, polarized arguments that counterpose a 'broad' and 'narrow' education produce more heat than light.

Historically, the appeal to broaden the curriculum is usually prompted by a degree of animosity towards the central status accorded to academic education. Schools that are devoted to the provision of subject-based academic teaching are often criticized for offering an impoverished curriculum. 'Surely, we should demand more from schools than to educate people to be proficient in reading and mathematics', argues an American supporter of the idea that teachers should 'educate the whole child'. To reinforce this point she adds that 'too many highly proficient people commit fraud, pursue paths to success marked by greed, and care little about how their actions affect the lives of others'.[2] No doubt there are many bad people who happen to be proficient in school subjects, but there is no causal or logical connection between an education in maths and reading and the anti-social behaviour of proficient adults. At a time when many schools fail to educate children to be proficient in maths and reading, downbeat attitudes towards the teaching of such fundamental subjects is misplaced. Schools that are struggling to teach the basics to their students are unlikely to improve matters by broadening out their curriculum.

Children in primary schools flourish best when they are exposed to a balanced curriculum. As long as the curriculum is founded on a subject-based and intellectually challenging ethos, there is a variety of ways to provide such an education. However, too often appeals for broadening the curriculum reflect a mood of disillusionment with the capacity of schools to motivate children to engage with maths, literature, history, the sciences and other subjects. The plea by some pedagogues for a broader or 'holistic' education is motivated, at least in part, by the belief that the so-called traditional subjects are irrelevant to children's lives. Numerous experts in primary education take the view that knowledge about a child is more important than knowledge about the subject. This sentiment, captured by the maxim, 'I teach children, not subjects', has great rhetorical influence in primary education. This tendency to regard the teaching of a child as the polar opposite of teaching a subject has the regrettable consequence of devaluing intellectual pursuits in primary schools. It has also promoted an ideal of a primary schoolteacher whose virtues are to do with 'feeling, intuition, sympathy, and empathy, rather than with intellectual capacity'. Marsden believes that, consequently, a 'de-intellectualized' and 'deficit view not only of primary children, but also of generalist primary teachers, was implanted'.[3]

In the past, the call to broaden out schooling was usually a euphemism to provide children with training in practical skills. In the twenty-first century such exhortations tend to advocate the adoption of therapeutic functions by schools. In recent years, reviews of the curriculum usually support lessons in emotional intelligence, well-being or happiness as a core mission of schools.[4] Some advocates of emotional education go so far as to assert that its institutionalization is the precondition for improving the academic performance of children.[5]

A good school will make every effort to attend to the moral, spiritual and emotional needs of a child, and good teachers recognize that the cultivation of the intellect is linked inextricably to the education of a child's dispositions and behaviour. As Bantock wrote:

At the end of the day, educating the emotions (as opposed to the application of therapy) does not involve any radically different approach from that inherent in educating any other aspect of the person. As the development of scientific awareness involves an induction into the conventions and traditions of scientific research, so the development of emotional refinement and awareness is assisted by a growing inwardness with those public vehicles of the emotions, the arts.[6]

Bantock makes a useful distinction between the education of the emotions and the application of therapy. The main foundation on which education of the emotions evolves is that of academic learning, whereas the application of therapy relies on psychological techniques. In contemporary times, what is called 'emotional education' has little to do with Bantock's idea of educating the emotions.

The recent institutionalization of lessons in happiness and emotional intelligence should be characterized as a form of therapeutic education.

Supporters of therapeutic education implicitly embrace a dogmatic counter-position of emotion to intellect. The construction of a distinct domain of emotional education is often justified on the grounds that it broadens out the classroom experience. However, the turn towards the therapeutic school is influenced by disenchantment with the purpose and effectiveness of an intellectually oriented curriculum. Supporters of the therapeutic turn often communicate an anti-academic sensibility. This sentiment is frequently shown through their self-conscious subordination of the acquisition of knowledge to the internalization of emotional skills. So an advertisement for a conference on emotional intelligence for Scottish teachers describes it as a 'master aptitude which profoundly affects all our abilities and ultimately determines how well we do in life'. This point is reiterated by the Chief Executive of the Health Promoting Schools Unit, who writes that the emotional agenda 'is central to better attainment and achievement'.[7] The central role allocated to the emotional agenda indicates that, rather than simply representing a 'broadening' out, this signals a redefinition of education.

Even the teaching of skills has become subordinate to the new therapeutic agenda. During the past decade the traditional idea of a skill that requires serious technical abilities has given way to an emphasis on a range of generic 'life skills'. This 'softening' of the meaning of skills has turned 'personality traits' into objects of therapeutic modification, with the result that 'the boundaries between skills, personal qualities and attitudes' has become 'increasingly fuzzy'.[8]

Arguments supporting the therapeutic turn frequently rely on the idea of multiple intelligences. Anthony Seldon, headmaster and a well-known advocate of the teaching of happiness to schoolchildren, argues his cause on the grounds that the 'purpose of education' is to nurture the 'eight "intelligences" – logical, linguistic, sporting, artistic, personal, social, oral and spiritual'.[9] In some instances the impulse to nurture these so-called intelligences is motivated by a genuine commitment to broaden out children's educational experience. But, as noted previously, the theory of multiple intelligences is frequently used to devalue the role of cognitive intelligence and the subject-based curriculum. In the first instance, the issue at stake is not whether schooling is 'narrow' or 'broad' but whether it is based on an academic curriculum. Debates that merely assess the curriculum in terms of how broad or narrow it is risk overlooking the content of what is being taught. In principle, children can be educated through a relatively small or relatively large number of subjects: what counts is the content of their education and how they are taught.

## Broadening out in historical perspective

Inevitably children experience school as somewhat artificial and different from their normal everyday experience. Contemporary pedagogy tries to minimize the unavoidable contrast between the formality of schooling and the informality of children's extra-educational experience by attempting to erode the distinction between the two. Since pedagogues feel uneasy about the capacity of formal education to engage with young people, they tend to opt for the informal. The call to broaden out education is to a significant degree motivated by the objective of making it more like non-school life.

Since the turn of the twentieth century, arguments in favour of broadening out education and criticism of the academic curriculum have been supported by two distinct constituencies. Industrialists and business leaders have often criticized the system of schooling for not training children to acquire the useful skills necessary for the running of an efficient economy. They demanded a pragmatic approach towards schooling – one that would help children gain the skills that they would need for the world of work. Criticism of the academic curriculum was also pursued by progressive child-centred educators. From the late nineteenth century onwards, this lobby was committed to the dethronement of the academic curriculum. The argument in favour of child-centred schooling was systematically elaborated by Dewey, who called for a shift of focus from the academic subject to the child's own social activities, and claimed that the 'true centre of correlation on the school subjects, is not science, nor literature, nor history, nor geography, but the child's own social activities'.[10] In the US, the new science of pedagogy was explicitly devoted to the project of broadening out education, and sought to encourage schools to 'replace traditional studies with practical studies', and base schools 'on the interest of children rather than the subject matter'.[11]

Many adherents of a child-centred school are not against an intellectually rigorous curriculum. However, the emphasis on the experience of the child fosters a mood of ambiguity about the role of academic learning, often leading to its subordination to the study of what is perceived as relevant to life. Hostility to academic subjects was pronounced among American curriculum engineers and psychologists in the early twentieth century, who denounced these subjects as both irrelevant to the experience of children and positively harmful to their health. The psychologist and child expert Stanley Hall criticized the 'ideal of knowledge for its own sake' and asserted that 'children's health and well-being were almost always jeopardized by traditional school studies'.[12] In a similar vein, Caroline Zachry, a leading progressive pedagogue, dismissed the academic curriculum as a 'relic that no longer served any useful purpose and that impaired students' personal development'.[13]

The assertion that academic learning can have an adverse impact on children's well-being and mental health is not new and is based on the conviction that much of what children do in school is unnatural and therefore stultifies their personal development. Often the very formality of education is condemned for curbing children's natural inclinations and causing them mental distress. Such concerns have been raised regularly in relation to the alleged risks to children caused by homework. As early as 1900 Edward Bok, editor of *The Ladies' Home Journal*, launched a campaign against homework, alleging that the 'mental health of American children was being destroyed' by it.[14] Others targeted discipline, rote learning and the inflexibility of the curriculum. Dewey took the view that too much focus on literacy caused 'undue nervous strain' and he warned of a 'sad record of injured nervous systems and muscular order and distortions'. In 1898 he denounced attempts to teach six- and seven-year-old children to read because it 'cripples rather than furthers later intellectual development'.[15]

In recent decades, the diseasing of the school experience has gone much further. A series of reports on primary education has claimed that children 'suffer stress' and that national examinations are to blame for making children anxious.[16] Virtually any school activity that subjects children to pressure or makes them feel uncomfortable is now diagnosed as the potential cause of a mental health problem. In 2008 it was reported that Whitminster Endowed Church of England Primary, near Stroud, no longer gives children spelling lists for homework, because the headteacher takes the view that 'many children find this activity unnecessarily distressing'.[17] A good school will do whatever it can to minimize the distress and insecurity that children will inevitably experience during their years of formal learning. However, it is unrealistic that feelings of anxiety can, or should, be abolished from the classroom, for the very simple reason that formal teaching and learning inevitably places students under pressure. As Vanhuysse and Sabbagh note, 'If teachers did not force students to study some mathematics and linguistic skills *beyond their immediate liking*, many students would probably come out of school unequipped for satisfying their own future needs.'[18]

The diseasing of the school experience has gained such formidable dynamic that the idea of 'forcing' students to do anything is often categorized as a form of emotional abuse. Consequently, there are strong pressures to avoid subjects and topics that are intellectually challenging and likely to stretch young people. John White remarks that 'Key Stage 3 tests on a Shakespeare play may be an example of the sort of thing to avoid', since if 'we want all pupils to want to go on learning, we should not opt for a system that alienates pupils, undermines confidence and makes them anxious, or feel that they are no good'.[19] From this perspective, the imperative of making children feel good appears to contradict the demands of an intellectually challenging curriculum. The rich, multi-layered texture of a Shakespeare play has to give way to confidence-boosting exercises. Ironically, this narrowing of the intellectual expectation we have of children is often described as the broadening of educa-tion. 'Why insist on maths and science for all?' asks Noddings in her call for a form of education that claims to give central place to children's well-being.[20]

As far back as 1900, child-centred curriculum experts had elaborated a mythology of academic schooling that endures to this day. According to this mythology, an academic curriculum was by definition a narrow one, which stultified children's creativity and prevented them from using their experience to explore and learn from life. This curriculum was castigated for being too formal, teaching outdated and irrelevant subjects, and for forcing children to learn by rote. It was accused of distorting children's emotional life, undermining their independence and causing numerous health problems and pathologies. By the 1930s, these criticisms corres-ponded to the outlook of many pedagogues. As William Bagley, a critic of progressive education, wrote in 1934:

> If you wish to be applauded at an educational convention, vocif-erous sentimental platitudes about the sacred rights of the child, specifying particularly his right to happiness gained through freedom. You are likely to get an extra 'hand' if you shed a few verbal tears over the cruelty of examinations and homework, while with eloquent condemnation you deftly bring into every other sentence one of the favourite stereotypes of abuse, such as Latin, mathematics (geometry especially), grammar, the tradi-tional curriculum, compartmentalization, 'chinks of the subject matter' to be memorized, discipline, formal discipline and the like, you may be fairly certain of an ovation.[21]

The 'sentimental platitudes' that Bagley identified in the 1930s have far greater resonance in the twenty-first century. In contrast to the 1930s, the 'cruelty of examinations' is a regular topic of public debate. Subject-based teaching has far more critics than before and 'formal discipline' and 'memorization' tend to be defined as bad practice.

Anti-intellectualism and animosity towards academic subjects has resulted in a pragmatic, even arbitrary, approach towards the content of learning. Consequently, the curriculum often turns into a battleground between competing aims and objectives. Ravitch notes that in the US, the 'definition of education itself was up for grabs, available for capture by any idea, fad, or movement that was advanced by pedagogical experts, popular sentiment or employers'.[22] Calls to broaden out education are justified on the ground that it must engage with life – either children's experiences, life in their community, or the world of work. Although opposition to academic learning involves different constituencies and political affiliations, they share the fundamental assumption that education needs to be relevant. Carl Rogers states this clearly – 'No one should ever be trying to learn something for which one sees no relevance.'[23] Throughout modern times the subjugation of knowledge to the dictates of relevance has been the hallmark of philistinism. As the well-known nineteenth-century German great man of letters, Goethe, observed, 'the philistine not only ignores all conditions of life which are not his own but also demands that the rest of mankind should fashion its mode of existence after his own'.

Probably the single most important driver of educational philistinism is the compulsive impulse to render education more and more relevant. In the name of relevance, the teaching of grammar gives way to the celebration of street language, and functional skills are preferred to theoretical knowledge. Relevance is counterpoised ideologically to the pursuit of the intellect. Rogers condemns education that has 'no personal meaning' for students on the grounds that 'such learning involves the mind only' and therefore it has 'no relevance for the whole person'.[24] The rhetorical construction of 'the mind only' is used to devalue the significance of cognition.

But is a curriculum that is constituted around a child's social life broader than one that is devoted to academic learning? The appeal to relevance is attractive; nobody, after all, would wish to provide children with an irrelevant education, and academic knowledge is often conveyed through clearly compartmentalized, formal and codified subjects. But such knowledge is anything but narrow: it is

'at least potentially universalizing knowledge' that allows children
to transcend their immediate experience and learn from the lives
of other cultural communities.[25] Potentially, an academic education
is more open-ended and provides more opportunities for children
to acquaint themselves with knowledge and experience gained from
a variety of sources than is an education devoted to relevance.

Take the subject of history, which is frequently portrayed as an
outdated and irrelevant relic of the nineteenth-century curriculum.
Outwardly, the study of this subject is entirely unnatural and un-
related to children's experience: how can the study of Ancient Greece
or medieval Europe be of relevance to twenty-first-century children
confronted with the challenges of a high-tech globalized world? Yet,
properly understood, history is the subject that probably contributes
most to the broadening out of the imagination. One of its purposes
is to help children transcend their own immediate experience and
gain an understanding about how humanity has evolved, changed
and developed an understanding of itself. It is ironic that, precisely
at a time when policy-makers are obsessed with training children
to adapt to change, they actually devalue the academic study of
change. What can be more narrow than the current emphasis on
programming children to internalize the correct personal and relationship skills? In contrast, the study of humanity's journey through
time provides children with the complex motives that make people
tick and with insights about the influences that make us who we are.
The Roman thinker Cicero understood far more about the relationship between education and personal development than our curriculum engineers when he stated that 'not to know what has been
transacted in former times is to continue always a child'. Current
thinking on rendering the curriculum broader and more relevant
infantilizes children rather than achieving its aim of assisting their
personal development.

Experience shows that the project of broadening out the curriculum can, in practice, narrow the potential for the intellectual
development of children. It is important to understand that just
about all the sins associated with a traditional academic education
– rote learning, formulaic and unimaginative teaching styles, lack

of opportunities for experimentation – are far more prevalent in the anti-subject, anti-intellectual curriculum.

The traditional liberal curriculum is frequently denounced for deadening children's natural curiosity with its insistence on rote learning: one critic looks forward to the day where 'rote learning of facts' gives 'way to nurturing through education of essential transferable skills that enable the next generation to navigate the information age'.[26] But the rhetoric of cultivating flexibility and personal development notwithstanding, template teaching and rote learning are embedded in the so-called 'holistic' and 'whole-child' therapeutic approach; and by comparison to the techniques and language used by therapeutic education – training, coaching, managing emotions – traditional rote learning appears as positively progressive. Anyone who examines the pedagogic aids available to teachers of emotional or happiness education will be struck by their prescriptive and didactic character. An influential proponent of happiness teaching writes that the 'secrets of happiness' can be learned through 'massive amounts of practice and repetition'. In passing, he praises the practice of effort through repetition of traditional religion, 'especially Buddhism'.[27] A guide written to help teachers to deliver a 'happiness programme' claims that 'we can train ourselves to be happier' and explains that 'training ourselves to be positive is a bit like training ourselves to be fit'. The children are offered a series of instructions on 'how to remember the good feelings and let go of the negative ones'; they are told that 'thinking about the good things that happen to us and writing them down helps each of us to build up our own individual store of happiness'. Teachers are given clear instructions on what children must do to train themselves happy: 'Ask pupils to open their Happiness Diary by writing down three things that happened today – things that make them feel happy and make them smile when they remember them.' The instructions are precise – children must write down three things that happened, not one or two, but three.[28]

Another manual also insists that children 'write down three things', because 'this deceptively simple exercise works by re-educating our attention to look for what is good in life'.[29]

The term 're-educating our attention' indicates that this is a training exercise that relies on indoctrinating children with the values
upheld by the person doing the re-educating. The entire programme depends on children internalizing a behavioural script
and performing it in public. They may not have to memorize the
instructions issued by their trainers but they have to mouth the
sentiments expected of a re-educated child. It is worth noting that
professionals who are rhetorically committed to child-centred
practices have no inhibitions about managing and re-educating
the feelings of young people. They claim disingenuously that
children are taught to be reflective, but then offer a formulaic form
of reflection that 'disguises strongly normative views about desirable attributes, attitudes and dispositions'.[30] These scripted forms
of emotional management reproduce the worst features of learning by rote. Moreover, by adopting the language of reflection and
openness, they hide their commitment to the micro-management
of children's internal life. This is not teaching but the programming of children.

One of the best-kept secrets of the pedagogy driving the anti-
knowledge, skills-oriented, whole-child approach is that it relies on
techniques that are unusually directive. Who could possibly object
to the following learning intention assigned to six- to eight-year-
old children in a recent version of the English school curriculum:
'to recognise, name and deal with feelings in a positive way'? But
who decides what is a positive way of dealing with feelings? The
child? The teacher? The psychologist? Imposing an emotional script
on a child is at least as prescriptive as practices associated with
religious indoctrination. The objective of teaching children to name
and deal with their feelings in practice constitutes a demand for
emotional conformism.

One reason why the illiberal and authoritarian impulse of this
form of training is rarely perceived is because of the mystifying language used to promote it. Terms like 'reflective learning', 'learning
to learn', and 'engaging with the whole child' self-consciously signal
a broad-minded and open-ended perspective on schooling. A clear

example of this mystification is one of the foundational concepts used by the new pedagogy – critical thinking skills. This concept is often upheld as a positive alternative to the outdated reliance on knowledge acquisition. But it should be noted that 'critical thinking skills' are anything but critical. These are taught as a formulaic technique as prescriptive as teaching six-year-olds to memorize their tables. Critical thinking skills are upheld as a means to develop students to become 'independent learners'; children do not learn how to think but are taught the so-called skills of thinking. Yet knowing how to think cannot be reduced to a skill. Thinking and reasoning exist in a relation of creative tension with the object of cognition. Our ability to think is not isolated from what we know, and it is mediated through our feelings. People cannot develop their ability to think in isolation from experience and learning. However, that is what thinking-skill coaches attempt to achieve. One advocate of this technical approach states that 'thinking skills need to be taught directly before they are applied to the content area'.[31]

The idea that thought can be taught without an object reduces thinking to a narrow technical formula. What is taught is not even a skill but a caricature of a skill. As the science educationalist David Perks argued:

> The attempt to train pupils to think is based on a cognitive model of the human being as a biological machine. The attempt to teach thinking skills implies that thought is a learned behaviour, like a dog learning a trick. Once the trick is learned, apparently it happens automatically and, by definition, needs no further thought. The promotion of thinking skills is an attack on intellectual life, on thought itself.[32]

The separation of knowledge from thought by reducing thinking to a form of skill acquisition is on par with the worst features of rote learning. Discouraging students from absorbing themselves in the content of a subject actually serves as a barrier to pupils learning to think for themselves.

## The therapeutic turn

Many of the ideas associated with anti-knowledge pedagogy – child-centred learning, teaching the whole child, the belief that formality stifles young people, the call to broaden out the curriculum and make it more relevant, the emphasis on skills – have, in one form or another, been around for a very long time. While these notions exercised significant influence over professional educators, their impact during most of the twentieth century was limited by the practical realities facing teachers in the classroom. However, the influence of these sentiments acquired momentum in the 1980s and today dominates the culture of policy-making in education. One of the clearest manifestations of this development is the regularity with which the acquisition of knowledge is explicitly subordinated to the goal of well-being and the happiness of the child.

The well-being of a child has always been of concern to enlightened educators but in recent times well-being itself is perceived as a problem that requires therapeutic intervention itself. Children's problems are medicalized and diagnosed in psychological terms, and this approach has been institutionalized to the point where 'emotional well-being, emotional literacy and emotional competence' are seen as 'some of the most important outcomes of the education system'.[33]

As noted previously, the education of the emotions constitutes an integral part of a good liberal education. There is, however, an important distinction between the *education of the emotions* and the current fad of *emotional education*. Since the Renaissance, the humanist tradition recognized the creative tension between cognition and feeling, and valued the education of the emotions. Humanists emphasized education as important in its own right but also because they believed that this possessed the power to cultivate feelings.[34] In contrast, twenty-first-century emotional education places the emphasis on the emotional and perceives it as a stand-alone therapeutic project. This project relies on therapeutic techniques that are quite distinct from, and provide a substitute for, education.

The therapeutic turn in education is underpinned by the sensibility of emotional determinism. The belief that the state of our emotion is the cause of most of our social and personal problems has become an integral part of western culture. Indeed, the way we feel about ourselves – our self-esteem – has become an important explanatory tool for making sense of the world.[35] Policy-makers and experts are often drawn towards explanations that link low educational achievement with psychological and emotional deficits. Emotion has become an object of cultural veneration, to the point that its management is perceived as the key to attaining educational success. Policy-makers still accept that children's socio-economic and cultural background influences their achievement in school. But more and more policies and school practices are informed by the view that the problem that needs to be addressed is some type of psychological deficit.

The therapeutic turn of education is based on the premise that attending to the emotional management of children is logically prior to educating them. Take the following leaflet handed out to parents on the first day of the new term at a primary school in Kent. It informs parents that '[this school] thinks every one of your children are [sic] of great importance and we believe that to be able to learn they need to be happy, confident, understand themselves and know how to get on with each other and make friends'. More or less the same semi-literate wording is used in numerous leaflets handed out in schools throughout England.[36] The reader may dismiss this letter as simply a rhetorical gesture echoing a desirable objective. But the idea that children are not able to learn unless they are happy and possess confidence, self-understanding and social skills, represents a clear statement of the ethos of therapeutic education: psychology first, education later.

Therapeutic intervention is often justified on the grounds that it provides the resources essential for educational success. So some advocates of this approach claim that SAT scores improve when children have participated in emotional education. A review of the literature on values education cites research that concludes that 'the government's own targets for raising educational achievement are more likely to be reached when opportunities exist to nurture children's self-esteem and space given for talking about their feelings and relationships'.[37] Sometimes it appears that emotional education is endowed with magical properties that can significantly enhance pupils' achievement. St Peter and St Paul Primary School in Carbrooke, Norfolk, reported that its SAT scores for writing doubled within 18 months after it introduced the Government's Social and Emotional Aspects of Learning Scheme.[38] Two American psychologists argue that when an average student enrols in a social and emotional learning programme, their scores are 'at least 10 percentile points higher on achievement test' than those who do not participate in such initiatives.[39]

Such strong claims have a distinctly ideological and anecdotal character, for there is no robust evidence that therapeutic intervention actually works towards the raising of educational standards. The ideological tone with which advocates of emotional education advertise their cause often has a quasi-religious character. Richard Layard, who is probably the most influential figure associated with the happiness crusade, writes that what 'we need is an educational revolution in which a central purpose of our schools becomes to help young people learn the secrets of the happy life and the happy society'. To realize this goal, Layard hopes to mobilize a 'cadre' of 'specialist teachers acting as proselytes and high priests of the movement'.[40] Apparently, the uncovering of these secrets by these high priests will draw on the resources of science. 'We live in a scientific age, and, although pockets of fundamentalism remain, only *science* can and should persuade the young about the routes to a happy society', writes Layard.[41] When high priests are called upon to convert non-believers about the virtues of the science of happiness, they are more likely to appeal to dogma than research.

## A motivational crisis

The embrace of therapeutic techniques by policy-makers and pedagogues is in the first instance a symptom of their loss of faith in the capacity of knowledge-based academic learning to inspire students. This loss of faith is particularly striking in relation to the task of motivating children to learn genuinely academic subjects. In part, this response is shaped by scepticism towards the authority of the academic subject. The absence of a strong cultural affirmation for authority of knowledge means that there is little pedagogic interest in attempting to reconcile the rigorous teaching of the subject with the need to motivate pupils. Instead, the general tendency is to opt for motivational techniques – usually drawn from psychology, therapy, management studies – that can be used in the classroom. For example, the American Institute of Education Sciences commissions research that 'seeks to reduce aggressive/disruptive and off-task behaviours via teacher-led instruction aimed at facilitating emotion regulation (particularly anger management), self-control, social problem-solving, and conflict resolution skills'.[42] This turn towards the regulation of children's emotions expresses a growing tendency to opt for technical solutions to the problem of education.

The swift endorsement of Gardner's Multiple Intelligences (MI) theory by policy-makers illustrates a constant search for techniques and schemes that can provide teachers with motivational resources. As Michael Barber indicates, 'If we are to design a curriculum that can motivate and make possible success for all young people, it will need to recognize the full breadth of Gardner's seven intelligences.' His belief that these intelligences have 'immense motivational potential' leads him to propose a curriculum that is consistent with Gardner's approach. [43] In recent years, positive psychology and the so-called science of happiness has emerged as the latest motivational fad in education. Its enthusiasts contend that experts using positive psychology and insights gained from neuroscience can help crack the problem of motivation. These counsellors can apparently 'assist teachers in better understanding the emotional connections that spur intrinsic motivation'.[44] One of the earliest calls to teach happiness in schools was based on the belief that it can counter children's negative experience of education and strengthen their motivation to learn.[45] Almost all the practices linked to the broadening out of the curriculum – personalized learning, making schooling more relevant, learning to learn – are devoted to boosting children's motivation to learn. It is worth noting that such practices are doomed to failure for the very simple reason that children are unlikely to become motivated in the abstract. Programming children to feel motivated distracts them from gaining an understanding of the relationship between effort and achievement.

The growing role of emotional education is bound up with wider societal and cultural trends. Schools are social and cultural institutions, and the issues and concerns that prevail at large have an impact on the way they work. Indeed, many problems that are characterized as educational are rooted in society itself and its struggle to transmit a clear system of meaning. Jürgen Habermas argues that the difficulties that society has in providing an account of itself results in what he calls a 'motivational crisis'. Debates about what values to teach children, how to socialize young people and what binds a community together can be interpreted as reflections of the difficulty that society has in motivating the public in accordance with a shared system of meaning. Habermas notes that 'the less the cultural system is capable of producing adequate motivation for politics, the education system and the occupational system, the more must meaning be replaced by consumable values'.[46] One of the ways in which western culture has sought to replace meaning is by attempting to motivate through therapeutic techniques.

Confusion about how to motivate people through a shared system of meaning provides the therapeutic world-view with considerable opportunity to gain influence. Consequently, today's cultural elite may be unsure about telling people what to believe, but it feels quite comfortable about instructing people how and what to feel.

The ascendancy of the project of happiness teaching constitutes one of the most vivid examples of the replacement of moral meaning by therapeutic values. Layard fears a catastrophic 'failure to develop a secular morality', and since 'people find it hard to talk about moral issues' a 'moral vocabulary is what is lacking for many children'. He recalls: 'I had an education that included a religious component and, even though I've become agnostic since then, I recognise that those with religious beliefs tend to be happier.'[47] With the weakening of religious beliefs, Layard hopes that positive psychology could contribute to the recovering of a moral vocabulary. Noddings, too, regards teaching happiness as a form of moral education that can make students better people.[48] Like most supporters of the happiness project, she adheres to the simplistic formula that being happy makes you good.

Layard and Noddings perceive the teaching of happiness as a form of moral education. However, it is far more accurate to characterize it as an attempt to recover moral meaning through the medium of psychology. Many educators and policy-makers have become sceptical about the possibility of teaching moral values in the classroom, and one response to this problem has been to recast morality in a grotesquely personal form. In schools the notion that children should 'feel good about themselves' has been turned into a moral principle of fundamental significance. Supporters of the happiness movement claim that happy children are likely to be 'good' and therefore behave more morally towards others – but feelings are not directly moral attributes. Therapeutic education in its various forms – increasing confidence, motivation, self-esteem, happiness – is actually amoral, for the simple reason that it perceives the 'treatment of the self as detached from fundamental commitments to beliefs and values'.[49] It is likely that the confusion of psychology with morality will simply diminish the capacity of a school to communicate a system of shared meanings.

The problem of motivation in schools and in wider society is indissolubly linked to the decline of authoritative behaviour. In this respect, therapeutic education can be seen as an attempt to by-pass this problem through substituting emotional management for authoritative conduct. Almost half a century ago, Kerlinger noted that an open display of authoritative behaviour in the classroom had become an object of scorn, and observed that the 'teacher who wants to play the boss role must now do it in a more covert and subtle fashion'. He believed that the introduction of what he called 'permissiveness' in education 'leads to the manipulation of pupils', and went so far as to argue that since emotional education tends to encourage a preoccupation with feelings, children lose their grounding in a stable and objective environment and become easy prey to manipulative techniques. 'When the central emphasis is on feelings, especially feelings toward other persons, objectivity, independence and autonomy become difficult to learn and to achieve', argued Kerlinger.[50]

The therapeutic turn represents not only the school's estrangement from its academic mission, but its estrangement from the exercise of educational authority. Emotional training and happiness classes are justified with reference to the authority of the psychological expert, the therapist or the scientist. The therapeutic turn implies the outsourcing of the authority of education to so-called experts and scientists. So, in the UK so-called behaviour experts are called upon by Government to sort out the problem of school discipline.[51] Therapeutic authority is based on the claim that therapy provides techniques that achieve results. 'Emotional intelligence can be used in a wide variety of areas, you can be using emotional intelligence to motivate', claims a website devoted to the promotion of this therapy.[52] Therapeutic education requires that teachers defer to the expert authority of behaviour managers. Such experts guide teachers and indirectly influence children's classroom experience. 'We often get calls from teachers who say they feel let down by the behaviour management training they received when they first qualified as teachers', notes David Allaway from Behaviour UK, an online training resource for teachers. He adds that 'we point them in the direction of behaviour training courses and conferences run by various suppliers across the UK'.[53] The authority of the therapist is also critical for the delivery of happiness education. In this case, cognitive behaviour therapists are invited to 'support' schools who have signed up to the happiness crusade.

Emotional education self-consciously eschews any open display of authority. Take the widely practised technique of circle time. This technique is used to gather children together in a circle to share their feelings and problems. Circle time is advertised as an effective way for motivating children to reflect and discuss their feelings about sensitive and difficult issues. Its advocates argue that it helps improve children's behaviour as well as their ability to communicate.[54] Circle time is used to stimulate children to divulge their feelings in public. Its practitioners often remark that children's participation is voluntary and that participants are free to keep quiet if they so choose. But as one critic stated, 'most circle time manuals recommend that children are asked to explain why they do not wish to contribute'.[55] Young primary schoolchildren are unlikely to challenge their teacher or stand up to the pressure to display their emotions.

Practitioners of circle time rarely reflect on the fact that the management of the emotions can be a distinctly authoritarian enterprise. Yet asking children to share their feelings in public and rewarding them for such behaviour cannot but send out the message that they should conform to the demands of their teacher. Even in the most permissive classroom, children are likely to feel defensive if they do not act in accordance with the emotional script communicated by the teacher. The promotion of certain emotional styles always contains the implication that other responses are inferior, and even illegitimate. In previous times, educators were charged with teaching children how to behave well. Good conduct was associated with clearly defined public acts such as politeness, acts of honesty and altruism. The regime of therapeutic education is wedded to a form of behaviour management that targets conduct, and attempts to shape feelings and emotions. Training a child how to feel is a far more intrusive and coercive project than educating a pupil how to behave. As one educational psychologist states, training children to become 'emotionally literate' is about 'reframing how we see ourselves'.[56]

To a significant extent, the turn towards therapeutic techniques represents an attempt to compensate for the erosion of teacher authority. Supporters of emotional education are convinced that their approach can contribute to the improvement of classroom behaviour. England's SEAL programme is designed to improve pupil behaviour and motivation through teaching children the emotional skills outlined in Goleman's model of emotional intelligence: self-awareness, managing feelings, motivation, empathy and social skills. Although the research commissioned to evaluate this programme indicates that it lacked impact on pupils' behaviour, supporters of SEAL insist on its potential to curb classroom disruption.[57]

Experience indicates that attempts to solve the motivational crisis through emotional management techniques tends to diminish the authority of the teacher rather than boost it. One teacher from the London borough of Hackney recalls that the introduction of a Behaviour Improvement Programme led to the outsourcing of the enforcing of discipline: during incidents of major disruption or when fights broke out, the teachers stood back and waited for the arrival of the Behaviour and Education Teams.[58] The more teachers are divested of their responsibility of managing their classroom, the more their authority is undermined. As one supply teacher stated:

> Children's behaviour is now absolutely outrageous in the majority of schools. I am a supply teacher, so I see very many schools and there are no sanctions. There are too many anger management people and their ilk who give children the idea that it is their right to flounce out of lessons for time out because they have problems with their temper.[59]

Many commentators have observed that schoolchildren's behaviour has deteriorated in recent decades. This may be so. But the problem in the first instance is not the behaviour of children but the difficulty that many teachers have in exercising authority. The adoption of behaviour management techniques complicates the open and honest exercise of authority. Many teachers frankly admit to their inability to deal with relatively minor challenges. In 2009 it was reported that many teachers found it difficult to deal with 'orchestrated coughing' and other forms of low-level disruption in the classroom. According to Tim Cox, a member of NASUWT's executive, his 'members frequently state that it is the constant low-level disruption that wears them down'. He added:

> It is the disrespect and the defiance that are the most difficult issues to deal with. It is the tap, tap, tap of the pen on the desk, the orchestrated coughing, the swinging back and forth on the chair, the refusal to comply with the simplest requests, wearing

coats, hoodies, sunglasses, the text messages and phone calls that disrupt lessons.[60]

Some teachers believe that the reason why they are ill-equipped to deal with classroom pranks is because their training courses did not prepare them for it. However, children have been testing the patience of their teachers since the beginning of the introduction of formal education. What has changed is that, in the absence of an unambiguous affirmation for the exercise of classroom authority, many teachers feel insecure about knowing when and how to hold the line. Experience indicates that motivational techniques do little to overcome the effects of the crisis of motivation. Projects that aim to make children feel good about themselves, raise their self-esteem or make them happy rarely achieve a consistent improvement in behaviour. There is no therapeutic alternative to the exercise of teacher authority.

## More than a distraction

Emotional education has become increasingly popular because it resonates with prevailing cultural norms that interpret the problems of existence through the idiom of psychology. Although there is a long-standing pedagogic tradition that regards formal education as potentially harmful to the well-being of children, in recent decades such sentiments have become far more omnipresent. Today, it is common to regard children as fragile, emotionally vulnerable things who cannot be expected to cope with pressure and real intellectual challenge. It was in this vein that in April 2007 England's School Minister instructed teachers to praise their pupils routinely. According to guidelines, teachers should reward children five times as often as they punish them for disrupting lessons.[61] That this simplistic formulation of the relationship between praise and punishment is circulated through the institution of education is a testimony to the impoverished intellectual and moral climate that prevails in this domain. But the exhortation to institutionalize the praising of children is not an isolated attempt to flatter the egos of young people.

Increasingly, the therapeutic objective of making children feel good about themselves is seen as the primary objective of schooling.

The consequences of this tendency to infantilize children have been enormously destructive. Making children feel good about themselves has been one of the main objectives of American schools during the past three decades. By the time they are seven or eight years old, American children have internalized the prevailing psychobabble and can proclaim the importance of avoiding negative emotions and of high self-esteem. Yet this has had no perceptible impact on their school performance. In Britain, too, educators who have drawn the conclusion that it is easier to help children feel good than to teach them maths, reading and science, have embraced the cause of emotional education. During the past decades they have also adopted a variety of gimmicks to improve classroom behaviour through helping children to relax. Some schools have opted for yoga, others use aromatherapy or chill-out music to improve concentration and learning.

Happiness education often turns into a caricature of itself. A report on the second annual European Happiness and Its Causes conference in October 2008 included a session where Kevin Hogston, deputy headteacher at Latchmere School in Surrey, talked about a 'feelings meter', peer massages and meditation in the classroom and other 'innovations' designed to improve student well-being. Others held forth on 'holistic spirituality' while the 'leading experts in the psychology of happiness' discussed how to make schools more happy.[62] The conference brochure succeeded in synthesizing the worst feature of American self-help psychobabble with a trendy western lifestyle version of Buddhism.

Self-help gimmicks are at best a waste of time. Although they are certainly not going to help raise educational standards, they do not necessarily have a negative impact on the classrooms. This is not the case with some of the other more intrusive initiatives which are designed to teach children how to be happy. The elevation of happiness into a classroom subject will consolidate the shift in focus from learning about the world to dwelling on the internal lives of pupils. Even by the confused standards of current educational policy, this is an unusually crass idea. Happiness cannot be taught. People have always pursued happiness. But until recently, happiness was not seen as an end in itself or something that could be promoted in its own terms. Teachers hoped that their students would be happy with their experience, but they did not set out to teach their pupils how to achieve this emotional state. Perversely, the more we try to make children feel good about themselves, the more we distract them from engaging in experiences that have the potential to give them a sense of achievement. These programmes encourage a mood of emotionalism in the school. An expansion of the resources that schools devote to managing the emotional life of children is likely to encourage them to become more inward-looking and less able to cope with the challenges that confront them. Promoting narcissism in the classroom is likely to encourage children to feel that they have a mental health problem.

Branding this therapeutic project as emotional education attempts to convey that new forms of behaviour management possess educational value. They do not. Currently, it is not the educational needs of children that shape the therapeutic curriculum, but the moral confusion of adults. Probably the most important driver of the happiness movement is the powerful mood of moral disorientation that prevails in western societies. Western culture finds it difficult to give meaning to everyday experience through a language that clarifies what is good and bad or right and wrong. Such a mood of disorientation creates a continuous demand for meaning. Proponents of the happiness movement understand this, which is why they often present the objective of their crusade as that of moral reform. However, it is not so much a moral project as a moralizing one. Its success will not be based on the growth of moral conviction but on the successful application of techniques of behaviour management. Policy-makers rely on the institutionalization of cognitive behavioural therapy, rather than on the clarification of the moral challenges that face us, to make us happy.

The crusade aims to normalize what, until now, has been a rare and fleeting experience: the state of happiness. But happiness is a state of mind that comes about through experiences that give us a special feeling of accomplishment or meaning about our lives. No one can help us to be happy, which is why policies that rely on the activity of therapists are far more likely to encourage us to conform to officially sanctioned forms of emotional behaviour. Teaching happiness to children – or to adults, for that matter – is also morally dubious. It is entirely acceptable for a teacher to tell your child what to do and what not to do, but is it really a teacher's job to instruct your child what to *feel*? The attempt to manage children's internal life is a highly intrusive enterprise with potentially authoritarian implications. How we feel and deal with our emotions should not be subject to policies implemented by so-called experts on behalf of confused officials.

It was Immanuel Kant who pointed out that making a man happy was quite different from making him good. The experience of history shows us that a good life is not always a happy one. People are often justified in being unhappy about their circumstances and surroundings. Discontent and ambition have driven humanity to confront and overcome the challenges it has faced. That is why the Controller in *Brave New World* wants people to live on a diet of 'feelies' and 'scent organs': an apposite metaphor as to why we should be suspicious of a crusade whose success depends on the colonization of our internal life.

It is important to realize that the institutionalization of happiness teaching is fundamentally an anti-educational process. Like other forms of therapeutic teaching, its emphasis on feelings and emotions undermines young people's critical engagement with knowledge and ideas. 'When the emphasis in a class is emotional, it is difficult for children to learn objective modes of thinking', writes Kerlinger. Yet children need to acquire this form of thinking if they are to gain the sense of intellectual independence they need to make their way in this world. More problematic is that emotional education encourages a one-sided focus on the self, with confusing consequences for children's relations to one another. 'This is because preoccupation with one's own and other people's feelings is an unstable and insecure ground on which to build a basis for learning to make objective and critical judgements of problems and issues since all of one's thinking becomes coloured and perhaps distorted by interpersonal affect', concludes Kerlinger.[63]

Since so much to do with children's feelings is influenced by their family circumstances, their relationship to others, and the role and influence of prevailing systems of values, schools can play only a modest role in helping them to feel good about themselves. But schools can made children feel good about *life*. Education has the capacity to excite the imagination and open children's eyes to the importance of knowledge and ideas. It introduces young people to the richness of human culture and encourages them to believe that life is something that they can genuinely understand. The wealth of human knowledge is the most important resource that we have for inspiring young people to gain an understanding of themselves as individuals and members of a wider community. And it is through the study of history, literature and the sciences that they acquire insights into the extraordinary emotional complexity of the human experience and learn to educate their own feelings. 'The arts', writes Bantock, 'constitute the means through which feelings can be refined, made conscious, articulated and defined.' The sciences are no less important in this respect, for they 'constitute ways in which an initial impulse which owes something to an emotional commitment can be transcended under the disciplined actualities of behaviour'.[64] A child's psychology tends to be active and creative. It is up to educators to stimulate it with knowledge rather than render it passive with therapy.

# Conclusion:
## Saving Education from Itself

Often debates about education are interpreted as being dominated by fundamentally different outlooks of left and right. No doubt there are some differences of emphasis among competing political interests, but it is striking that, rhetoric aside, the political outlook of recent governments has made very little difference to how education works. Since the 1970s, debates on education have focused on the need to raise standards, yet one government after another has failed to make serious headway on this front. The Thatcher and Blair regimes in the UK, and the Reagan and Clinton governments in the US, were all committed to raising standards of education: despite their different policies and emphasis they all proved ineffective in tackling the problem. At various times, right-wing or left-wing governments, business interests or the teaching professions have been blamed for the failure to reform education. Political differences on education revolve mainly around issues such as how it should be organized and how its benefits should be distributed. There are many reasons for this, but the most important relate to a reluctance to acknowledge the questions posed by the erosion of adult authority and a lack of focus on the issue of what education is for.

Over the decades the anti-intellectual and anti-traditionalist sentiments of curriculum engineers have converged with the instrumentalist and managerial ethos of business and social engineering policy-makers. Within education there is a powerful consensus that embraces progressive child-centred experts, policy-makers interested in improving the skills of the workforce, social engineers devoted to using schools to solve society's problems, and advocates of training and lifelong learning. They all show an indifference to subject knowledge-based education and embrace the idea that education is a means to realize some external objective. And parties on both left and right have been happy to oversee the steady expansion of education into new areas of life.

Yet the expansion of the institution of education invariably produces meagre results. The ineffectiveness of instrumentalist policies is not surprising, since education is not simply a stand-alone institution that can be improved or reformed through the injection of cash or the introduction of new techniques. Resources can provide books, computers, classroom equipment and even new teachers. But what happens in the classroom is influenced by many other variables. It is shaped by cultural attitudes towards knowledge and ideas. Education is linked to, and influenced by, the quality of intergenerational relationships. And, of course, it depends on the status, authority and quality of teachers. Current policies rarely address the fundamental problems, and resources are often wasted on limiting the damage caused by evading them. As a result, a significant proportion of people employed in education does very little educating. It is no longer the case that the adults working in schools are necessarily front-line teachers: increasingly, teachers are required to share their authority with a growing body of managers and experts. One British Government publication cites the following 'best practice' from a school that it portrays as a model for managing the behaviour of children:

> In addition to the five learning mentors a full service school team consists of a school health worker, who also manages the Child and Adolescent Mental Health Services (CAHMS) programme, a school based social worker and assistant social worker who also work in the partner primary schools, an attendance officer, five heads of year, two assistant headteachers, the SENCO and a senior manager for administration and finance.[1]

This representation of best practice implicitly redefines the role of the teacher from that of an educator to that of a behaviour manager or social worker.

One of the most disturbing consequences of the trends outlined in the previous chapters is the gradual decoupling of schooling from the provision of education. Not surprisingly, this reorientation of the role of the school has important implications for the status and authority of the teacher. There are powerful institutional pressures on teachers to think of themselves as one among a variety of children's service providers. Even bodies representing the teaching profession have acquiesced to this transformation in professional identity. The General Teaching Council for England (GTC) advises teachers to 'communicate and establish productive working relations with other professionals'. This organization's *Code of Conduct and Practice* warns teachers to know their limits and 'always act within their own competence and responsibilities'. That's another way of saying, 'Defer to the expert, limit your role, and do not take full responsibility for the situation.' The GTC cites with approval a school governor who states that 'the worst and most damaging attitude a teacher can possibly have is the attitude that they "know it all" and therefore won't reach out for help from other professionals when they need it'.[2]

The criticism levelled at the teacher who possesses the attitude of 'knowing it all' represents an indirect attempt to limit authority. A serious educator will want to take responsibility for every dimension of a child's education. Through exercising the insights gained through their relationship with their class, they are usually best placed to make judgements about how to respond to specific problems. Teachers need the freedom to make professional judgements if they are to be effective educators. By advocating the involvement of numerous professionals and so-called partnerships in the management of a school, the GTC has achieved the perverse outcome of discouraging teachers from seeing problems through and taking responsibility. The more teachers are expected to 'reach out for help from other professionals', the less effective they become as educators.

The demand that teachers share responsibility with other experts and professionals cannot but weaken the authority of the educator. Teachers who draw on the support of a behaviour manager or a 'hard core cover supervisor' to help control the classroom are likely to find it difficult to gain respect for their professional authority. In many cases the outsourcing of teachers' authority and responsibility for managing behaviour has turned some schools into community centres, where real education has become a part-time activity. This diversification of the activities of the school wastes not only resources but also the time available for real teaching.

It is time for society to conduct a grown-up conversation about what we mean by a teacher. It is worth noting that none of the eight 'core values of the teaching profession' outlined in the GTC's *Code of Conduct* touch upon the role of an educator. The focus of this 33-page document is on the role of the teacher as a childminder, manager and therapist. Society needs to take a reality check and decide what it wants from the teaching profession. It is widely recognized that the teaching profession does not enjoy the respect that it deserves. There are many reasons for this regrettable trend, the most important of which is the tendency to perceive the teacher as a child professional rather than as an educator. While it is perfectly legitimate to adopt this emphasis in a pre-school and early primary school setting, at a certain point teachers need to think of themselves as educators first and foremost. The restoration of the status and authority of the educator requires that the teaching profession takes itself, and is taken, more seriously. That requires a fundamental rethinking of the meaning of teacher training. Institutions undertaking teacher training need to replace their existing narrow-minded curriculum with one that is more intellectually challenging. We need teachers who have a competent grasp of an academic discipline and who can therefore gain authority from their ability to educate their students in a particular subject. Although not the topic of this book, it should be evident to all that the future of the school is intimately linked to the quality of teacher training.

## 'The emperor has no clothes'

Before society can establish a harmonious and a creative engagement with education, it needs to be clear about what education
means. This requires a fundamental rethink about an institution
that has lost its way. Since education has become society's one big
hope, it is difficult to acknowledge that so many of the claims made
on its behalf have the character of wishful thinking. For a start, the
very language with which experts and educators talk about schools
is mystifying and confusing. Modern societies have allowed themselves to be overawed by an obscurantist technical-sounding
language that has little or no content. It is not surprising that the
public switches off when they hear experts hold forth about learning
outcomes, learning to learn, personalized learning, variant understanding or experiential learning.

Many policy documents and pedagogic statements addressing
school-related issues seem inane. It is hard to know whether the
authors are attempting to deceive or are simply incorrigible
windbags. The following passage provided by an official report on
*21st Century Schools* illustrates the workings of the language of
mystification:

> This twenty-first-century school system, which is beginning to
> develop, will look and feel very different to the one we have been
> used to. It will be one in which, to achieve their core mission of
> excellent teaching and learning, schools look beyond traditional
> boundaries, are much more outward-facing, working in closer
> partnership with children, young people and parents; other
> schools, colleges, learning providers and universities; other chil-
> dren services; the third sector, the private sector and employers;
> and the local authority and its Children's Trust partners.[3]

What this passage actually means is that what goes on in school will
be less significant for children's education in the future than today.
Terms like 'outward-facing' and 'partnership' attempt to provide a
semblance of coherence to what is really a project without direction.

As far as the authors of this report are concerned, how the 'mission of excellent teaching' is to be realized through partnerships with a bewildering list of constituencies is best left to the imagination.

One journalist who looked at the language used to describe the aims of the English National Curriculum concluded that 'very little of it means anything at all'. Philip Hensher asked, 'Can the government really complain if the general public has the impression that education in schools nowadays appears to consist of a lot of pious nothing-in-particular?' He added: 'Nobody understands what their children are supposed to be learning, or how these ludicrous aims are supposed to be achieved.'[4] That education lacks a coherent language through which it can express its mission indicates that this is an institution that is struggling to give itself meaning.

Take a term like 'learning society'. Outwardly, this widely acclaimed metaphor conveys the idea that society is devoted wholly to the business of learning and acquiring knowledge. Yet this is a term that lacks both precision and meaning. According to one review of this metaphor, 'It is an extraordinarily elastic term that provides politicians and policymakers with something that can seem profound, but on close inspection is largely vacuous.'[5] Of course policy-makers often attempt to evade problems through resorting to platitudes and empty rhetoric. But sometimes such words are also part of a vocabulary of mystification and deception. Through conveying the idea that learning takes place everywhere, the idea of 'learning society' succeeds in devaluing the role of formal education. When every experience can be construed as a learning activity, the status of serious formal study becomes negotiable and is ultimately compromised. The best that can be said about this term is that it resonates with the aspiration to learn. But aspiration transmitted through a language of mystification only invites cynicism about the meaning of education.

Now and again we discover that even the experts sometimes comprehend that the emperor has no clothes. In 2008, the British public was informed that the House of Commons Children's Committee has been trying to find out the meaning of 'personalized learning'. Since personalized learning constitutes one of the main planks of current government policy, it is a little surprising that after years of deliberation, policy-makers are still unclear about what it means. The experts – including the leading figure associated with personalized learning – were surprisingly candid and indicated that it was a 'total waste of time trying to find a definition'. Professor David Hargreaves added that the vague definition used in a new government guide for schools was 'well-intentioned waffle'[6]: a charitable way of saying that experts and politicians haven't got a clue what they are talking about. However, the rhetoric of education is not just well-intentioned waffle: sometimes it is charged with the explicit objective of deceiving the public.

What are we to make of the following statement by Mick Waters, the QCA's former director of the Key Stage 3 curriculum for 11- to 14-year-olds?

> The challenge for schools is to work out which ingredients need to be taught separately, so that children quarry learning in real depth; which ingredients need to be taught by the drip-feed method for a few minutes every day: and which can be taught jointly.[7]

In one sense the passage can be interpreted as an example of the banal attempting to represent itself as clever and profound. But the attempt to peddle the virtues of lessons that are a few minutes long – the so-called drip-feed method – as an exercise in learning in 'real depth' requires precisely this kind of language of mystification.

Occasionally it takes little boys to shout out that 'the emperor has nothing on'. In February 2009 I was talking to a group of 12-year-old boys about their life at school. One of them gazed at me with a puzzled demeanour and asked, 'Why do teachers call thick children gifted?' The entire group looked at me knowingly, indicating that they possessed sufficient sophistication to understand that often their teachers use words that self-consciously obscure the truth. In a world where experts use an incomprehensible language to describe children, youngsters do not get the clarity that they deserve. Patronizing education talk avoids having to confront some uncomfortable realities, but it also undermines the potential for conducting a genuine open conversation between generations.

The bombastic turn of educational rhetoric corresponds to the practices and techniques that they describe. And yet educational policies and pedagogic techniques are often presented as evidence-based and products of scientific reflection. However, the scientific claims made on behalf of the different practices associated with current pedagogic methods are rarely substantiated by rigorous research. Most research cited as proof that a particular policy works reveals little more than what happened at a certain time at a certain school. Educational research works best when charged with the task of explaining what is going on in the classroom, and at its best this can guide thinking and illuminate experience. It is far less effective as an instrument of policy-making that can tell policy-makers 'what works'. Effective policy requires deliberation on fundamental cultural, moral and philosophical questions about the world we inhabit. Experience indicates that what works in a specific setting cannot be simply replicated in another. As David Olson argues, 'The reputation of educational research is tarnished less by the lack of replicable results than by the lack of any deeper theory that would explain why the thousands of experiments that make up the literature of the field appear to have yielded so little.'[8]

It is entirely legitimate for policy-makers to utilize the insights of research. But it is entirely illegitimate for policy to influence and drive research. One reason why so much of educational research has yielded so little insight is because it is not disinterested research. Its focus on 'what works' implicitly assumes what is the desirable outcome, and its role is to provide the evidence required by policy-makers. Often research is treated as an afterthought by experts who are already convinced of the best way forward. For example, the 2004 report *A Literature Review of the Evidence Base for Culture, the Arts and Sport Policy*, written for the Scottish Government, notes that 'although no research has demonstrated a *causal* relationship between participation in arts, culture and sport activities and a reduction in offending behaviour, national and international research and evaluation has demonstrated a link between the two'.[9]

That's another way of saying that all that is lacking is proof of a causal connection. Or take the example of self-esteem. Raising the self-esteem of children is one of the key objectives of educational experts. Yet a study of this concept sponsored by the British Government was forced to concede there is not even agreement on the meaning of self-esteem. The study noted that 'self-esteem has received more attention than almost any other concept as a barometer of coping and adaptation', before stating that research is 'not robust enough to justify any substantive conclusions being drawn'.[10] Yet very, very strong conclusions have been drawn by the experts. Absence of clarity about its meaning does not prevent the dogmatic promotion of self-esteem as a core value among schoolchildren. Curriculum engineers frequently characterize it as a 'core skill' – whatever that means!

Through the manipulation of research, officials attempt to avoid the consequences of failed policies or acknowledge the dimension of the problems facing schools. So Sir Alan Steer, the British Government's behaviour expert, can write that 'while there is a legitimate concern in society about standards of behaviour of young people (as in earlier generations) there is strong evidence from a range of sources that the overall standard of behaviour achieved by schools is good and has improved in recent years'.[11] The 'strong evidence' turns out to be not so strong, and is contradicted by other sources contained in Sir Alan's report. Indeed, although research is used to minimize the scale of the problem, the report itself implicitly recognizes it.

Those involved in some of the most high-profile debates on education rarely acknowledge that what is at stake is not much more than a clash of personal opinion. For example, everyone involved in education appears to have strong views on whether testing children has positive or negative consequences. Sometimes arguments for one side or another claim the authority of research, but in reality what they offer is opinion. Most of the time such views are based on a combination of common sense, prejudice and insights gained from research, and interpreted through the prism of moral and political values. Although many experts are unaware of it, their evidence-based recommendations are little more than prejudice masquerading as research. The American sociologist Joel Best writes about how, at different times, competing reading techniques are justified on the grounds that their efficacy is based on 'an exhaustive review of the research literature on how children learn to read'.[12] He tells the story that when his oldest son started school in California, the principal informed parents that research demonstrated that the 'most effective teaching method' for reading was whole language instruction. Ten years later, when his younger child started school, the preferred technique for teaching reading was phonics. Both techniques could draw on research to justify themselves. Which is why it is best to tread cautiously and start from the needs of a specific classroom rather than assume that a technique – even one that appears effective, such as phonic – possesses magical properties.

The profusion of educational fads is fuelled by the dogmatic project of turning education into an all-purpose saviour of society. Such policies frequently fail to realize their objectives and turn out to be a serious waste of resources and effort. For example, a £3 billion programme designed to improve the achievements of pre-school children in England has had no discernible effect on the development levels of those entering primary school, according to a University of Durham study.[13] In reality, the failure of a policy to improve the achievement of children is not surprising, since levels of attainment cannot be automatically improved through injecting more cash into the classroom. The belief that standards can be increased overall through the implementation of the right mix of policies is based on a simplistic and technocratic idea of how education works. Education is basically a cultural institution inhabited by young people who are influenced by their family, peers and community. In such a complex environment, the effect of policies tends to be indirect and will only become discernible after a considerable period of time.

Public debates about the standards and quality of education tend to be dominated by the idea that exam results, surveys and other official statistical information provide an accurate representation of the situation. Some of this information can provide some useful insights into the workings of broad trends. However, a two per cent increase or one per cent decrease in the achievement of children taking a particular test should not be interpreted as evidence that standards are rising or falling. It is far from evident what is being measured. Children can be coached to pass exams without being educated, and a fall in achievement in percentage terms does not necessarily signify a fall in standards. It is important to comprehend that formal educational achievements provide, at best, indirect evidence of the quality of knowledge, cultural and moral outlook transmitted to children. Everyone knows that formal educational achievement has dramatically expanded in recent decades. However, it is not at all obvious how to interpret the contribution of the dramatic increase in paper qualifications to the intellectual, cultural and moral life of society. As the previous chapters suggest, what has expanded is not simply education but initiatives that are driven by imperatives that are external to it.

Of course it is possible to raise an individual child's achievement through a clearly focused and intensive strategy that cultivates interest in learning and attempts to raise expectations. Such an approach can also be applied in a specific school, and there is some evidence that carefully targeted and locally oriented experiments can make a difference – at least for a period of time. By contrast, highly centralized top-down attempts to reform education invariably fail to realize their objectives. The most important reason for this record of failure is the tendency to opt for pedagogic fixes for what are cultural and social problems. Over the decades, government-initiated educational reforms have failed for the very simple reason that the problems of the school cannot be overcome through technical solutions. More government investment in infrastructure or industry can often yield positive results. However, such investments tend to lead to the *extensive*, rather than the *intensive*, growth of education.

The extensive growth of education is usually expressed through a quantitative increase in the time people spend in a formal institutional environment. The expansion of paper qualifications, higher education and formal achievements is a symptom of the extensive growth of education. The extensive growth of education is usually realized through the instrument of training. The intensive growth of education involves a qualitative cultural change in attitudes which cannot be measured statistically. It is a cultural change that can be seen through a growing valuation of learning, ideas, and of the belief that education is important in its own right. Such a change is invariably linked to the attitudes and expectations that prevail in the wider community and is therefore stimulated by influences that are local. That is why policies that are committed to the intensive development of education need to provide considerable freedom for the exercise of local initiative and influence.

Education, which involves human relationships and culture, is not directly responsive to the initiatives of central government. 'A policy of more education will not automatically deliver the results the government seeks', notes one analysis of this subject.[14] The most important contribution that governments can make is to help create a climate of high expectations for young people through a mix of solid leadership and effective policies.

Since many policy-makers demand swift results and dramatic improvements in outcomes, the education system has become too focused on short-term solutions. Often, success for a school means being able to demonstrate that government targets have been met and that the achievement of pupils has been raised by so many percentage points. This means a school can meet a target for literacy while doing little to cultivate children's love of reading. In turn, examiners help out by packaging results in ways that flatter the educational system. Government turns a blind eye to dubious practices such as the dilution of standards of exams.[15] The ethos of target-setting and measuring achievement fosters a culture of self-deception throughout the institution of education. From primary to higher education, teachers spend far too much time filling in forms and ticking boxes. This is not simply a waste of time: it breeds institutional cynicism which, in some cases, borders on organized fraud. Is it any surprise that from time to time we discover cases where teachers have been caught cheating in national exams? Teachers in schools facing pressure to meet externally imposed targets have changed pupils' answers or have coached them to answer questions that they knew would come in a test.[16]

One of the perverse consequences of target-focused education is that it diminishes the quality of the classroom experience. In such circumstances, teachers have little opportunity to exercise their professional judgement and respond to the needs of their pupils they have to teach to the curriculum. The dominance of a bureaucratic imperative forces teachers to react to externally imposed demands while keeping their eyes on the classroom. Under such circumstances, the quality of their interaction with pupils suffers, as does the intellectual life of the school. That is why the current addiction to educational reform represents a recipe for failure – and why such failure serves as an invitation for yet another round of policy-making. So in March 2009 it was reported that England's Schools Secretary Ed Balls was seeking new powers to overlook the content of every public exam in the country in order to ensure that standards are maintained. This impulse to micro-manage schools is the inexorable consequence of the politicization of education. Unsuccessful initiatives create a demand for new policies which, in turn, further erode the integrity of education, thus guaranteeing their failure. This vicious circle of educational reforms represents an enormous waste: of resources, of teachers' energies and creativity, and of pupils' opportunity to acquire knowledge.

When education becomes an instrument of social policy, it is easy to lose sight of what education should look like. When education is detached from an inter-generational conversation, it acquires significance for extrinsic reasons. In this politicized form, education has become an ever-expanding institution that has lost sight of what it is really about. Education needs to be saved from itself in order to realize the potential of the younger generations. Saving education requires that we depoliticize it, and allow far more independence for education to discover its future direction for itself.

## A word to parents

With so much hope invested in the institution of education, it is not surprising that it really matters to individuals. People rightly regard educational qualifications and degrees as essential for improving their social and economic status. From this perspective, educational qualifications also serve as a marker for social status. People understand that employers use qualifications to screen potential recruits. They also believe that as more and more people acquire higher levels of educational attainment, they will need even more qualifications to stand out and gain the attention of an employer. But one outcome of this trend is the devaluation of paper qualifications. For those with ambition, a good secondary school education does little to provide them with special status. Even a university degree fails to supply a mark of distinction. 'As the university sector has ballooned, simply having been to university no longer serves as much of a distinguishing mark', notes one astute commentator.[17] In the end, credential inflation represents a waste of effort for everyone concerned. As Moore points out, 'credentialization' increases 'the demand for credentials but deflates their labour market value'.[18]

Yet the diminishing status of qualifications that were once held in esteem has not decreased the public's appetite for obtaining more and more educational certificates. Although many realize that formal qualifications do not open the really important doors, they still continue to invest hope and resources in obtaining them. Such a response is entirely understandable since, for an individual, education offers the prospect of important opportunities. And education continues to serve as a mark of status – a culturally sanctioned way of ranking people.

Precisely because educational achievement is used to rank people by employers, public institutions, and the community at large, parents tend to take the schooling of their children very seriously. Indeed, for a significant group of parents their children's education has become a source of constant anxiety and preoccupation. Schooling has become a focus of intense competition among parents. Some parents devote considerable resources to get their children into a 'good' school and often feel at a loss to know what to do if their children are not accepted to such an institution. In the UK, a growing number of mothers and fathers have resorted to employing lawyers to secure school places for their offspring. Reports indicate that this reliance on legal intervention is a 'sign of desperation' of some parents.[19] Many parents go so far as to move house in order to live in the catchment area of a desirable school. Others feign religious conviction and regularly attend church services in order to help their child gain admission to a church-run school. It is now common for parents to spend significant amounts of money for private tutors to help their children improve their examination results. Not surprisingly, the number of children entering private education has grown during the past decade. Once the children are in the 'right' school their parents play an active role in helping them with their homework and projects. According to a recent report by the Qualifications and Curriculum Authority (QCA), two-thirds of parents help their children with GCSE coursework. And many of them do far more than 'help': it is often parents, not the students, who are busy looking for information on the internet or at the library.[20]

Inevitably, many parents who want to help their children to do well and achieve the highest possible grades find it difficult to draw the line that separates helpful 'encouragement' from getting stuck into the project themselves. Some cannot confine their input to a few helpful remarks. They begin by working out a project structure with their child, but before too long they are busy filling in the details. Soon, without giving it very much thought, they adopt the role of the family search engine and direct their children to the relevant sources. Sometimes they end up all but writing the project. Round two begins once the project has reached draft stage. Now parents really come into their own. Having rediscovered their literary skills, they give instructions on re-drafting and correcting the grammar and spelling. Often, very little of the final submission is the child's own work.

The education system is complicit in promoting the growing trend towards what should be called the outsourcing of education by schools. To put it bluntly, in their efforts to demonstrate improved standards, schools manipulate parents' concern for their children by drawing them in as unpaid teachers. From day one in primary school, parents are told that the performance of their child is intimately linked to how much support he or she gets at home. The official meaning of 'support' is not confined to a few encouraging words. Parents are expected to play an active pedagogic role in the educational life of their children. Schemes have even been introduced to train them to participate directly in their children's homework.

Further education colleges offer evening classes concerned with 'Helping Your Child to Read', 'Helping Your Child with GCSE Maths', or 'Helping Your Child Through GCSE English'. Many parents who are anxious about their children's future now regard homework as a joint enterprise: surveys indicate that, on average, parents spend between six and seven hours a week on homework duties.

Government-sponsored guidelines go through the motions of advising parents to hold back from actually doing the homework and not to 'take over too much'. But once parents have internalized the message that their children's performance is regarded as a direct reflection of the quality of support they receive at home, it is difficult not to get involved 'too much'.

Once homework becomes an informal instrument for assessing parental behaviour, anxious fathers and mothers find it difficult to draw the line between helping and cheating.

Expanding the role of parents in education has become a key policy of recent governments, and underscores ministers' lack of faith in their ability to confront the problems in schools. But mobilizing parents' instinctive love for their children to shore up the institution of education does not solve deep-seated problems. What it does do is encourage parents to become their children's advocates in their dealings with teachers, leading to the widespread adoption of the 'My child, right or wrong' attitude. It is difficult to avoid the conclusion that for the sake of political advantage, parental insecurities are often manipulated by policy-makers.

Parents can play a valuable role by providing a stimulating

environment for their children. The best form of parental involvement in a child's education is positive encouragement, and sometimes this involves discussion of issues and problems raised in
school. But homework and coursework need to be the independent
effort of the child.

The absorption of parental energies into the work of schools is
symptomatic of a wider loss of clarity about the lines which ought
to be drawn between the generations. Such a confusion is not always
the outcome of the high esteem that parents attach to the values of
education. The competitive grasping for opportunities suggests that
people strive for social advantages rather than a stimulating intellectual environment for their children. This is a form of education
that is detached from an inter-generational conversation. The
reasons why it is an object of parental ambition are entirely extrinsic
to education. It is its functioning as a mode of social selection that
is the main driver of parental obsession with education.

Although it is entirely understandable that mothers and fathers
possess strong ambitions regarding their children's future, the current
climate of competitive parenting has the effect of undermining
the purpose of education. It lends weight to the anti-intellectual
influences that impact on the life of schools and reinforces the
tendency to perceive education as an instrument for achieving a
purpose external to itself. The investment of parental hope in the
ability of education to serve as a vehicle for social mobility runs in
parallel with the policy-maker's desire to use education to solve
society's problems. Both of these trends reinforce one another to
distract schools from getting on with the job of education.

Naturally parents and children will seek to use education to
pursue their private interests. In principle, the pursuit of such
interests can contribute to the development of cultural attitudes that
genuinely value education. But education can never work as merely
a private transaction – it works most effectively as part of an inter-
generational conversation, and it requires a degree of commitment
by adults to support one another in the realization of this project.
That is, the precondition for the emergence of a future-oriented and
intellectually challenging institution of education is the promotion

of cultural affirmation for the exercise of adult solidarity and authority. It is in this context that teachers can acquire the kind of professional authority that they need to educate young people effectively.

## Where next?

One of the most regrettable consequences of the confusions that surround the exercise of adult authority is the tendency to interpret the failures of education through the prism of the behaviour, capacity or attitudes of children. By contrast, the implications of the devaluation of adult authority for the classroom are rarely explored. Curriculum engineers regard lack of motivation and poor behaviour as synonymous with the crisis in education rather than a symptom of problems with teaching and the authority of teachers. The tendency to confuse a symptom of this crisis with the cause is most striking in relation to the debate on behaviour. Arguments about whether children's behaviour has improved or declined have overtaken the logically prior issue of why adults and teachers find it difficult to manage the conduct of children in the first place. The failure of adult society to contain the behaviour of the young is overlooked. Invariably such issues are extracted from their generational context, and uncontained behaviour is recast as the character trait of children. Frequently they are diagnosed with a label. So we now have 'hard to place' and 'hard to reach' children. Many education experts believe that children have a very short attention span and will switch off unless entertained and constantly stimulated through different forms of digital technology. As a result, short lessons are upheld as best practice. The belief that children cannot pay attention to more complex and ideas-driven lessons dominates the thinking of curriculum experts. It seems that the adult world avoids confronting the implications of its reluctance to behave authoritatively by harbouring a loss of faith in children's capacity to take education seriously.

One of the most destructive prejudices influencing curriculum engineering is the fatalistic belief that children are what they are.

Classroom techniques are influenced by the conviction that children are limited by their family and social circumstances and lack the intellectual and moral resources to cope with a challenging educational environment. This sentiment is particularly damaging to the development of children from disadvantaged communities, who are perceived as lacking the motivation to study subjects that are not directly relevant to their lives. No doubt children from economically disadvantaged or marginalized families do not enjoy the advantages of those whose parents possess considerable cultural capital. But it is precisely for that reason that educators should try to raise their expectations by stimulating their intellect and curiosity.

The fundamental premise of a liberal–humanist system of education is the belief that there is nothing fixed about the attitude, behaviour and motivation of a child. Children, who are in the process of becoming more mature individuals, develop unexpected characteristics as they respond to their education. Whatever their genetic abilities, children can make significant progress, and the vast majority of them are able to acquire knowledge in any subject. When children acquire knowledge, they are capable of becoming independent intellectually in a range of subjects. When children fail to realize this potential, it is due often to the low expectations that society has of their abilities.

Liberal education regards children as the rightful heirs to the achievements of human society. It takes responsibility for ensuring that this inheritance is handed over to the young. It is also concerned for preparing children for the world ahead. The main question it needs to address now is what, ideally, an educated citizen should know in order to deal with the challenges of today. In the first instance, public deliberation on this matter must consider what we wish every child to become if they are to play a responsible role in a democratic society. Such a discussion involves a consideration of values and the ideals that we associate with an educated citizen. Working towards such an ideal is the beginning of an inter-generational conversation, and it therefore needs to be directed towards the cultivation of a common aspiration among children. The current ideal of personalized education directly contradicts the meaning of an inter-generational conversation. That is why, the more that schooling is personalized, the less it is likely to educate the young.

Education cannot, and should not, be changed through clever techniques and policies. In the first instance, education should be taken out of the domain of party politics. Governments must recognize that, with the best intention in the world, their policies will at best yield meagre results. They are much more likely to distract schools from educating and complicate the life of teachers unnecessarily. Governments must resist the temptation of dumping the problems of society on schools. Schools can cultivate desirable intellectual and moral qualities and prepare children for the world they face, but they cannot provide solutions to problems that originate in adult society. Hopefully, children can be educated to assume responsible adult roles and contribute to the welfare of society. But they should not be treated as instruments for social reform which must be entirely the responsibility of the adult world. Confusing the roles of different generations only leads to the consolidation of the evasion of adult responsibility.

Throughout the previous chapters, a great emphasis was placed on the regrettable consequences of the erosion of adult authority. The failure to acknowledge this issue is the fundamental issue facing education, to which almost every problem facing schools is either directly or indirectly linked. Unfortunately this problem is overlooked in public deliberations. To make matters worse, curriculum engineers and experts readily acquiesce to it and in some cases celebrate it. The normal ambiguities associated with the exercise of adult authority have become codified into a cultural script that represents it in extremely negative terms. The term 'authority figure' is used in such a way that it continually conveys the implication of an abuse of power – increasingly the emphasis is on containing it and regulating it. Challenging the pathologization of the authority figure is a precondition for saving education from itself and providing teachers with the cultural resources to behave in an authoritative manner in the classroom.

Government and society have a legitimate right to outline what education should mean and how it should work. Every society benefits from an intelligent debate about the meaning of education. The consensus that emerges from such a conversation should influence the institutional foundation of education. Such a consensus can be transmitted through a National Curriculum or another system of guidance, but it is important that such a system should not be too prescriptive. Society needs to learn to trust schools and teachers to work out how they should get on with the task of educating their pupils. We need a fundamental realignment away from the excessive influence and control exercised by government and towards local initiative and direction.

It is very difficult to promote and implement effective educational policies without addressing the fundamental question of what schools are for and what values should influence proceedings in the classroom. In Chapters 4 and 5 we discussed this issue in relation to the question of socialization. How we socialize children pertains to wider cultural matters that must be clarified explicitly through an ongoing process of public deliberation. But the question of values is also relevant for directing the work of teachers and shaping the ethos of schools. At present the values that are meant to guide schools have a perfunctory and rhetorical character. Take the following list of 'core values of the teaching profession' proposed by the GTC:

- Excellence and continual development.
- Commitment and empathy.
- Reflection and self-regulation.
- Honesty and integrity.
- Respect, equality, diversity and inclusion.
- Involvement and empowerment.
- Collegiality and co-operation.
- Responsiveness to change.

This list, which reads as though it has been lifted from a bureaucrat's human resources management textbook, contains not a single value that is specific to the domain of education. How are these core values of the teaching profession any different from those of dentists, accountants or soldiers? It begs the question of what the values of education and educators are. The core value of the teaching profession needs to be subject expertise and the responsible exercise of authority and judgement in the classroom.

Yet if we get the values right, we can begin to sort out education. The valuation of education as something that is important in its own right is the precondition for it to flourish. One of the principal characteristics of education is its lack of interest in an ulterior purpose. That does not mean that it is uninterested in developments affecting children and society: it means that it regards the transmission of cultural and intellectual achievements of humanity to children as its defining mission. Once society is able to affirm an education system that values itself and the acquisition of knowledge, then policy-makers and the public can begin to determine the practical steps required to go forward.

It is urgent that the current confusion of learning with education is overcome. Learning is not an activity specific to education. Human beings learn throughout their lives, but what they learn is not necessarily knowledge. Conversely, many of the lessons and insights that people need to learn – how to conduct relationships, communicate their problems, deal with challenges – cannot be taught. But children do require that schools teach them the knowledge they need in order to be educated. Instead of wasting precious resources on trying to teach what cannot be taught, schools need to be orientated towards the task of providing subject-based knowledge to children.

Education needs to be saved from the influence of curriculum experts. It will take a long time for teachers to recover their confidence and begin to think of themselves as educators rather than as learners. There are too many vested interests that play the game of ticking the right boxes, micro-managing the classroom, and promoting social engineering schemes. Many of the prevailing practices – inspections, examinations, teaching to the curriculum – encourage the process of standardization instead of improving standards. In principle, the formal assessment of children's assessment can play an important role in providing insights into a child's level of attainment and performance. However, assessment – especially of primary schoolchildren – requires the kind of sensitivity and subtlety that is alien to the current forms of formalized testing. Worse still, the formal processes introduced in schools encourage the unimaginative scripting of students in the art of passing exams. The fault lies not with the principle of examining children but with the blight of rote-learning encouraged by an anti-educational school culture that lives on a diet of worksheets and technical gimmicks.

No doubt many readers of this book have strong views about topics such as what subjects should be taught and assessed, how the curriculum should be framed and how children ought to be socialized and disciplined. There are a number reasons why *Wasted* has resisted the temptation to formulate a set of policies for schools. Although a lot of time is wasted in the classroom on instructing children on the wrong things, the situation would not improve if teachers were empowered just to teach a more educationally oriented curriculum. The real issue at stake is not simply whether a child should study history or media studies, but the need to confront the most fundamental challenge facing society: to gain clarity about the meaning of education. Schools that are devoted to pursuing education as something that is important in its own right are likely to formulate an effective approach towards the specific needs of their pupils. More widely, the affirmation of adult authority in and out of the classroom is essential for providing a sturdy cultural foundation for education. The depoliticization of education and the insulation of schools from the influence of social engineers is also a precondition for transforming schools

In principle, children can be educated through a variety of different strategies and through different subjects. There are many ways of teaching children, and only someone who is wedded to a dogma would insist that only their pedagogic technique works. What we need is a tolerant and open-minded ethos towards education rather than a prescriptive approach towards schooling. To save education from itself, it is necessary to provide greater independence to schools and allow teachers to exercise their professional judgement. It is difficult to see how much headway can be made as long as education is run on highly centralized institutional and ideological models. Central government has a legitimate role in outlining a basic common curriculum through which children gain access to their rightful intellectual inheritance. But how this curriculum is taught, and through what subjects, is best decided by local schools and communities. A genuinely pluralist approach can both counter the influence of curriculum experts and social engineers, and provide new opportunities for discovering what works best for schooling children.

# *Notes*

Preface

1 See comment by Wes Sterling, NUS National President, NUS Press Office: www.nus.org.uk/News/Media-Centre/A-level-results-2008/.

**Introduction: The Paradox of Education**

1 Arendt (2006 [1961]) p. 196.

2 The growing disconnection between generations is discussed in Furedi and Bristow (2008).

3 Sean Coughlan, 'School is the "last moral force"', *BBC News*, 9 March 2009.

4 See National Commission on Excellence in Education (1983) *A Nation at Risk: The Imperative for Education Reform*, US Government Printing Office: www.ed.gov/pubs/NatAtRisk/risk.html, p. 35.

5 McCaslin and Infanti (1998) p. 280.

6 Justin Parkinson, 'Parents create feckless youths', *BBC News*, 31 March 2005.

7 'Parents to be hit with penalties if children misbehave at school', *The Daily Telegraph*, 15 April 2009; and 'Schools are "employing bouncers"', *BBC News*, 12 April 2009.

8 Mary Bousted, 'Don't blame teachers when it's parents who are failing', *The Observer*, 5 April 2009.

9 Cited in 'Pupils playing up? Let them play bingo, says Sir Alan Steer', *The Times*, 16 April 2009.

10 'We need pushy parents to improve failing schools, says education minister', thislondon.co.uk, 25 August 2008.

11 Robert Winnett, 'Schools to be graded by parents and pupils', *The Daily Telegraph*, 11 March 2009.

12 The Department for Children, Schools and Families (2008) *The Independent Review of the Primary Curriculum*, p. 45.

13 See 'Parents to be hit with penalties if children misbehave at school', *The Daily Telegraph*, 15 April 2009; and 'Schools are "employing bouncers"', *BBC News*, 12 April 2009.

14 See for example 'Bright schoolchildren take back seat to "social misfits", says head teacher', *The Daily Telegraph*, 12 March 2009.

15 Katherine Sellgren, 'Expectations "too high" say heads', *BBC News*, 13 March 2009.

16 Tanya Byron, 'We see children as pestilent', *The Guardian*, 17 March 2009.

17 Young and Muller (2007) p. 181.

18 See 'Behaviour experts to help schools', *BBC News*, 16 April 2009.

19 The Department for Children, Schools and Families (2008) *The Independent Review of the Primary Curriculum*, p. 29.

20 'Books disappearing from schools, says Michael Rosen', *The Daily Telegraph*, 3 March 2009.

21 Polly Curtis, 'Ofsted's new mission to get rid of boring teachers', *The Guardian*, 5 January 2009.

22 'Ofsted tells on school teachers', *BBC News*, 20 January 2006.

23 See for example Helen Rumbelow, 'A master class in bribery; pay your school kids', *The Times*, 3 April 2009.

24 Cited in Polly Curtis, 'Ofsted's new mission to get rid of boring teachers', *The Guardian*, 5 January 2009

25 Cited in Ravitch (2000) p. 293.

26 These points are developed in Furedi (2008).

27 Katherine Sellgren, 'Warning over narcissistic pupils', *BBC News*, 14 March 2009.

28 See for example Gary Eason, '"Toxic cycle" of family breakdown', *BBC News*, 18 March 2008.

29 Louise Tickle, 'Tears for fears', *The Guardian*, 3 March 2009.

30 Speech made on 18 November 2005: www.number10.gov.uk/output/Page8547.asp.

31 Wolf (2002) calls into question the association between education and economic growth.

32 Katherine Sellgren, 'Expectations "too high" say heads', *BBC News*, 13 March 2009.

33 For an interesting case study of Scotland, see Iannelli and Paterson (2007).

34 Iannelli and Paterson (2007) p. 231.

35 Moore (2007) p. 120.

## Chapter 1: Throwaway Pedagogy

1 Statement by ASCL General Secretary Dr John Dunford, 14 May 2008: www.ascl.org.uk//MainWebSite/SearchResultsd24452490f5d494.aspx?Map=0014830DE8403804B0E0833ED4F2E002&NewsItemID=143&NewsGroupID=.

2 See www.demos.co.uk/media/pressreleases/educationepidemic.

3 Hargreaves (2003).

4 Tony Blair, 'Speech on Education', 24 October 2005: http://www.number10.gov.uk/Page8363.

5 *2020 Vision: Report of the Teaching and Learning in 2020 Review Group*, London, 2006, p. 11.

6 Estelle Morris, 'Change, but don't lose the constants', *The Guardian*, 23 September 2008.

7 Department for Education and Skills (2004) p. 4.

8 QCA (2005) p. 4.

9 Bill Law, 'A new focus for the curriculum': www.nesta.org.uk/a-new-focus-for-the-curriculum/.

10 QCA (2005) p. 4.

11 Cited in Ball (2008) p. 11.

12 John Dewey (1902) 'The school as social center'.

13 Ravitch (2000) p. 335.

14 Cited in Ravitch (2000) p. 292.

15 Schön (1967) p. 28.

16 UNESCO (1972) pp. 90–1.

17 Coombs (1985) p. 250.

18 'Foreword' by David Blunkett, *The Learning Age: A Renaissance for a New Britain*: www.lifelonglearning.co.uk/greenpaper/summary.pdf.

19 Bentley (1998) p. 177.

20 Barber (1997) p. 160.

21 Edwards and Nicoll (2006) p. 118.

22 Dewey (1897) p. 6.

23 Ryan (1995) pp. 134–5.

24 *2020 Vision: Report of the Teaching and Learning in 2020 Review Group*, London, 2006, p. 8.

25 B. Levin (1998) p. 131.

26 Rob Moore (2008) 'Schimatism, The Pursuit of Difference and the Tradition of the New', p. 4 (unpublished chapter).

27 *A Nation At Risk*: www.ed.gov/pubs/NatAtRisk/index.html (1983).

28 Sir Claus Moser, 'Introductory Paper', given at the conference 'The Knowledge Society: Changing the shape for the 21st century', 8–16 September 2000.

29 Hargreaves (2003) p. 19.

30 Sir Claus Moser ,'Introductory Paper'.

31 DfEE (1998) 'Introduction' to *The Learning Age: A Renaissance for a New Britain*, available online at: www.leeds.ac.uk/educol/documents/000000655.htm.

32 Beck (2002) p. 621.

33 Beck (2002) p. 623.

34 Lester Smith (1971) p. 127.

35 Schön (1967) p. 217.

36 See DfEE (1997) *Excellence in Schools*, p. 12.

37 Bentley (1998) pp. 135–6.

38 Keith Bloomer (2001) *Learning to Change: Scottish Education in the Early 21st Century*, Scottish Council Foundation, p. 28: www.scottishcouncilfoundation.org/pubs_more.php?p=14.

39 Cited in Phillips (1997) p. 160.

40 Phillips (1997) p. 160.

41 Cited in Coffield (1999) p. 482.

42 DfEE (1998) *The Learning Age: A Renaissance for a New Britain*.

43 For example see Ball (2008) p. 11.

44 Wheelahan (2008) p. 206.

45 Bentley (1998) p. 4.

46 Bentley (1998) p. 4.
47 Beck (2002) p. 624.
48 Hargreaves (2003) p. 27.
49 Bentley (1998) p. 176.
50 Bentley (1998) pp. 124–5.
51 QCA (2005) p. 4.
52 See for example John White 'Towards an aims-led curriculum', QCA: www.qca.org.uk/futures/.
53 Rogers (1983) p. 137. Originally published in 1969.
54 Arendt (2006 [1961]) pp. 187–8.
55 Levinson (1997) p. 7.

## Chapter 2: The Meaning of Education

1 Cited in Jones (2003) pp. 23–4.
2 Anthony Seldon, 'Schools must pay more attention to children's well-being', *The Daily Telegraph*, 30 November 2008.
3 Ecclestone and Hayes (2008) p. 34.
4 Peters (1959) p. 17.
5 Oakeshott (1989) p. 65.
6 Arendt (2006 [1961]).
7 Arendt (2006 [1961]) p. 171.
8 Dewey (1938 [1916]) section 1,
9 Arendt (2006 [1961]) p. 192.
10 QCA (2007) p. 8.
11 Dewey (1934) vol. 12, p. 4, available at: www.the-philosopher.co.uk/dewey.htm.
12 Arendt (2006 [1961]) p. 182.
13 Arendt (2006 [1961]) p. 188.
14 See Gordon (1999) p. 10 for an exposition of this argument.
15 Gordon (1999) p. 10.
16 Cited by Entwistle (1979) p. 44.
17 Arendt (2006 [1961]) pp. 188–9.
18 Arendt (2006 [1961]) p. 189.
19 Levinson (1997) p. 7.
20 Arendt (2006 [1961]) pp. 189–90.
21 Arendt (2006 [1961]) p. 173.
22 Arendt (2006 [1961]) pp. 191–2.
23 Gordon (1999) p. 256.
24 Crosland made this remark in 1974. Republished in Finch and Scrimshaw (1982) p. 27.
25 Paulo Freire, 'Education: Domestication or Liberation?' in Finch and Scrimshaw (1982) p. 39 (originally published in 1972).
26 G. Paton, 'Universities have a duty to promote "social justice", says John Denham', *The Daily Telegraph*; 30 September 2008.
27 Oakeshott (1989) p. 68.
28 Oakeshott (1989) p. 68.
29 Arendt (2006 [1961]) p. 192.

30 Oakeshott (1989) p. 68.
31 Young (2008) p. 67.
32 Oakeshott (1989) p. 68.
33 Peters (1982) p. 15.
34 Young (2008) p. 82.
35 Ravitch (1985) p. 40.
36 Young (2008) p. 84.
37 Christopher Ray, 'The Retreat From Scholarship' in Lovelock (2008).
38 Ecclestone and Hayes (2008) p. 141.
39 Ecclestone and Hayes (2008) p. 141
40 White (2005) p. 132.
41 White (2006) p. 2
42 Bentley (1998) p. 8.
43 Bentley (1998) p. 9.
44 Arendt (2006 [1961]) p. 192.
45 Arendt (2006 [1961]) p. 179.
46 See Oakeshott (1989) pp. 81, 83.
47 White (2005) p. 137.
48 White (2005) p. 137.
49 'Rose denounces impact of testing', *BBC Online*, 20 October 2008: http://news.bbc.co.uk/1/hi/education/7680895.stm.

## Chapter 3: Confusions about Adult Authority

 1 Jessica Shepherd, 'What does Britain expect?', *The Guardian*, 17 July 2007.
 2 Robert Pigott, 'Call for "post-9/11" RE teaching', *BBC News Education*, 17 June 2008.
 3 Chris Hastings and Julie Henry, 'National song-book project falls flat', *The Daily Telegraph*, 4 May 2008.
 4 See Habermas (1976) who wrote that 'there is no administrative production of meaning', p. 70.
 5 'Adults give young "bad example"', *BBC News*, 11 July 2008.
 6 'Teachers being bullied in schools': http://news.bbc.co.uk/go/pr/fr/-/cbbcnews/hi/newsid_7260000/newsid_7268300/7268342.stm, 28 February 2008.
 7 Hannah Goff, 'Spoilt children "disrupt schools"', *BBC News*, 25 March 2008.
 8 See 'Staff fears in toddler exclusion', *BBC News Education,* 7 November 2008.
 9 See 'Teachers report widespread abuse', *BBC News*, 6 April 2009.
10 'Staff fears in toddler exclusion', *BBC News Education,* 7 November 2008.
11 G. Paton, 'Hundreds of schoolchildren under five children are suspended in a year', *The Daily Telegraph*, 7 November 2008.
12 Ravitch (1985) p. 13.
13 Arendt (2006 [1961]) 'What is Authority', p. 91.
14 Bantock (1952) p. 189.
15 Arendt (2006 [1961]) p. 193.
16 Phillips (1997) p. 64.
17 See Nisbet (2000) for a sociological account of this development.

18 Arendt (2006 [1961]) p. 2.
19 On the project of undermining parental confidence see Furedi (2008).
20 Dewey (1946) p. 97.
21 Dewey (1936) p. 605.
22 Dewey (1936) p. 605.
23 Bentley (1998) p. 2.
24 Dewey (1966) p. 60.
25 Freire (1972) pp. 58–9.
26 See Richard DuFour, 'The Learning-Centred Principle', *Beyond Instructional Leadership*, 59 (8), May 2002: http://cursa.ihmc.us/rid=1206976613786_1901503955_1669/DuFour-%20Learning%20Centered%20Principal.pdf.
27 Lionel Elvin in Peters (1969) p. 87.
28 The 'anxious concern with motivation' also 'allowed behavioural psychology to yet again find its way into ideas of teaching and learning'. See Lovlie and Standish (2002) pp. 327–8.
29 Hofstadter (1964) p. 328.
30 See Barber (1997) p. 169.
31 Barber (1997) pp. 169, 170.
32 Postman (1996) p. 26.
33 Bentley (1998) p. 79.
34 Bentley (1998) p. 188.
35 Bentley (1998) p. 80.
36 Bentley (1998) p. 80.
37 Bentley (1998) p. 163.
38 Bentley (1998) p. 162.
39 For a discussion of the therapeutic cultural trends that influence this development see Furedi (2004).
40 Bentley (1998) p. 162.
41 Rogers (1983) p. 3.
42 Rogers (1983) p. 189.
43 Ravitch (2000) p. 459.
44 White (2005) p. 141.
45 Crawford (1995) pp. 434–5.
46 Ravitch (2000) p. 341.
47 White (2006) p. 11.
48 This point is coherently argued by Phillips (1997).
49 Bentley (1998) pp. 6, 7.
50 Whitty and Wisby (2007)
51 Lovlie and Standish (2002) p. 327.
52 Dewey (1956) p. 18.
53 Burkard (2007) p. 3.
54 Burkard (2007) pp. 4–5.
55 Whitty and Wisby (2007) p. 305.
56 Julie Henry, 'School pupils rate teachers in speed-dating style interviews', *The Daily Telegraph*, 25 October 2008.
57 Julie Henry, 'School pupils rate teachers in speed-dating style interviews',

*The Daily Telegraph*, 25 October 2008.

58 'Union denounces pupil interviews', *BBC News UK*, 20 June 2007.

59 Cook-Sather (2006) p. 369.

## Chapter 4: Socialization in Reverse

1 See *Headliners*, October 2007: www.headliners.org/storylibrary/stories/2007/sat+group+climate+change.htm?id=5852289142420909396.

2 Porritt (1998) p. 82.

3 Cited in 'Adults give young "bad example"', *BBC News*, 11 July 2008.

4 Prensky (2001) p. 3.

5 Heyting, Kruithof and Mulder (2002) p. 383.

6 See E. G. West, 'Liberty and Education: John Stuart Mill's Dilemma', *Philosophy*, April 1965.

7 Durkheim (1956) p. 71.

8 Cited in Giddens (1986) p. 176.

9 Durkheim (1956) p. 70.

10 Durkheim (1956) p. 123.

11 The Hadow Report (1926) *The Education of the Adolescent*, London, HM Stationery Office.

12 Kessen (1979) p. 817.

13 Loseke and Cahill (1994) p. 174.

14 Kessen (1979) p. 818.

15 Ayling (1930) pp. 204, 213.

16 See Chapter 10 in Furedi (2008).

17 Dewey (1934) pp. 2–3.

18 Ravitch (2000) p. 80.

19 Dewey (1966) p. 20

20 Dewey and Dewey (1962) p. 81.

21 Kessen (1979) p. 818.

22 Marsden (1997) p. 228.

23 Chung and Walsh (2000) p. 226.

24 Ravitch (2000) p. 276.

25 See for example Bentley (1998) p. 26.

26 Kessen (1979) p. 818.

27 Hofstadter (1964) p. 337.

28 Arendt (2006 [1961]) p. 174.

29 'Children and their Primary Schools (1967), A Report of the Central Advisory Council for Education (England)', London: Her Majesty's Stationery Office, Vol. 1, chapter 15, paragraph 500, available online: www.dg.dial.pipex.com/documents/plowden15.shtml.

30 See Sean Coughlin, 'School is "the last moral force"', *BBC News Education*, 3 September 2008.

31 Cotgrove (1972) p. 74.

32 Bantock (1965) p. 134.

33 See Zachry (1940) p. 394.

34 Ravitch (2000) p. 427.

35 See Furedi (2004) pp. 62–3.

36 http://curriculum.qca.org.uk/key-stages-1-and-2/Values-aims-and-purposes/index.aspx.

37 White (2006) p. 3.

38 Bentley (1998) p. 160.

39 See 'Call for skills lessons in school', *BBC News*, 24 September 2008.

40 'Call for skills lessons in school', *BBC News*, 24 September 2008.

41 See Graeme Paton, 'Schools should teach skills not subjects', *The Daily Telegraph*, 3 June 2008.

42 For examples of this trend, see Furedi (2008) chapter 7.

43 Ball (2008) p. 177.

44 Gewitz (2001) p. 366.

45 'Parents "ignorant" on five-a-day', was the headline of a story published by *BBC News*, 23 June 2008.

46 www.schoolcouncils.org/schools/School-Councils-UK/case_studies/school-council-teach-parents-a-lesson.

47 'Letter: Children, teach your parents well', *Taunton Gazette*, 8 April 2008: www.tauntongazette.com/archive/x1272965790/Letter-Children-teach-your-parents-well.

48 Home Office Press Release: 'Children Remind Adults to Act Responsibly on our Streets', 4 April 2007: http://press.homeoffice.gov.uk/press-releases/children-remind-asbo-adults.

49 See David Benady, 'The plus side of pestering', 24 January 2008, www.mad.co.uk/Main/Search/MadSearchResults/Articles/ba0fc996cf7e4195b876ba555bc3e2fc/The-plus-side-of-pestering.html.

50 Caroline Stacey, 'Positive side of pester power', *The Times*, 3 November 2007.

51 Cited in Bibi van der Zee, 'Pester power', *The Guardian*, 1 February 2007.

52 Energy Saving Trust, 'The role of education and schools in shaping energy-related consumer behaviour', October 2007: www.energysavingtrust.org.uk/uploads/documents/aboutest/Schools%20report.pdf.

53 Lisa Fedarado, 'Pint-size eco-police, making parents proud and sometimes crazy', *New York Times*, 10 October 2008: www.nytimes.com/2008/10/10/nyregion/10green.html.

54 Speech by Malcolm Wicks MP, June 2006: www.dti.gov.uk/about/dti-ministerial-team/page31126.html.

55 David Miliband, February 2007: www.defra.gov.uk/news/2007/070202b.htm.

56 Alan Johnson, 'Children must think differently', *The Independent*, 2 February 2007: www.independent.co.uk/opinion/commentators/alan-johnson-children-must-think-differently-434686.html.

57 Energy Saving Trust, *The Role of Education and Schools in Shaping Energy-related Consumer Behaviour*, October 2007: www.energysavingtrust.org.uk/uploads/documents/aboutest/Schools%20report.pdf.

58 Cited in Bibi van der Zee, 'Pester power', *The Guardian*, 1 February 2007.

59 DTI, 'Our energy challenge: power from the people – microgeneration strategy', March 2006: www.berr.gov.uk/whatwedo/energy/sources/sustainable/microgeneration/strategy/page27594.html.

60 Russell (2007).
61 See www.number10.gov.uk/Page633.
62 'Parents must do better – Johnson', *BBC News*, 11 July 2006.
63 'Parents must do better – Johnson', *BBC News*, 11 July 2006.
64 'Parents must do better – Johnson', *BBC News*, 11 July 2006.

**Chapter 5: Social Engineering**

 1 In Lovelock (2008) p. 140.
 2 See www.musicmanifesto.co.uk/key-aims.
 3 See *Diversity and Citizenship Curriculum Review* (2007), Department for Education and Skills: London, p. 68 (otherwise known as the Ajegbo report after its author Sir Keith Ajegbo).
 4 See 'Statement of Values by the National Forum for Values in Education and the Community', available on: http://curriculum.qca.org.uk/uploads/Statement-of-values_tcm8-12166.pdf.
 5 'Editorial', *Prospero: A Journal of New Thinking in Philosophy for Education*, 13 (4), 2007, p. 4.
 6 Durkheim, 'The Role of the State in Education', republished in Giddens (1986) p. 177.
 7 Durkheim, 'The Role of the State in Education', p. 178.
 8 See *Diversity and Citizenship Curriculum Review* (2007) p. 68.
 9 Heyting et al. (2002) p. 396.
10 Heyting et al. (2002) p. 396.
11 Standish (2009) p. 32.
12 Bentley (1998) p. 160.
13 Winnie Hu, 'Gossiping, girls and boys get lessons in empathy', *The New York Times*, 5 April 2009.
14 See Clarke (1940) p. 70. He added that 'England was secure in its own identity, and the furnace of war could only reinforce that faith'.
15 Habermas (1976) p. 47.
16 Editorial', *Prospero; A Journal of New Thinking in Philosophy for Education*, 13 (4), 2007, p. 4.
17 McCulloch, Goodman and Richardson (2007) p. 105.
18 Halsey (1978) pp. 133–4.
19 Arendt (2006 [1961]) p. 193.
20 Barber (1997) p. 17.
21 Zieger (2004) p. 87.
22 Zieger (2004) p. 91.
23 Snow (2007) p. 50.
24 See The National Commission on Excellence in Education (1983), *A Nation at Risk: The Imperative for Educational Reform*, p. 1, Washington, DC, available at: www.ed.gov/pubs/NatAtRisk/index.html.
25 Davies et al. (2005) p. 343.
26 The Department for Children, Schools and Families (2008) *The Independent Review of the Primary Curriculum*, p. 6.
27 See: www.dcsf.gov.uk/consultations/downloadableDocs/Duty%20to%20

Promote%20Community%20Cohesion%20Gu.

28 Habermas (1976) p. 71.

29 'Schools told to close gender gaps', *BBC News*, 17 April 2007.

30 'Pupils "must learn about nappies"', *BBC News*, 28 July 2006.

31 Alan Johnson, 'Children must think differently', *The Independent*, 2 February 2007.

32 'Schools "must tackle homophobia"', *BBC News*, 7 July 2008.

33 'Call for sex lessons at age four', *BBC News*, 14 July 2008; Kate Devlin, 'Sex education "must become compulsory in schools"', *The Daily Telegraph*, 28 July 2008; and '"Emotions" urged in sex education', *BBC News*, 5 May 2005.

34 'Boys will learn to be good dads at 11', *The Sunday Times*, 21 September 2008.

35 Mike Baker, 'Do we ask too much of teachers?', *BBC News*, 10 October 2008.

36 'Nursery alert for racist toddlers', *BBC News*, 7 July 2008.

37 'Anti-racism lessons in nurseries', *BBC News*, 6 February 2008.

38 Standish (2009) pp. 76–7.

39 'Citizenship in secondary schools: evidence from Ofsted inspections (2003/04)', HMI 2335, February 2005.

40 'Warning over citizenship classes', *BBC News*, 2 February 2008.

41 See 'Patriotism "should not be taught at school"', *The Daily Telegraph*, 4 February 2008.

42 Alexander (2001) p. 17.

43 Anthony Crosland, 'Comprehensive education' (1974) in Finch and Scrimshaw (1982) p. 27.

44 John Denham, 'Be fair to adults as well as young people', *The Guardian*, 16 September 2008.

45 See Graeme Paton, 'Class divisions still blight education', *The Daily Telegraph*, 27 July 2008.

46 Claire Fox, 'The Philosophy Gap' in Hayes (2004) p. 24.

**Chapter 6: The Loss of Faith in Education**

1 Burton (2007) pp. 8–9.

2 See www.standards.dfes.gov.uk/eyfs/site/profile/index.htm.

3 Finlay et al. (2007) p. 6.

4 Teaching and Learning in 2020 Review Group (2007) p. 5.

5 Finlay et al. (2007) p. 5.

6 Simon (1981) p. 139.

7 Young (2008) p. 36.

8 Johnson et al. (2007) p. 8

9 Graeme Paton, 'Schools should teach skills, not subjects', *The Daily Telegraph*, 3 June 2008.

10 See Simon (1981) p. 138.

11 Entwistle (1979) p. 102.

12 See Entwistle (1979) p. 31.

13 Johnson et al. (2007) pp. 25, 41.

14 Johnson et al. (2007) p. 32.

15 Moore and Young (2001) p. 457.

16 'Introduction' by Dr Mary Bousted to Johnson et al. (2007) p. 9.
17 Association of Teachers and Lecturers Position Statement, 'Subject to Change: New Thinking on the Curriculum' (2006): www.atl.org.uk/Images/Subject%20to%20change%20-%20curriculum%20PS%202006.pdf.
18 Beck and Young (2005) p. 190.
19 Johnson et al. (1997) p. 35.
20 'Fertile minds need feeding', *The Guardian*, 10 February 2009.
21 Bill Law, 'A new focus for the curriculum': www.nesta.org.uk/a-new-focus-for-the-curriculum/.
22 Sellinger and Yapp (2001).
23 Bill Law, 'A new focus for the curriculum': www.nesta.org.uk/a-new-focus-for-the-curriculum/.
24 Bentley (1998) p. 25.
25 Johnson et al. (1997) p. 27.
26 Macdonald (2003) p. 144.
27 Qualifications and Curriculum Authority (2007) 'Analysis of evidence from sixty stakeholder events during 2008': www.qca.org.uk/qca_18487.aspx.
28 G. H. Bantock, 'The Discovery Methods' in Cox and Dyson (1969) p. 115.
29 Bentley (1998) p. 74.
30 Tight (1998) p. 483.
31 See 'TLRP's evidence-informed pedagogic principles': www.tlrp.org/themes/tenprinciples.html.
32 Cited in Entwistle (1979) p. 36.
33 Young (2008) pp. 164–5.
34 Wheelahan (2008).
35 Simon (1981) p. 143.
36 Bentley (1998) p. 6.
37 Barber (1998) p. 26.
38 'TLRP's evidence-informed pedagogic principles': www.tlrp.org/themes/tenprinciples.html.
39 Kennedy (1997) p. 25.
40 Altheit and Dausien (2002) p. 6.
41 Crowther (2004) p. 130.
42 Rogers (1983) p. 137.
43 Department for Children, Schools and Families, *Personalised Learning*: https://czone.eastsussex.gov.uk/sites/gtp/library/professional/Documents/assessment/Personalised%20learning.pdf.
44 Teaching and Learning in 2020 Review Group (2007) p. 46.
45 Leadbeater (2004) p. 69.
46 Teaching and Learning in 2020 Review Group (2007).
47 Mike Baker, 'Let's not get personal', *BBC News*, 21 November 2008.
48 Teaching and Learning in 2020 Review Group (2007) pp. 39, 48.
49 '"Reluctance" to identify gifted', *BBC News*, 30 January 2009.
50 Johnson et al. (2007) p. 72.
51 'Conversations with Howard Gardner', *The Herald*, 10 October 1998.
52 Helene Guldberg, 'Class Divisions': www.spiked-online.com, 21 July 2004.

53 Simon (1981) p. 138.
54 Simon (1981) p. 140.
55 See Pring (2007) p. 504.
56 Burton (2007) p. 9.
57 See www.thegrid.org.uk/learning/gifted/policies/definition.shtml.
58 See Gardner (1993).
59 Barber (1997) p. 172.
60 Helene Guldberg, 'Class divisions': www.spiked-online.com, 21 July 2004.
61 Bentley (1998) p. 23.
62 Burton (2007) p. 10.
63 Bentley (1998) p. 24.
64 Cited in Ecclestone and Hayes (2008) p. 16.
65 'TLRP's evidence-informed pedagogic principles': www.tlrp.org/themes/tenprinciples.html.

## Chapter 7: The Unhappy Turn to Happiness

1 See *Towards a New Primary Curriculum: A Report from the Cambridge Primary Review*: www.primaryreview.org.uk/Downloads/Curriculum_report/CPR_Curric_rep_Pt1_Past_Present.pdf.
2 Nel Noddings, 'What does it mean to educate the whole child?', *Education Leadership*, September 2005.
3 Marsden (1997) pp. 234–5.
4 See for example 'Lessons in being happy proposed', *BBC News*, 8 December 2008.
5 Timothy Shriver and Roger Weissberg, 'No emotion left behind', *The New York Times*, 16 August 2005.
6 Bantock (1986) pp. 138–9.
7 'Diary Date', Emotional Intelligence Conference, 21 June 2003: www.sehd.scot.nhs.uk/publications/well2/well2-04.htm.
8 Payne (2000) pp. 355–6.
9 Anthony Seldon, 'Teaching happiness is no laughing matter', *The Daily Telegraph*, 24 May 2007.
10 Dewey (1897) 'My Pedagogic Creed' in Dworkin (1967) p. 25.
11 Ravitch (2000) p. 53.
12 Cited in Ravitch (2000) p. 70.
13 Cited in Ravitch (2000) pp. 274–5.
14 Cited in Ravitch (2000) p. 90.
15 Cited in Ravitch (2000) p. 357.
16 See 'Primary children "suffer stress"', *BBC News*, 12 October 2007.
17 'Pupils "distressed over spelling"', *BBC News*, 2 October 2008.
18 Vanhuysse and Sabbagh (2005) p. 399.
19 White (2006) p. 13.
20 Noddings (2003) p. 200.
21 Cited in Ravitch (2000) p. 288.
22 Ravitch (2000) p. 89.
23 Rogers (1983) p. 137.

24 Rogers (1983) p. 20.

25 Young and Muller (2007) p. 175.

26 'Introduction' by Mary Bousted to Johnson et al. (2007) p. 9.

27 See Richard Layard, 'Happiness and the teaching of values', *CentrePiece*, Summer 2007, p. 20.

28 See 'Session 1: What Works Well': www.teachingexpertise.com/files/Happiness%20programme%20-%20What%20Works%20Well%20part%201.pdf.

29 'Promoting students' happiness': www.teachingexpertise.com/articles/promoting-students-happiness-3910.

30 Ecclestone and Hayes (2008) p. 43.

31 Cited in Burkard (2007) p. 189.

32 David Perks, 'I'd like to teach the world to think . . .', *Spiked-online*, 23 April 2008.

33 Ecclestone and Hayes (2008) pp. ix–x.

34 For an excellent discussion of this subject see Bantock (1986) p. 124.

35 For a discussion of emotional determinism see Furedi (2004) pp. 25–7.

36 The leaflet titled SEAL advertises the UK Government's SEAL programme.

37 Jelfs (2001) p. 12.

38 See 'Seal of approval for feelgood factor', *The Guardian*, 7 October 2008.

39 Timothy Shriver and Roger Weissberg, 'No emotion left behind', *The New York Times*, 16 August 2005.

40 See Layard (2007) .

41 Richard Layard, 'Happiness and the teaching of values', *CentrePiece*, Summer 2007, p. 22.

42 'A Randomized Controlled Trial of the Combination of Two Preventive Interventions': http://ies.ed.gov/funding/grantsearch/details.asp?ID=649.

43 Barber (1997) pp. 172, 191.

44 Sue A. Stickel and Yvonne L. Callaway, 'Neuroscience and Positive Psychology – Implications for School Counsellors', 9 March 2007: www.eric.ed.gov/ERICDocs/data/ericdocs2sql/content_storage_01/0000019b/80/33/59/a8.pdf.

45 Noddings (2003).

46 Habermas (1976) p. 93.

47 Cited in Stuart Jeffries, 'Will this man make you happy?', *The Guardian*, 24 June 2008.

48 Noddings (2003).

49 Wylie (2005) p. 16.

50 Kerlinger (1960) p. 125.

51 See 'Behaviour experts to help schools', *BBC News*, 16 April 2009.

52 www.emotionalintelligencearticles.org/emotional-intelligence-to-motivate.html.

53 Cited in 'Managing challenging behaviour with CPD': www.teachingexpertise.com/articles/managing-challenging-behaviour-3336.

54 Revell (2004) p. 56.

55 Revell (2004) p. 56.

56 Cited in Furedi (2004) p. 198.

57 See Hannah Richardson, 'Behaviour classes "lack impact"', *BBC News*,

2 December 2008.

58 Personal communication, 15 April 2003.

59 Graeme Paton, 'Caning pupils "can be effective behaviour control"', *The Daily Telegraph*, 26 February 2009.

60 Graeme Paton, 'Teachers rattled by hums and coughs in class', *The Daily Telegraph*, 26 March 2009.

61 See 'Schools discipline and pupil behaviour guidelines: guidance for schools' on Teachernet; and Richard Garner, 'Teachers told to praise the unruly as strike looms over discipline', *Independent*, 11 April 2007.

62 Teacher Support Network, press release, 14 October 2008: http://teachersupport.info/news/press-releases/2008-Happiness-Conference.php.

63 Kerlinger (1960) p. 125.

64 Bantock (1986) p. 137.

**Conclusion: Saving Education from Itself**

1 Cited in Steer (2009) p. 51.

2 General Teaching Council for England, *Draft Code of Conduct and Practice*, November 2008.

3 DCSF (2008) *21st Century Schools: A World Class Education for Every Child*: publications.dcsf.gov.uk/eOrderingDownload/DCSF-01044-2008.pdf.

4 Philip Hensher, 'Does anyone really understand the National Curriculum', *The Independent*, 3 April 2009.

5 Smith (2000).

6 Mike Baker, 'Let's not get personal', *BBC News*, 21 November 2008.

7 Devika Bhat and Alexandra Frean, 'Mandarins propose Mandarin for new curriculum', *The Times*, 5 February 2007.

8 Olson (2003) p. 2.

9 Ruiz (2004) p. 1.

10 Cited in Furedi (2004) p. 157.

11 Steer (2009) p. 2.

12 Best (2006) p. 129.

13 Alexandra Frean, '£3bn scheme to help pre-school children learn "has had no effect"', in *The Times*, 28 August 2007.

14 Stedward (2003) p. 146.

15 See for example Tom Clark and Polly Curtis, 'Dumbing down disguised', *The Guardian*, 20 January 2009.

16 James Lyons, 'Test teachers', *The Daily Mirror*, 6 December 2007.

17 Wolf (2002) p. 202.

18 Moore (2007) p. 123.

19 See Polly Curtis, 'More parents use lawyers to secure school places', *The Guardian*, 23 October 2008.

20 Frank Furedi, 'Who's doing the homework', *The Daily Telegraph*, 8 February 2006.

# Bibliography

Alexander, T. (2001) *Citizen Education*, London: Campaign for Education.

Altheit, P. and Dausien, B. (2002) 'The "double face" of lifelong learning: Two analytical perspectives on a "silent revolution"', *Studies in the Education of Adults*, 34 (1).

Arendt, H. (2006 [1961]) *Between Past and Future*, London: Faber & Faber.

Ayling, J. (1930) *The Retreat from Parenthood*, London: Kegan Paul, Trench, Trubner & Co.

Bagnall, R. G. (2000) 'Lifelong learning and the limitations of economic determinism', *International Journal of Lifelong Education*, 19 (1).

Ball, S. (2008) *The Education Debate*, Bristol: Policy Press.

Bantock, G. H. (1952) *Freedom and Authority in Education: A Criticism of Modern Cultural and Educational Assumptions*, London: Faber & Faber.

—— (1965) *Education and Values: Essays in the Theory of Education*, London: Faber & Faber.

—— (1986) 'Educating the emotions: An historical perspective', *British Journal of Educational Studies*, 2.

Barber, M. (1997) *The Learning Game: Arguments for an Education Revolution*, London: Indigo.

Beck, J. (2002) 'The sacred and the profane in recent struggles to promote official pedagogic identities', *British Journal of Sociology of Education*, 23 (4).

Beck, J. and Young, M. (2005) 'The assault on the professions and the restructuring of academic and professional identities: A Bernsteinian analysis', *British Journal of Sociology of Education*, 26 (2).

Bentley, T. (1998) *Learning Beyond the Classroom: Education for a Changing World*, London: Routledge.

Best, J. (ed.) (1994) *Troubling Children: Studies of Children and Social Problems*, New York: Aldine de Gruyter.

—— (2006) *Flavour of the Month: Why Smart People Fall for Fads*, Berkeley: University of California Press.

Burkard, T. (2007) *Inside the Secret Garden: The Progressive Decay of Liberal Education*, Buckingham: The University of Buckingham Press.

Burton, D. (2007) 'Psycho-pedagogy and personalised learning', *Journal of Education for Teaching*, 33 (1).

Chung, S. and Walsh, D. (2000) 'Unpacking child-centredness: a history of meanings', *Journal of Curriculum Studies*, 32 (2).

Cladis, M. S. (1995) 'Education, virtue and democracy in the work of Emile Durkheim', *Journal of Moral Education*, 24 (1).

Clarke, F. (1940) *Education and Social Change: An English Interpretation*, London: The Sheldon Press.

Coffield, F. (1999) 'Breaking the consensus: Lifelong learning as social control', *British Educational Research Journal*, 25 (4).

Collins, R. (1979) *The Credential Society: An Historical Sociology of Education and Stratification*, New York: Academic Press.

Cook-Sather, A. (2006) 'Sound, presence, and power: "Student Voice" in educational research and reform', *Curriculum Inquiry*, 36 (4).

Coombs, P. (1985) *The World Crisis In Education: The View from the Eighties*, New York: Oxford University Press.

Cotgrove, C. (1972) *The Science of Society: An Introduction to the Science of Society*, London: George Allen & Unwin.

Cox, C. B. and Dyson, A. E. (eds) (1969) *Black Paper Two: The Crisis in Education*, London: The Critical Quarterly Society.

—— (1970) *Black Paper Three: The Crisis in Education*, London: The Critical Quarterly Society.

Cox, C. B. and Boyson, R. (1977) *Black Paper*, London: Temple Smith.

Crawford, K. (1995) 'A history of the right: The battle for control of National Curriculum history 1989–1994', *British Journal of Education Studies*, 43 (4).

Crowther, J. (2004) '"In and against" lifelong learning: flexibility and the corrosion of character', *International Journal of Lifelong Education*, 23 (2).

Davies, I, Godard, S. and McGuinn, N. (2005) 'Citizenship education and character education: Similarities and contrasts', *British Journal of Educational Studies*, 53 (3).

Department for Children, Schools and Families (2008) *The Independent Review of the Primary Curriculum*, http://publications.teachernet.gov.uk/default.aspx?PageFunction=productdetails&PageMode=publications&ProductId=BLNK-01010-2008&.

Department for Education and Skills (2004) *Five Year Strategy for Children and Learners*, presented to Parliament by the Secretary of State for Education and Skills, July, Cm6272.

Dewey J. (1897) 'My pedagogic creed' in Dworkin, M. (ed.) (1967) *Dewey on Education*, New York: Teachers College Press.

—— (1902) 'The school as social center', *The Elementary School Teacher*, 3 (2).

—— (1934) 'Individual psychology and education', *The Philosopher*, 12.

—— (1936) 'Authority and freedom', *Survey Graphic*, November, 25 (11).

—— (1938) [1916] *Democracy and Education*, New York: The Free Press.

—— (1946) *Problems of Men*, New York: The Philosophical Library.

—— (1956) [1902] *The Child and the Curriculum*, Chicago: University of Chicago Press.

—— (1966) *Democracy and Education*, New York: Free Press.

Dewey, J. and Dewey, E. (1962) [1915] *Schools for Tomorrow*, New York: E. P. Dutton Co. Ltd.

DfEE (1997) *Excellence in Schools*, London: Stationery Office Limited.

DfEE (1998) 'Introduction' to *The Learning Age: A Renaissance for a New Britain*, available online at: www.leeds.ac.uk/educol/documents/000000655.htm.

DfES (2003) *The London Challenge: Transforming London Secondary Schools*, London: DfES.

Durkheim, E. (1956) *Education and Sociology*, New York: The Free Press.

—— (1986) 'The role of the state in education', republished in Giddens (1986) p. 177.

Dworkin, M. (ed.) (1967) *Dewey on Education*, New York: Teachers College Press.

Ecclestone, K. and Hayes, D. (2008) *The Dangerous Rise of Therapeutic Education*, London: Routledge.

Edwards, R. and Nicoll, K. (2006) 'Expertise, competence and reflection in the rhetoric of professional development', *British Educational Research Journal*, 32 (1).

Entwistle, H. (1979) *Antonio Gramsci: Conservative Schooling for Radical Politics*, London: Routledge & Kegan Paul.

Fallows, S. and Steven, C. (eds) (2000) *Integrating Key Skills in Higher Education*, London: Kogan Page Ltd.

Finch, A. and Scrimshaw, P. (eds) (1982) *Standards, Schooling and Education*, London: Hodder and Stoughton.

Finlay, I., Spours, K., Steer, R., Coffield, F., Gregson, M., Hodgson, A. and Edward, S. (2007) '"The heart of what we do": Policies on teaching, learning and assessment in the new learning and skills sector', http://www.ioe.ac.uk/schools/leid/lss/Report4.pdf.

Francis, L. and Grindle, Z. (1998) 'Whatever happened to progressive education? A comparison of primary school teachers' attitudes in 1982 and 1996', *Educational Studies*, 24 (3).

Freire, P. (1972) *Pedagogy of the Oppressed*, New York: Herder and Herder.

Furedi, F. (2004) *Therapy Culture: Cultivating Vulnerability in an Anxious Age*, London: Routledge.

—— (2006) *Where Have All the Intellectuals Gone?*, 2nd edn, London: Continuum.

—— (2008) *Paranoid Parenting: Why Ignoring the Experts May Be Best for Your Child*, London: Continuum.

Furedi, F. and Bristow, J. (2008) *Licensed to Hug*, London: Civitas.

Gardner, H. (1993) *Frames of Mind: The Theory of Multiple Intelligences*, London: Fontana.

Gewitz, S. (2001) 'Cloning the Blairs: New Labour's programme for the resocialisation of working-class parents', *Journal of Education Policy*, 16.

Giddens, A. (1986) (ed.) *Durkheim on Politics and the State*, Cambridge: Polity Press.

Gill, B. and Schlossman, S. (2003) 'Parents and the politics of homework: Some historical perspectives', *Teachers College Record*, 105 (5).

—— (2004) 'Villain or saviour? The American discourse on homework, 1850–2003', *Theory Into Practice*, 43 (3).

Gordon, M. (1999) 'Hannah Arendt on authority: Conservatism in education reconsidered', *Educational Theory*, 49 (2).

—— (1998) 'John Dewey on authority: A radical voice within the liberal tradition', *Educational Philosophy and Theory*, 30 (3).

Habermas, J. (1976) *Legitimation Crisis*, London: Heinemann.

Halsey, A. H. (1978) *Change in British Society*, Oxford: Oxford University Press.

Hargreaves, D. (2003) *Education Epidemic*, London: Demos.

Hayes, D. (ed.) (2004) *The RoutledgeFalmer Guide to Key Debates in Education*, London: RoutledgeFalmer.

Heyting, F., Kruithof, B. and Mulder, E. (2002) 'Education and social integration: On basic consensus and the cohesion of society', *Educational Theory*, 52 (4).

Hofstadter, R. (1964) *Anti-intellectualism in American Life*, London: Jonathan Cape.

Hyland, T. (2006) 'Vocational education and training and the therapeutic turn', *Educational Studies*, 32 (3).

Iannelli, C. and Paterson, L. (2007) 'Education and social mobility in Scotland', *Research in Social Stratification and Mobility*, 25.

Jelfs, H. (2001) *Identifying and Utilising Values: Spiritual, Moral, Social and Cultural Development and Citizenship in a Primary School*, London: Department for

Education and Skills.

Johnson, M., with Ellis, N., Gotch, A., Ryan, A., Foster, C., Gillespie, J. and Lowe, M. (2007) *Subject to Change: New Thinking on the Curriculum*, London: ATL.

Jones, K. (2003) *Education in Britain: 1944 to the Present*, Cambridge: Polity.

Kennedy, H. (1997) *Learning Works*, Coventry: The Further Education Funding Council.

Kerlinger, F. (1960) 'The implications of the permissiveness doctrine in American education', *Educational Theory*, 10 (2).

Kessen, W. (1979) 'The American child and other cultural inventions', *American Psychologist*, 34 (10).

Kounine, L., Marks, J. and Truss, E. (2008) *The Value of Mathematics*, London: Reform.

Labaree, D. L. (2005) 'Progressivism, schools and schools of education: An American romance', *Paedogogica Historica*, 41 (1 & 2).

Layard, R. (2007) 'The teaching of values', the 2007 Ashby Lecture, University of Cambridge.

Leadbeater, C. (2004) *Personalisation Through Participation: A New Script for Public Services*, London: Demos.

Leatherwood, C. (2005) 'Assessment policy and practice in higher education: Purpose, standards and equity', *Assessment & Evaluation in Higher Education*, 30 (3).

Lester Smith, W. O. (1971) *Government of Education*, Harmondsworth: Penguin Books.

Levin, B. (1998) 'An epidemic of education policy: (What) can we learn from each other?', *Comparative Education*, 34 (2).

Levinson, N. (1997) 'Teaching in the midst of belatedness: The paradox of natality in Hannah Arendt's educational thought', *Educational Theory*, 47 (4).

Loseke, D. and Cahill, S. (1994) 'Normalizing the child daycare discourse in popular magazines, 1900–1990' in Best, J. (ed.) (1994) *Troubling Children: Studies of Children and Social Problems*, New York: Aldine de Gruyter.

Lovelock, J. (ed.) (2008) *The Head Speaks: Challenges and Visions in Education*, Buckingham: The University of Buckingham Press.

Lovlie, L. and Standish, P. (2002) 'Introduction: *Bildung* and the idea of a liberal education', *Journal of Philosophy of Education*, 36 (2).

Macdonald, D. (2003) 'Curriculum change and the post-modern world: Is the school curriculum-reform movement an anachronism?', *Journal of Curriculum Studies*, 35 (2).

Marsden, W. E. (1997) 'Contradictions in progressive primary school ideologies and curricula in England: Some historical perspectives', *Historical Studies in Education*, 9 (2).

McCaslin, M. and Infanti, H. (1998) 'The generativity crisis and the "scold war": What about those parents?', *Teacher College Record*, 100 (2).

McCulloch, G., Goodman, J. and Richardson, W. (2007) 'Editors' introduction: Social change in the history of education', *History of Education*, 36 (4–5).

Moore, R. (2000) 'For knowledge: Tradition, progressivism and progress in education – reconstructing the curriculum debate', *Cambridge Journal of Education*, 30 (1).

—— (2007) *Sociology of Knowledge and Education*, London: Continuum.

Moore, R. and Young, M. (2001) 'Knowledge and the curriculum in the sociology of education: towards a reconceptualisation', *British Journal of Sociology of Education*, 22 (4).

Morris, M. and Griggs, C. (eds) (1988) *Education: The Wasted Years? 1973–1986*, London: The Falmer Press.

Nicholl, K. (2005) 'Getting at the facts: The fabrication and action of truth within lifelong learning policy'. Paper presented to the AARE Conference, Parramatta, November. Online at: http://www.aare.edu.au/05pap/nic05434.pdf (accessed 19 May 2006).

Nicoll, K. and Edwards, R. (2004) 'Lifelong learning and the sultans of spin: Policy as persuasion?', *Journal of Education Policy*, 19 (1).

Nisbet, R. (2000) *Twilight of Authority*, Indianapolis: Liberty Fund Inc.

Noddings, N. (2003) *Happiness and Education*, Cambridge: Cambridge University Press.

Oakeshott, M. (1989) *The Voice of Liberal Learning: Michael Oakeshott on Education*, New Haven: Yale University Press.

O'Byrne, A. (2005) 'Pedagogy without a project: Arendt and Derrida on teaching, responsibility and revolution', *Studies in Philosophy and Education*, 24.

Olson, D. (2003) 'The triumph of hope over experience in the search for "what works": A response to Slavin', *Educational Researcher*, http://aera.net/uploadedFiles/Journals_and_Publications/Journals/Educational_Researcher/Volume_33_No_1/ERv33n1_OLSON.pdf.

Payne, J. (2000) 'The unbearable lightness of skill: The changing meaning of skill in UK policy discourses and some implications for education and training', *Journal of Education Policy*, 15 (3).

Peters, R. S. (1959) *Authority, Responsibility and Education*, London: George Allen & Unwin Ltd.

—— (1969) (ed.) *Perspectives on Plowden*, London: Routledge & Kegan Paul.

—— (1982 [1967]) 'What is an educational process?', in Finch and Scrimshaw (1982).

Phillips, Melanie (1997) *All Must Have Prizes*, London: Warner Books.

Porritt, J. (1998) *Captain Eco and the Fate of the Earth*, New York: Dorling Kindersley, Inc.

Postman, N. (1996) *The End of Education: Redefining the Value of School*, New York: Vintage Books.

Prensky, M. (2001) 'Digital natives, digital immigrants', *On the Horizon*, 9 (5), October.

Pring, R. (2007) 'The common school', *Journal of Philosophy of Education*, 41 (4).

Qualifications and Curriculum Authority (2005) *A Curriculum for the Future*, London: QCA.

Qualifications and Curriculum Authority (2007) *The Curriculum: Taking Stock of Progress*, London: QCA.

Ravitch, D. (1985) *The Schools We Deserve: Reflections on the Educational Crises of Our Times*, New York: Basic Books.

—— (2000) *Left Back: A Century of Failed School Reforms*, New York: Simon & Schuster.

Revell, L. (2004) 'Circle Time' in Hayes, D. (ed.) (2004) *The RoutledgeFalmer Guide to Key Debates in Education*, London: RoutledgeFalmer.

Rogers, C. (1983) *Freedom to Learn*, Columbus, Ohio: Charles E. Merrill Publishing Company.

Ruiz, J. (2004) *A Literature Review of the Evidence Base for Culture, the Arts and Sport Policy*, Education Department Research Programme, Edinburgh: Scottish Executive.

Russell, J. (2007) *How to Turn Your Parents Green*, Bristol: Tangent Books.

Ryan, A. (1995) *John Dewey and the High Tide of American Liberalism*, New York: W. W. Norton & Company.

Schön, D. (1967) *Technology and Change: The New Heraclitus*, Oxford: Pergamon Press.

Sellinger, M. and Yapp, C. (2001) *IC Teachers*, London: IPPR.

Simon, B. (1981) 'Why no pedagogy in England?', in B. Simon and W. Taylor (eds) (1981), *Education in the Eighties: The Central Issues*, London: Batsford.

Smith, M. K. (2000) 'The theory and rhetoric of the learning society', *The Encyclopedia of Informal education*: www.infed.org/lifelonglearning/b-lrnsoc.htm. Last update 2 July 2008.

Smith, R. (2002) 'Self-esteem: The kindly apocalypse', *Journal of Philosophy of Education*, 36 (1).

Snow, C. P. (2007) *The Two Cultures*, Cambridge: Cambridge University Press.

Standish, A. (2009) *Global Perspectives in the Geography Curriculum: Reviewing the Moral Case for Geography*, New York: Routledge.

Stedward, G. (2003) 'Education as industrial policy: New Labour's marriage of the social and the economic', *Policy & Politics*, 31 (2).

Steer, A. (2009) *Learning Behaviour: A Review of Behaviour Standards and Practices in our Schools*, Nottingham: DCSF Publications.

Teaching and Learning in 2020 Review Group (2007) *2020 Vision: Report of the Teaching and Learning in 2020 Review Group*, London: Department of Education and Skills.

Tight, M. (1998) 'Education, education, education! The vision of lifelong learning in the Kennedy, Dearing and Fryer reports', *Oxford Review of Education*, 24 (4).

—— (1994) 'Crisis, what crisis? Rhetoric and reality in higher education', *British Journal of Educational Studies*, 42 (4).

UNESCO (1972) *The World of Education Today and Tomorrow: Learning to Be*, Paris: UNESCO.

Vanhuysse, P. and Sabbagh, C. (2005) 'Promoting happiness, respecting difference? New perspectives on the politics and sociology of education in liberal democracy', *British Educational Research Journal*, 31 (3).

Wheelahan, L. (2008) 'A social realist alternative for curriculum', *Critical Studies in Education*, 49 (2).

White, J. (2005) 'Reassessing 1960s philosophy of the curriculum', *London Review of Education*, 3 (2).

—— (2006) *The Aims of School Education*, London: IPPR, http://www.ippr.org/uploadedFiles/research/projects/Education/The%20Aims%20of%20School%20Ed%20FINAL.pdf.

Whitty, G. and Wisby, E. (2007) 'Whose voice? An exploration of the current policy interest in pupil involvement in school decision making', *International Studies in Sociology of Education*, 17 (3).

Wolf, A. (2002) *Does Education Matter: Myths About Education and Economic Growth*, London: Penguin Books.

Wylie, K. (2005) 'The moral dimension of personal and social education', *Pastoral Care*, September.

Young, M. (2003) 'Durkheim, Vygotsky and the curriculum of the future', *London Review of Education*, 1 (2).

—— (2008) *Bringing Knowledge Back In: From Social Constructivism to Social Realism in the Sociology of Education*, London: Routledge.

Young, M. and Muller, J. (2007) 'Truth and truthfulness in the sociology of educational knowledge', *Theory and Research in Education*, 5.

Zachry, C. B. (1940) *Emotion and Conduct in Adolescence*, New York: Appleton-Century.

Zieger, R. (2004) '"Uncle Sam wants you . . . to go shopping": A consumer society responds to national crisis, 1957–2001', *Canadian Review of American Studies*, 34 (1).

# Index